She-Hulk

Secret Invasion

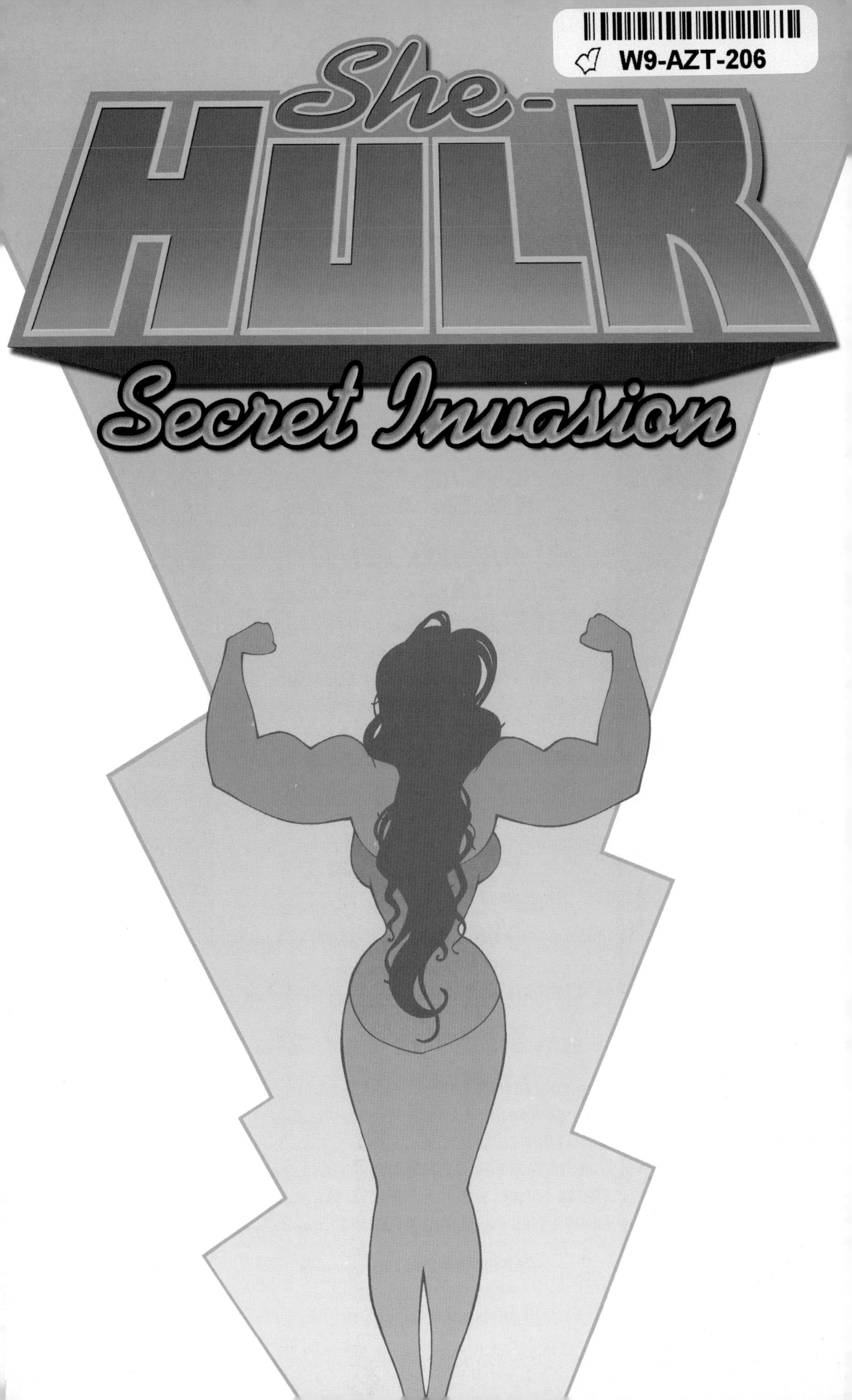

She-HULK
Secret Invasion

WRITER: Peter David

SHE-HULK #31-33:
PENCILER: Vincenzo Cucca
INKER: Vincenzo Acunzo
COLORIST: Barbara Ciardo
GG STUDIO TEAM COORDINATOR:
Giuliano Monni
LETTERS: Dave Sharpe
COVER ART: Mike Deodato & Rain Beredo
ASSISTANT EDITOR: Lauren Sankovitch
EDITOR: Bill Rosemann

X-FACTOR #33-34:
PENCILER: Larry Stroman
INKER: Jon Sibal
COLORIST: Jeromy Cox
LETTERS: Virtual Calligraphy's Cory Petit
COVER ART: Boo Cook
EDITORS: Will Panzo & Aubrey Sitterson

COLLECTION EDITOR: Jennifer Grünwald
EDITORIAL ASSISTANT: Alex Starbuck
ASSISTANT EDITORS: Cory Levine & John Denning
EDITOR, SPECIAL PROJECTS: Mark D. Beazley
SENIOR EDITOR, SPECIAL PROJECTS: Jeff Youngquist
SENIOR VICE PRESIDENT OF SALES: David Gabriel

EDITOR IN CHIEF: Joe Quesada
PUBLISHER: Dan Buckley
EXECUTIVE PRODUCER: Alan Fine

PREVIOUSLY IN SHE-HULK:

Freed from her recent incarceration in the Cleveland City Jail, She-Hulk teamed with a road-tripping Hercules to defeat a 50-foot-tall Celtic demigod (the guard-for-hire Bran in his true form), who was rampaging through the city. Meanwhile, Jen's bounty-hunting partner **Jazinda** (who just happens to be the shape-shifting daughter of Kl'rt the Super-Skrull), learned that Bran had been working with an unnamed group who have "taken an interest" in our green glamazon.

Afterwards, Jazinda had a sudden premonition concerning a mysterious "Talisman" that led her and She-Hulk to Detroit, Michigan...

PREVIOUSLY IN X-FACTOR:

Having left Mutant Town behind as a smoldering wreck, X-Factor has relocated to Detroit, promptly lowering the property value of Larry Stroman's house. Calling themselves XF Investigations, they have quickly developed a reputation for being the go-to agency for cases that are somewhat unusual. Meanwhile the team is convinced that they have left the threats of Val Cooper and the O*N*E behind, unaware that Val knows exactly where they are and has been insisting on Madrox's cooperation lest she make XF's life extremely difficult.

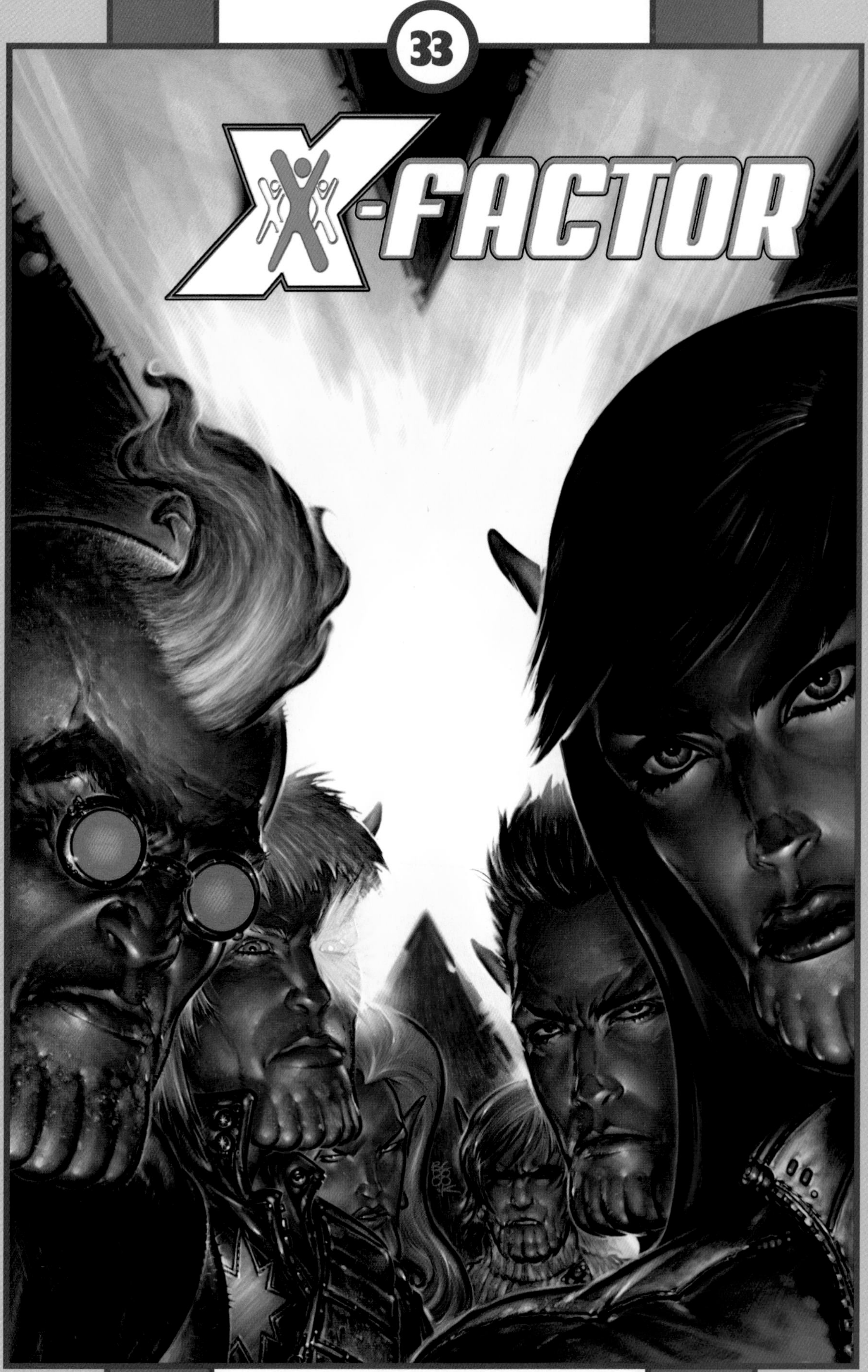
33
X-FACTOR

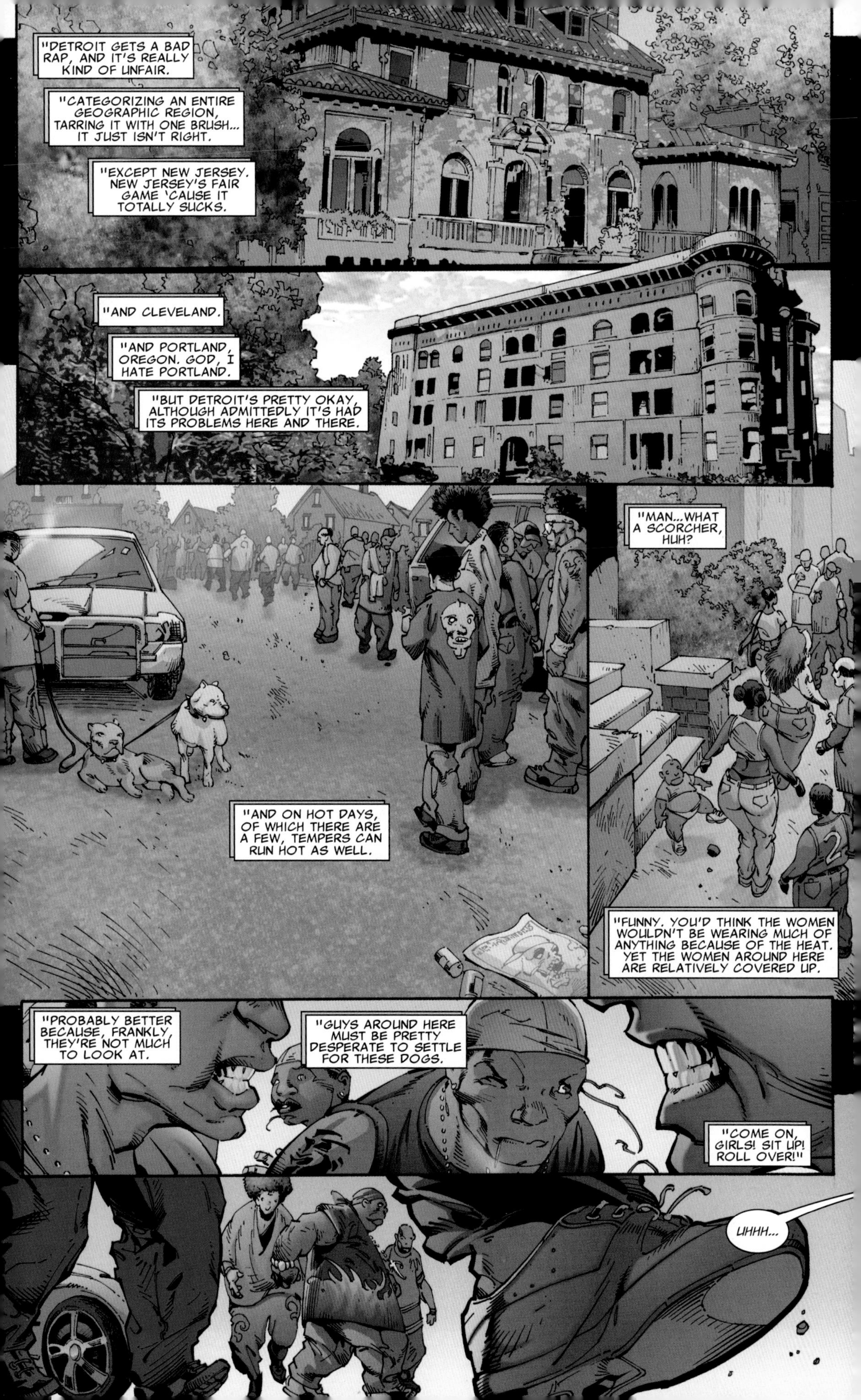
"DETROIT GETS A BAD RAP, AND IT'S REALLY KIND OF UNFAIR.
"CATEGORIZING AN ENTIRE GEOGRAPHIC REGION, TARRING IT WITH ONE BRUSH... IT JUST ISN'T RIGHT.
"EXCEPT NEW JERSEY. NEW JERSEY'S FAIR GAME 'CAUSE IT TOTALLY SUCKS.
"AND CLEVELAND.
"AND PORTLAND, OREGON. GOD, I HATE PORTLAND.
"BUT DETROIT'S PRETTY OKAY, ALTHOUGH ADMITTEDLY IT'S HAD ITS PROBLEMS HERE AND THERE.
"AND ON HOT DAYS, OF WHICH THERE ARE A FEW, TEMPERS CAN RUN HOT AS WELL.
"MAN...WHAT A SCORCHER, HUH?
"FUNNY. YOU'D THINK THE WOMEN WOULDN'T BE WEARING MUCH OF ANYTHING BECAUSE OF THE HEAT. YET THE WOMEN AROUND HERE ARE RELATIVELY COVERED UP.
"PROBABLY BETTER BECAUSE, FRANKLY, THEY'RE NOT MUCH TO LOOK AT.
"GUYS AROUND HERE MUST BE PRETTY DESPERATE TO SETTLE FOR THESE DOGS.
"COME ON, GIRLS! SIT UP! ROLL OVER!"
UHHH...

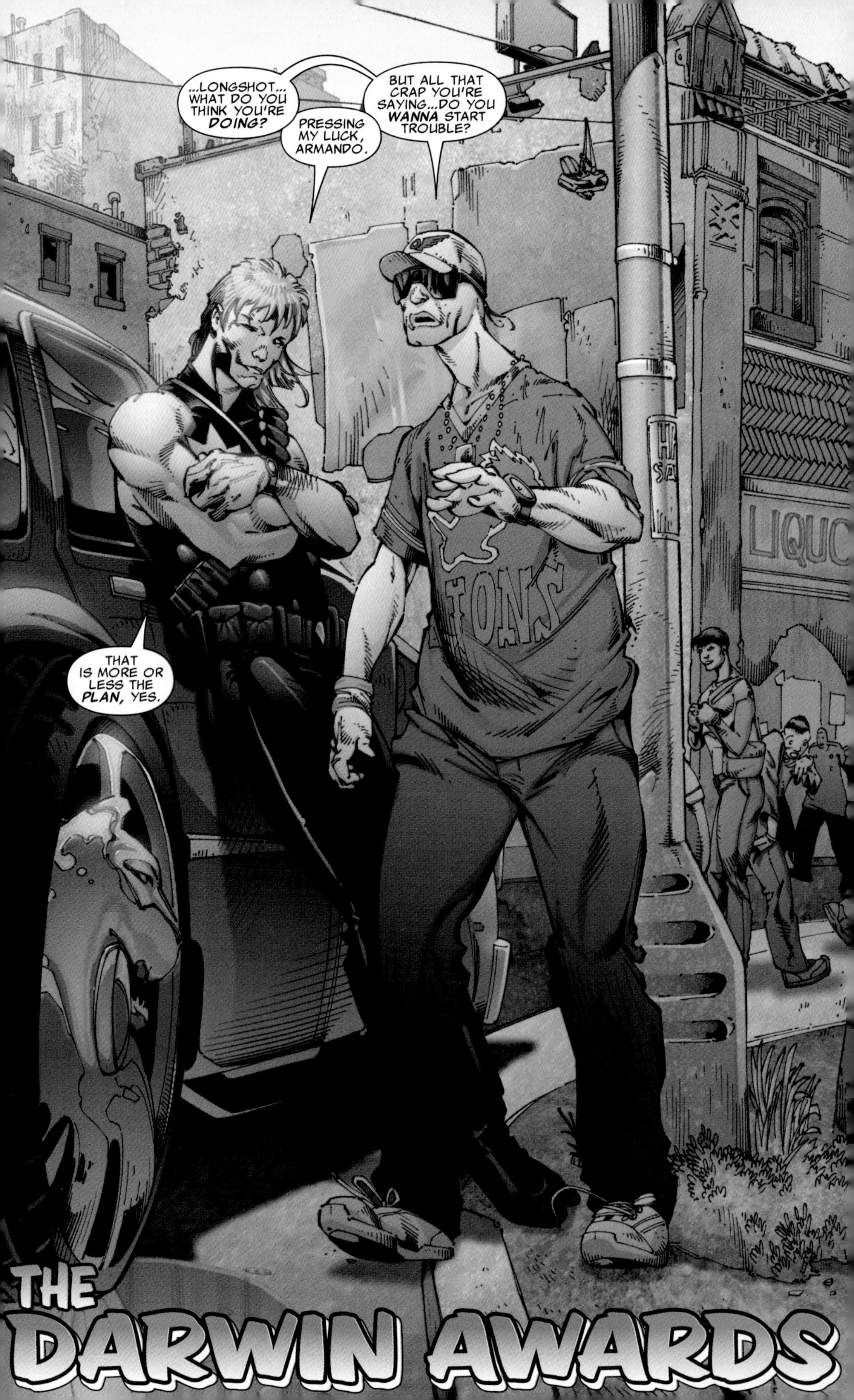
...LONGSHOT... WHAT DO YOU THINK YOU'RE DOING?
BUT ALL THAT CRAP YOU'RE SAYING...DO YOU WANNA START TROUBLE?
PRESSING MY LUCK, ARMANDO.
THAT IS MORE OR LESS THE PLAN, YES.
THE DARWIN AWARDS

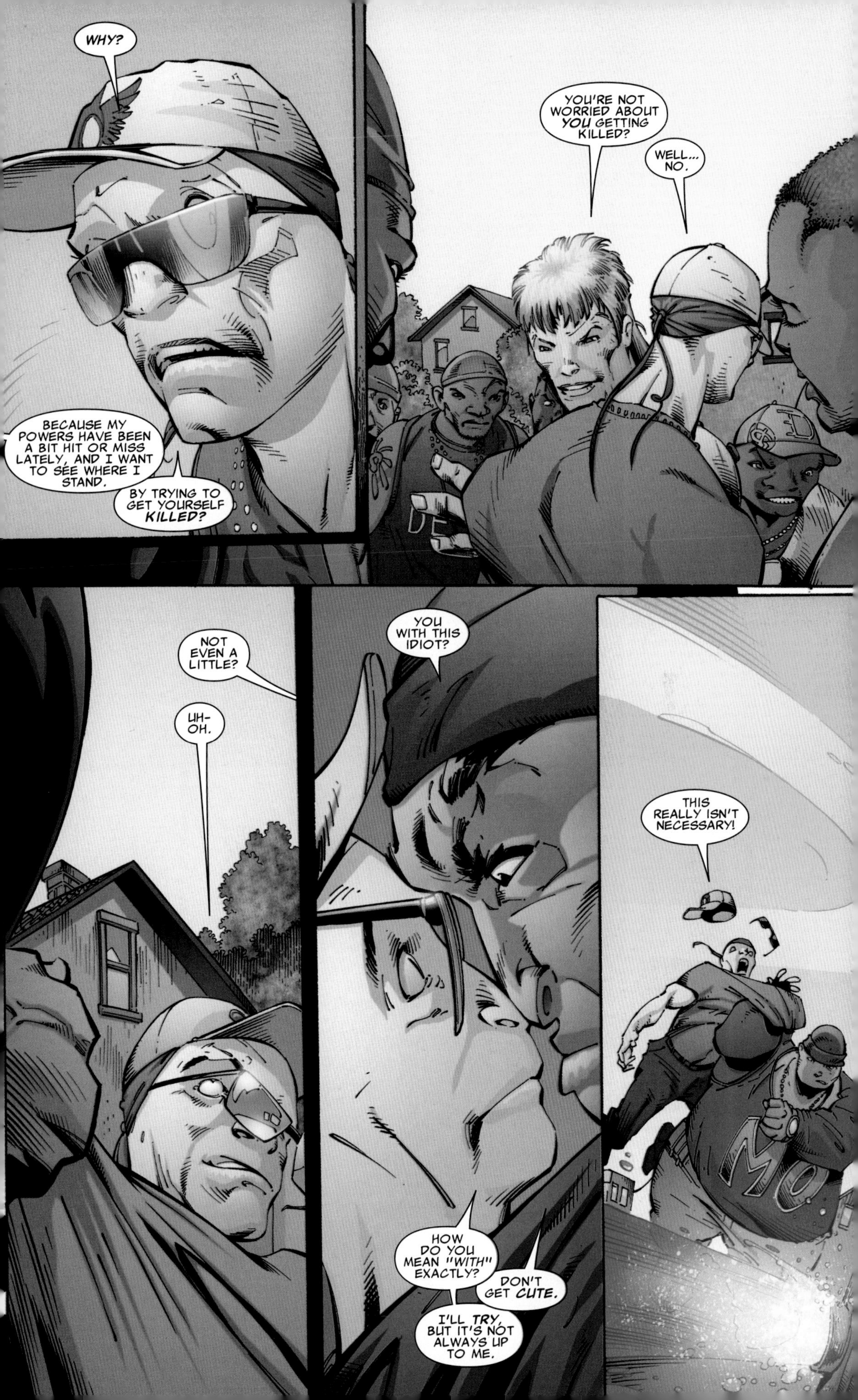
WHY?
BECAUSE MY POWERS HAVE BEEN A BIT HIT OR MISS LATELY, AND I WANT TO SEE WHERE I STAND.
BY TRYING TO GET YOURSELF KILLED?
YOU'RE NOT WORRIED ABOUT YOU GETTING KILLED?
WELL... NO.
NOT EVEN A LITTLE?
UH-OH.
YOU WITH THIS IDIOT?
HOW DO YOU MEAN "WITH" EXACTLY?
DON'T GET CUTE.
I'LL TRY, BUT IT'S NOT ALWAYS UP TO ME.
THIS REALLY ISN'T NECESSARY!

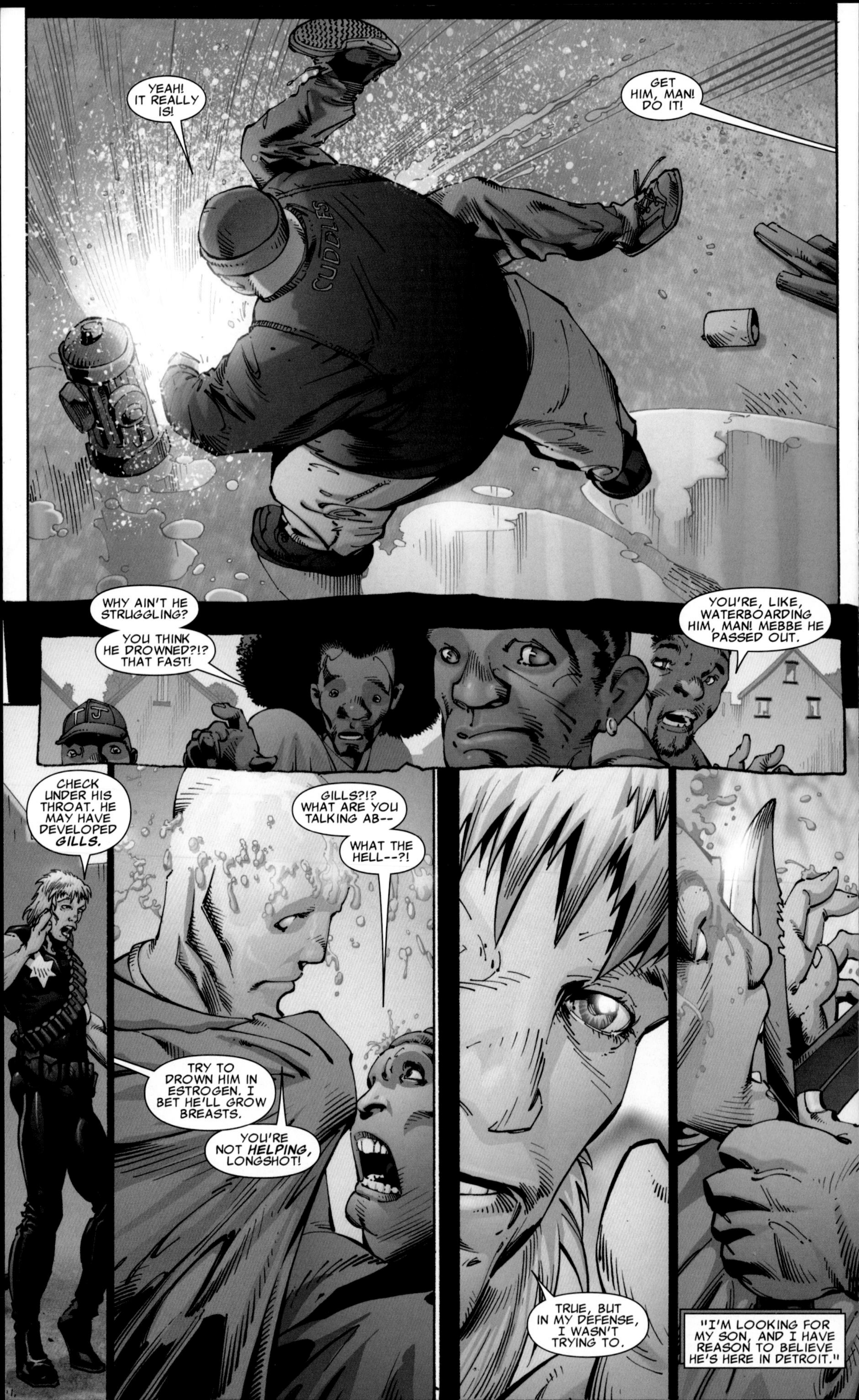
YEAH! IT REALLY IS!
GET HIM, MAN! DO IT!
CUDDLES
WHY AIN'T HE STRUGGLING?
YOU THINK HE DROWNED?!? THAT FAST!
YOU'RE, LIKE, WATERBOARDING HIM, MAN! MEBBE HE PASSED OUT.
TJ
CHECK UNDER HIS THROAT. HE MAY HAVE DEVELOPED GILLS.
GILLS?!? WHAT ARE YOU TALKING AB--
WHAT THE HELL--?!
TRY TO DROWN HIM IN ESTROGEN. I BET HE'LL GROW BREASTS.
YOU'RE NOT HELPING, LONGSHOT!
TRUE, BUT IN MY DEFENSE, I WASN'T TRYING TO.
"I'M LOOKING FOR MY SON, AND I HAVE REASON TO BELIEVE HE'S HERE IN DETROIT."

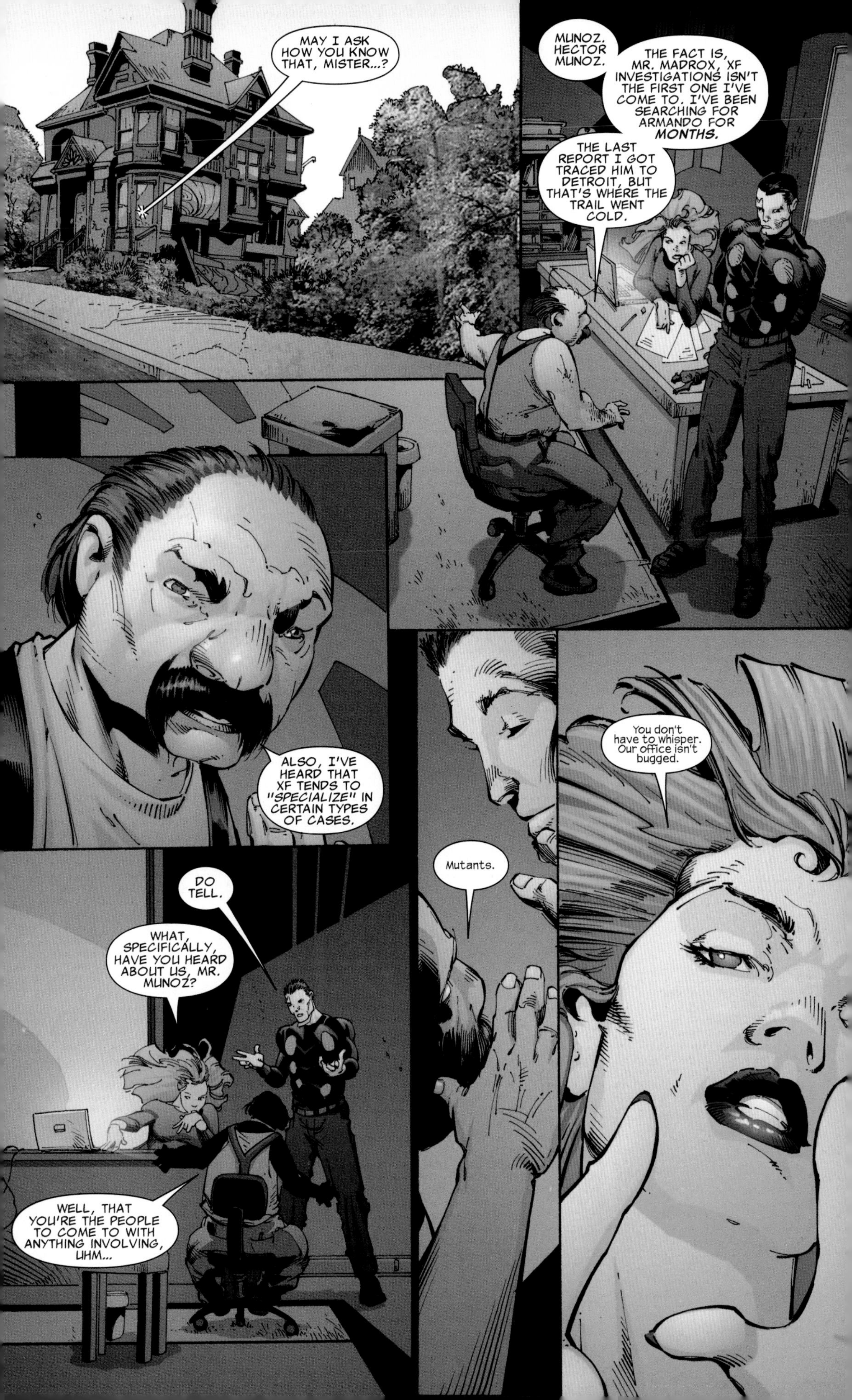
MAY I ASK HOW YOU KNOW THAT, MISTER...?
MUNOZ. HECTOR MUNOZ.
THE FACT IS, MR. MADROX, XF INVESTIGATIONS ISN'T THE FIRST ONE I'VE COME TO. I'VE BEEN SEARCHING FOR ARMANDO FOR **MONTHS.**
THE LAST REPORT I GOT TRACED HIM TO DETROIT, BUT THAT'S WHERE THE TRAIL WENT COLD.
ALSO, I'VE HEARD THAT XF TENDS TO *"SPECIALIZE"* IN CERTAIN TYPES OF CASES.
DO TELL.
WHAT, SPECIFICALLY, HAVE YOU HEARD ABOUT US, MR. MUNOZ?
WELL, THAT YOU'RE THE PEOPLE TO COME TO WITH ANYTHING INVOLVING, UHM...
Mutants.
You don't have to whisper. Our office isn't bugged.

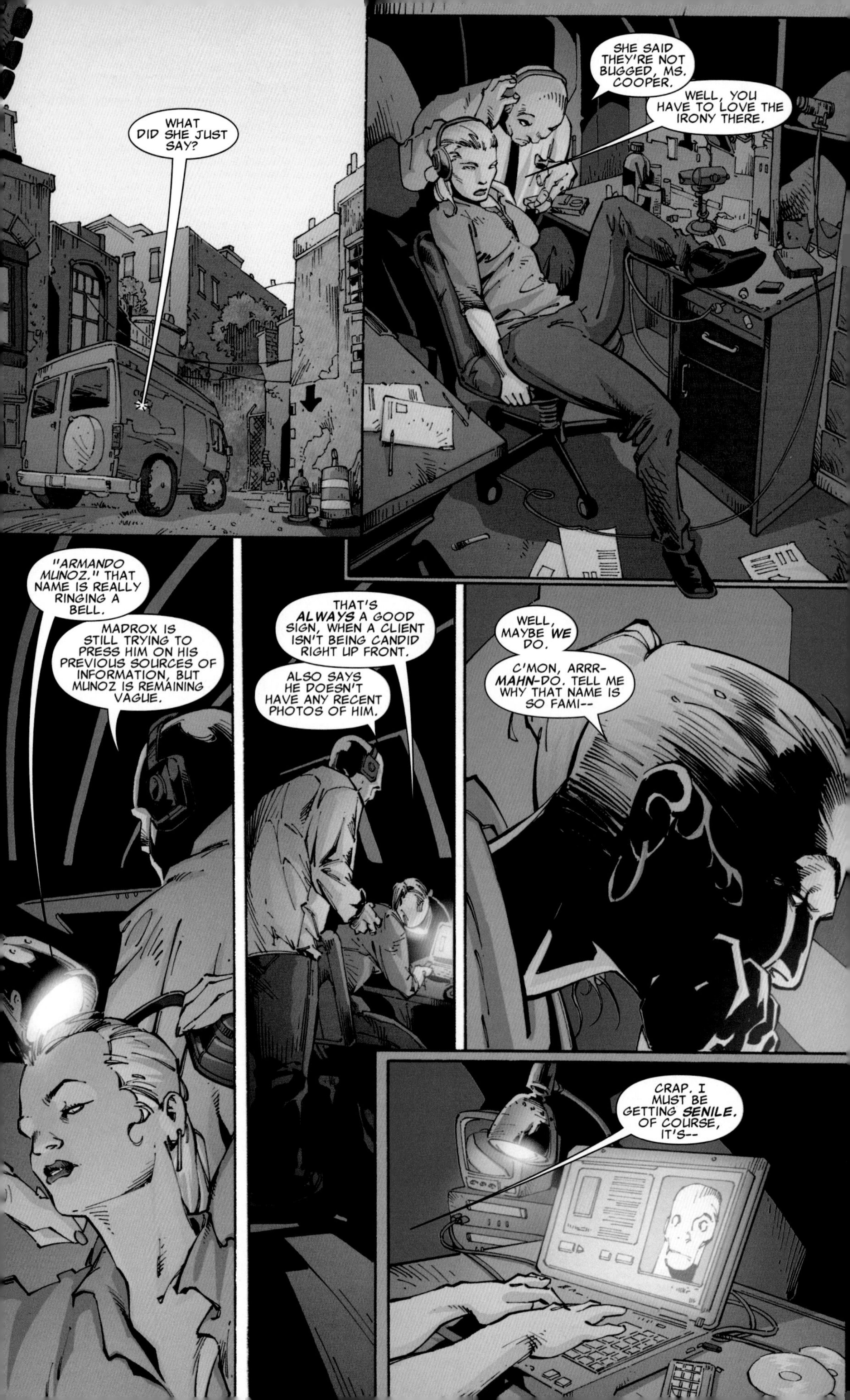
WHAT DID SHE JUST SAY?
SHE SAID THEY'RE NOT BUGGED, MS. COOPER.
WELL, YOU HAVE TO LOVE THE IRONY THERE.
"ARMANDO MUNOZ." THAT NAME IS REALLY RINGING A BELL.
MADROX IS STILL TRYING TO PRESS HIM ON HIS PREVIOUS SOURCES OF INFORMATION, BUT MUNOZ IS REMAINING VAGUE.
THAT'S ALWAYS A GOOD SIGN, WHEN A CLIENT ISN'T BEING CANDID RIGHT UP FRONT.
ALSO SAYS HE DOESN'T HAVE ANY RECENT PHOTOS OF HIM.
WELL, MAYBE WE DO.
C'MON, ARRR-MAHN-DO. TELL ME WHY THAT NAME IS SO FAMI--
CRAP. I MUST BE GETTING SENILE. OF COURSE, IT'S--

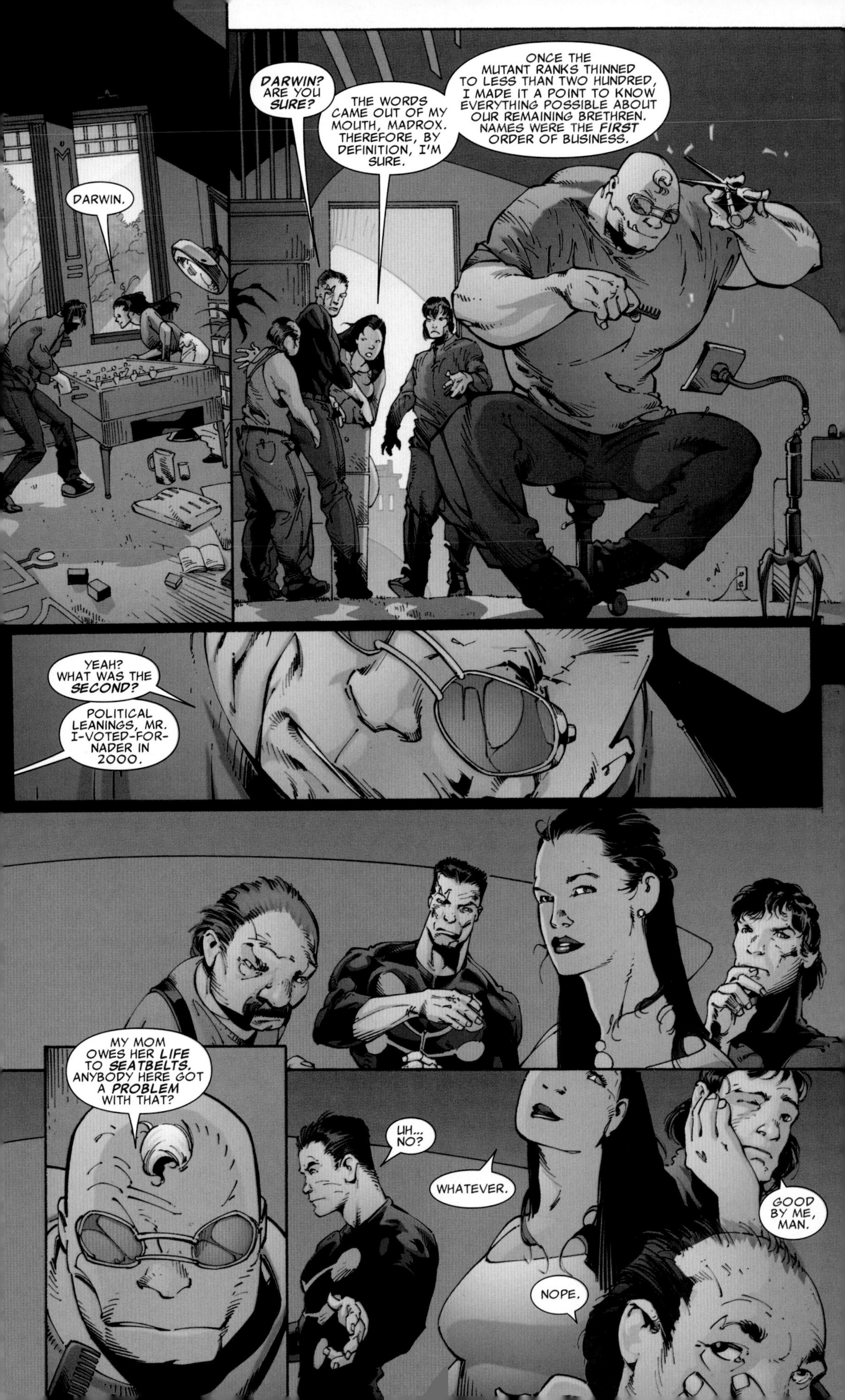
DARWIN.
DARWIN? ARE YOU SURE?
THE WORDS CAME OUT OF MY MOUTH, MADROX. THEREFORE, BY DEFINITION, I'M SURE.
ONCE THE MUTANT RANKS THINNED TO LESS THAN TWO HUNDRED, I MADE IT A POINT TO KNOW EVERYTHING POSSIBLE ABOUT OUR REMAINING BRETHREN. NAMES WERE THE FIRST ORDER OF BUSINESS.
YEAH? WHAT WAS THE SECOND?
POLITICAL LEANINGS, MR. I-VOTED-FOR-NADER IN 2000.
MY MOM OWES HER LIFE TO SEATBELTS. ANYBODY HERE GOT A PROBLEM WITH THAT?
UH... NO?
WHATEVER.
GOOD BY ME, MAN.
NOPE.

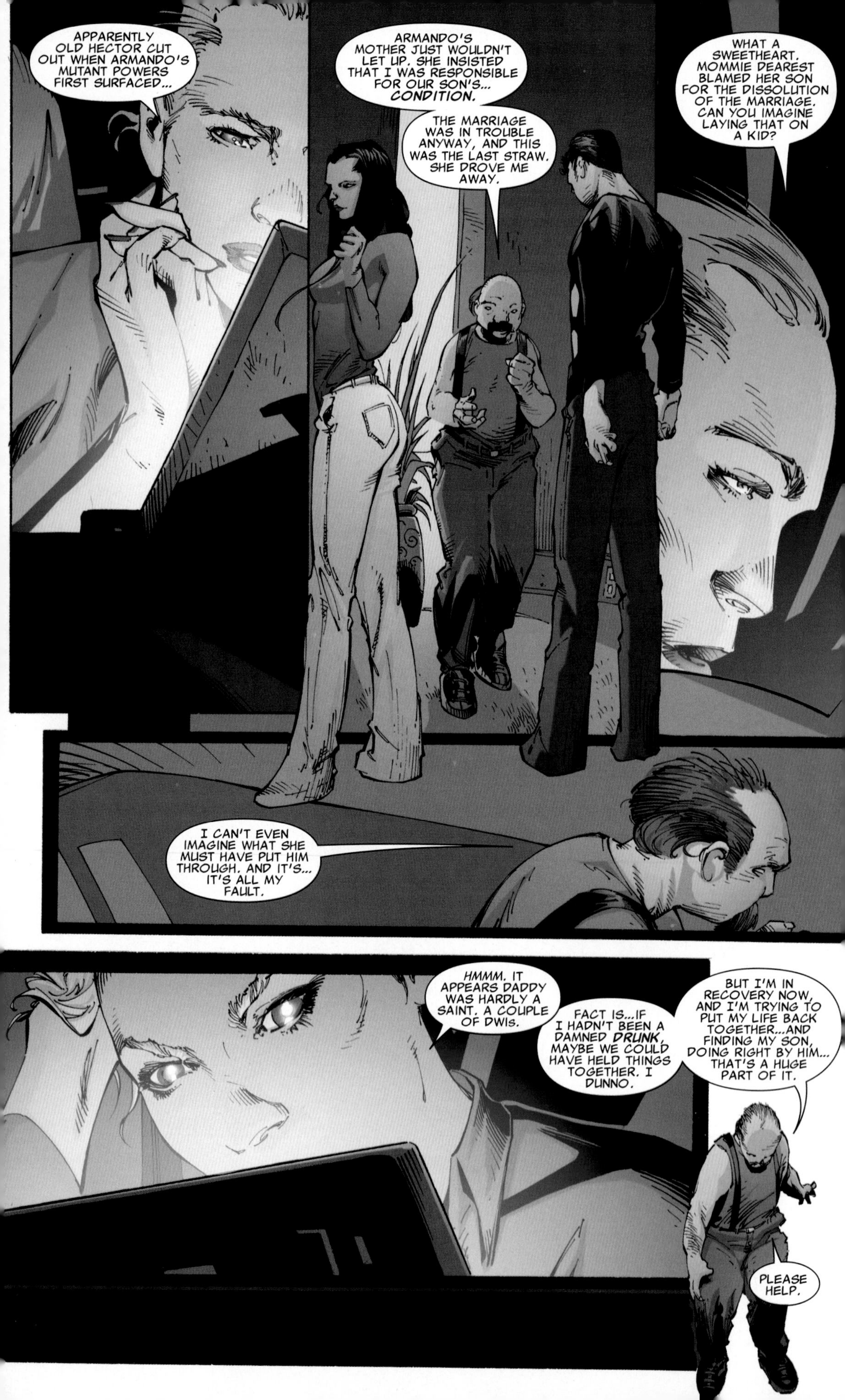
APPARENTLY OLD HECTOR CUT OUT WHEN ARMANDO'S MUTANT POWERS FIRST SURFACED...
ARMANDO'S MOTHER JUST WOULDN'T LET UP. SHE INSISTED THAT I WAS RESPONSIBLE FOR OUR SON'S... CONDITION.
THE MARRIAGE WAS IN TROUBLE ANYWAY, AND THIS WAS THE LAST STRAW. SHE DROVE ME AWAY.
WHAT A SWEETHEART. MOMMIE DEAREST BLAMED HER SON FOR THE DISSOLUTION OF THE MARRIAGE. CAN YOU IMAGINE LAYING THAT ON A KID?
I CAN'T EVEN IMAGINE WHAT SHE MUST HAVE PUT HIM THROUGH. AND IT'S... IT'S ALL MY FAULT.
HMMM. IT APPEARS DADDY WAS HARDLY A SAINT. A COUPLE OF DWIS.
FACT IS...IF I HADN'T BEEN A DAMNED DRUNK, MAYBE WE COULD HAVE HELD THINGS TOGETHER. I DUNNO.
BUT I'M IN RECOVERY NOW, AND I'M TRYING TO PUT MY LIFE BACK TOGETHER...AND FINDING MY SON, DOING RIGHT BY HIM... THAT'S A HUGE PART OF IT.
PLEASE HELP.

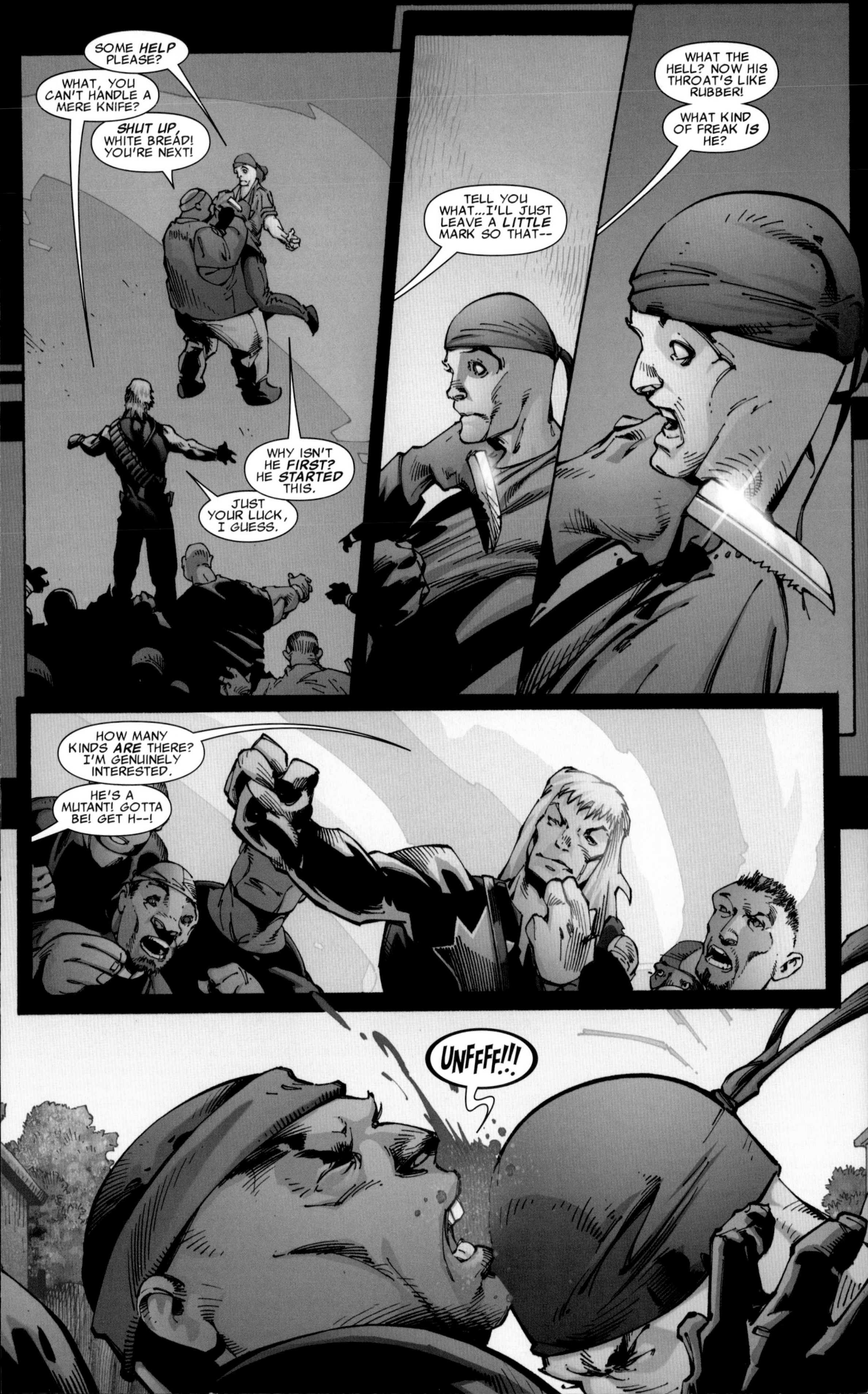
SOME HELP PLEASE?
WHAT, YOU CAN'T HANDLE A MERE KNIFE?
SHUT UP, WHITE BREAD! YOU'RE NEXT!
WHY ISN'T HE FIRST? HE STARTED THIS.
JUST YOUR LUCK, I GUESS.
TELL YOU WHAT...I'LL JUST LEAVE A LITTLE MARK SO THAT--
WHAT THE HELL? NOW HIS THROAT'S LIKE RUBBER!
WHAT KIND OF FREAK IS HE?
HOW MANY KINDS ARE THERE? I'M GENUINELY INTERESTED.
HE'S A MUTANT! GOTTA BE! GET H--!
UNFFFF!!!

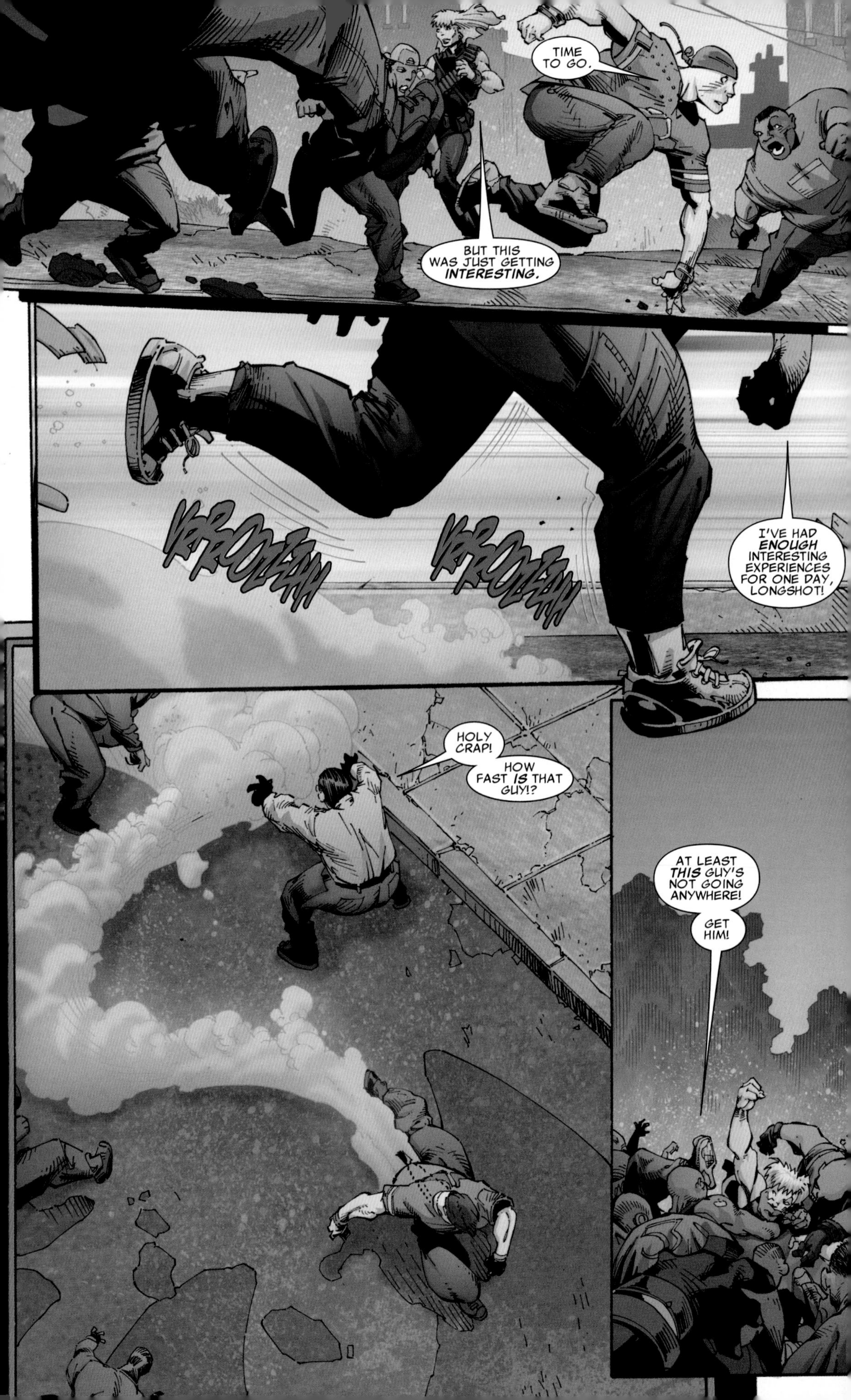
TIME TO GO.
BUT THIS WAS JUST GETTING INTERESTING.
VRROOZAM
VRROOZAM
I'VE HAD ENOUGH INTERESTING EXPERIENCES FOR ONE DAY, LONGSHOT!
HOLY CRAP!
HOW FAST IS THAT GUY!?
AT LEAST THIS GUY'S NOT GOING ANYWHERE!
GET HIM!

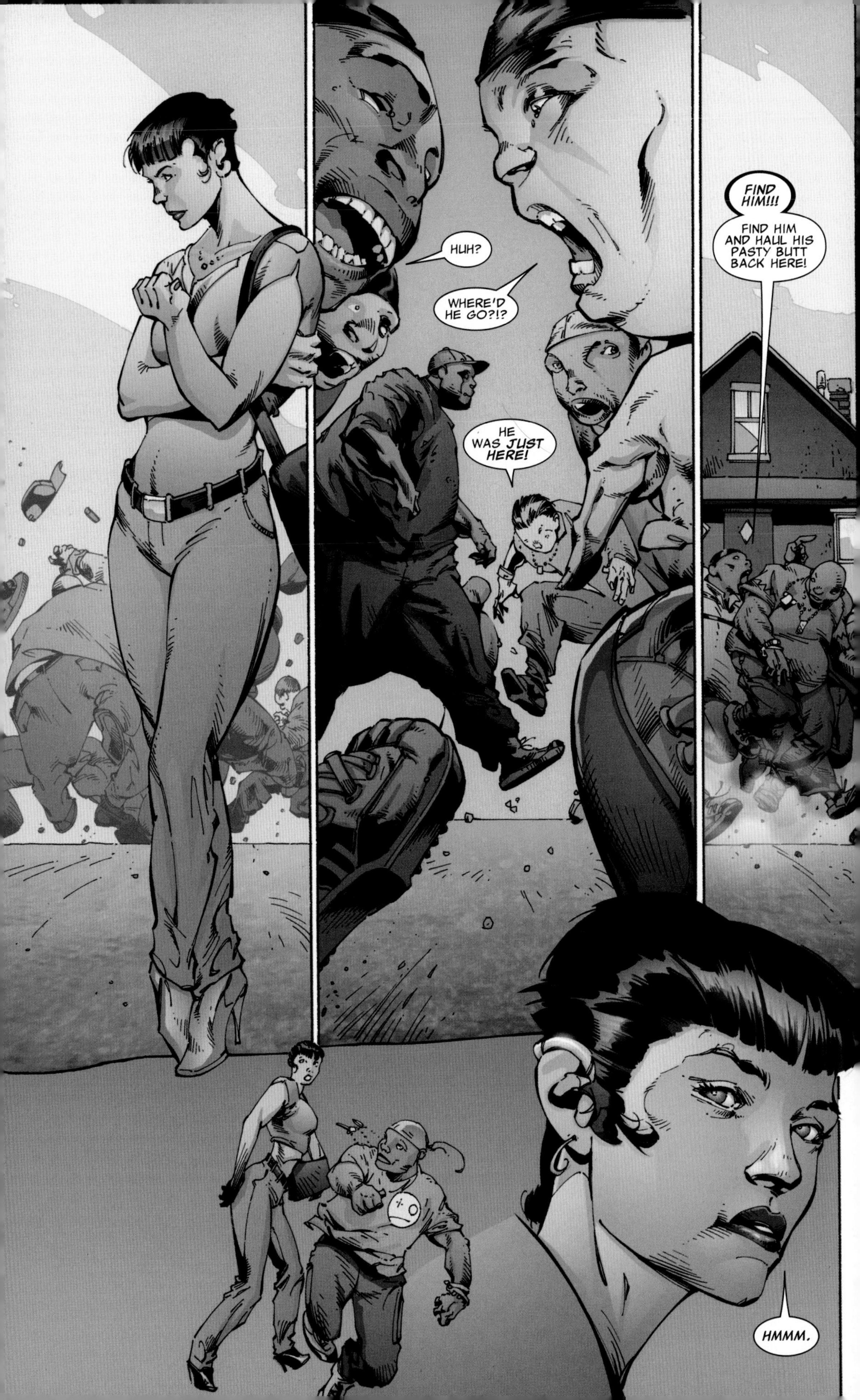
HUH?
WHERE'D HE GO?!?
HE WAS JUST HERE!
FIND HIM!!!
FIND HIM AND HAUL HIS PASTY BUTT BACK HERE!
HMMM.

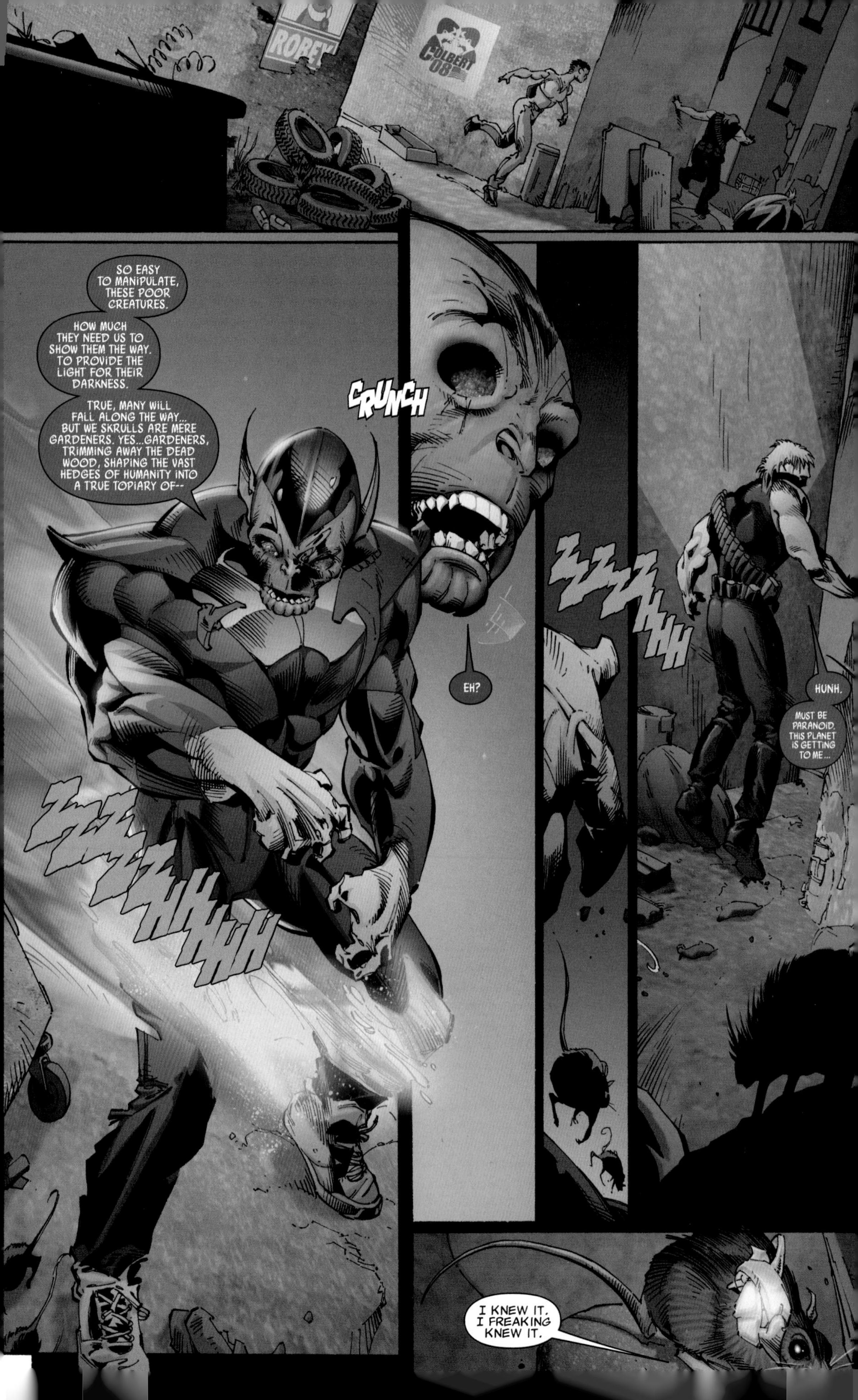
ROREY
COLBERT '08
SO EASY TO MANIPULATE, THESE POOR CREATURES.
HOW MUCH THEY NEED US TO SHOW THEM THE WAY. TO PROVIDE THE LIGHT FOR THEIR DARKNESS.
TRUE, MANY WILL FALL ALONG THE WAY... BUT WE SKRULLS ARE MERE GARDENERS. YES...GARDENERS, TRIMMING AWAY THE DEAD WOOD, SHAPING THE VAST HEDGES OF HUMANITY INTO A TRUE TOPIARY OF--
CRUNCH
ZZZZZHHHHHH
EH?
ZZZZZHHHH
HUNH.
MUST BE PARANOID. THIS PLANET IS GETTING TO ME...
I KNEW IT. I FREAKING KNEW IT.

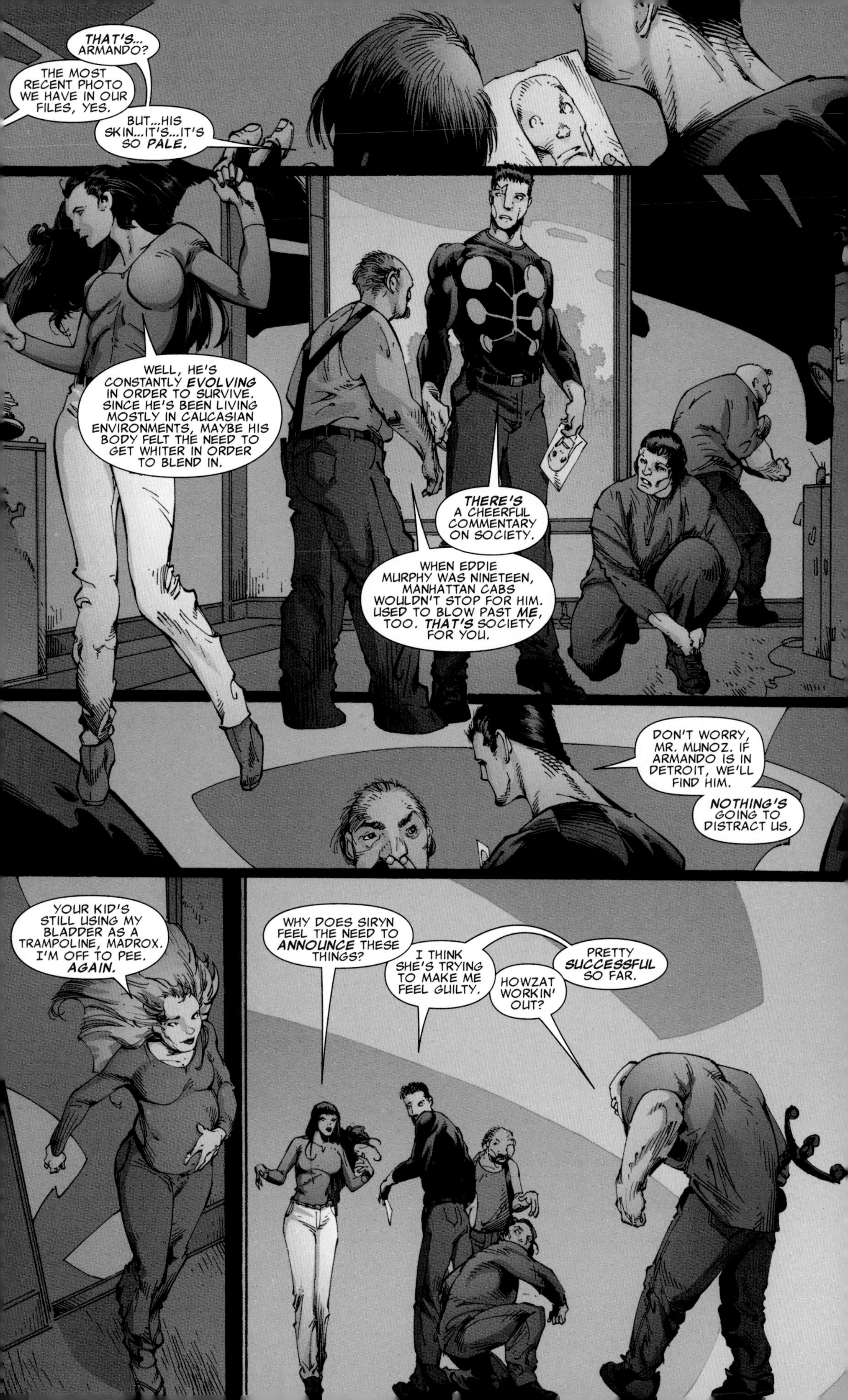
THAT'S... ARMANDO?
THE MOST RECENT PHOTO WE HAVE IN OUR FILES, YES.
BUT...HIS SKIN...IT'S...IT'S SO PALE.
WELL, HE'S CONSTANTLY EVOLVING IN ORDER TO SURVIVE. SINCE HE'S BEEN LIVING MOSTLY IN CAUCASIAN ENVIRONMENTS, MAYBE HIS BODY FELT THE NEED TO GET WHITER IN ORDER TO BLEND IN.
THERE'S A CHEERFUL COMMENTARY ON SOCIETY.
WHEN EDDIE MURPHY WAS NINETEEN, MANHATTAN CABS WOULDN'T STOP FOR HIM. USED TO BLOW PAST ME, TOO. THAT'S SOCIETY FOR YOU.
DON'T WORRY, MR. MUNOZ. IF ARMANDO IS IN DETROIT, WE'LL FIND HIM.
NOTHING'S GOING TO DISTRACT US.
YOUR KID'S STILL USING MY BLADDER AS A TRAMPOLINE, MADROX. I'M OFF TO PEE. AGAIN.
WHY DOES SIRYN FEEL THE NEED TO ANNOUNCE THESE THINGS?
I THINK SHE'S TRYING TO MAKE ME FEEL GUILTY.
PRETTY SUCCESSFUL SO FAR.
HOWZAT WORKIN' OUT?

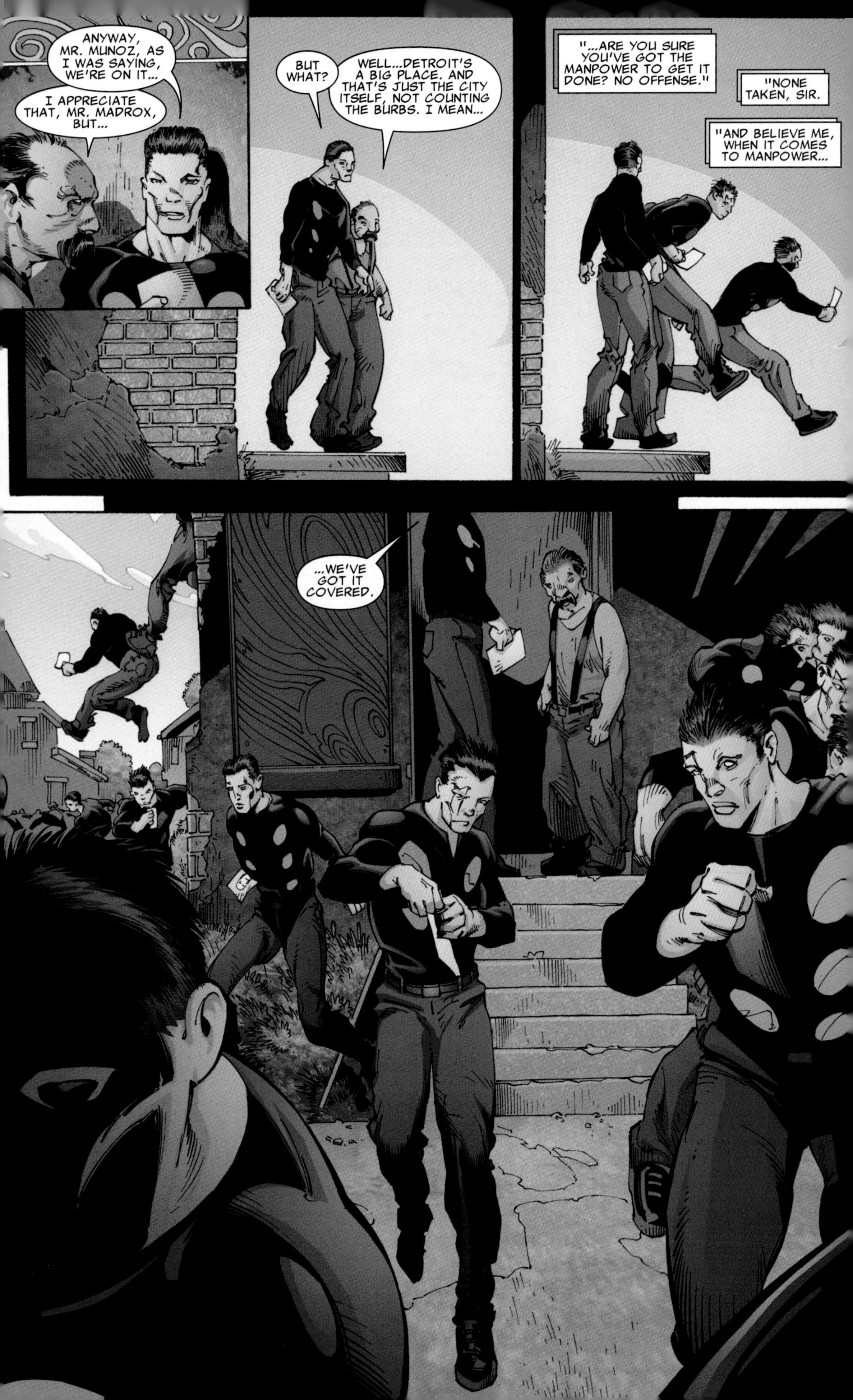
ANYWAY, MR. MUNOZ, AS I WAS SAYING, WE'RE ON IT...
I APPRECIATE THAT, MR. MADROX, BUT...
BUT WHAT?
WELL...DETROIT'S A BIG PLACE. AND THAT'S JUST THE CITY ITSELF, NOT COUNTING THE BURBS. I MEAN...
"...ARE YOU SURE YOU'VE GOT THE MANPOWER TO GET IT DONE? NO OFFENSE."
"NONE TAKEN, SIR.
"AND BELIEVE ME, WHEN IT COMES TO MANPOWER...
...WE'VE GOT IT COVERED.

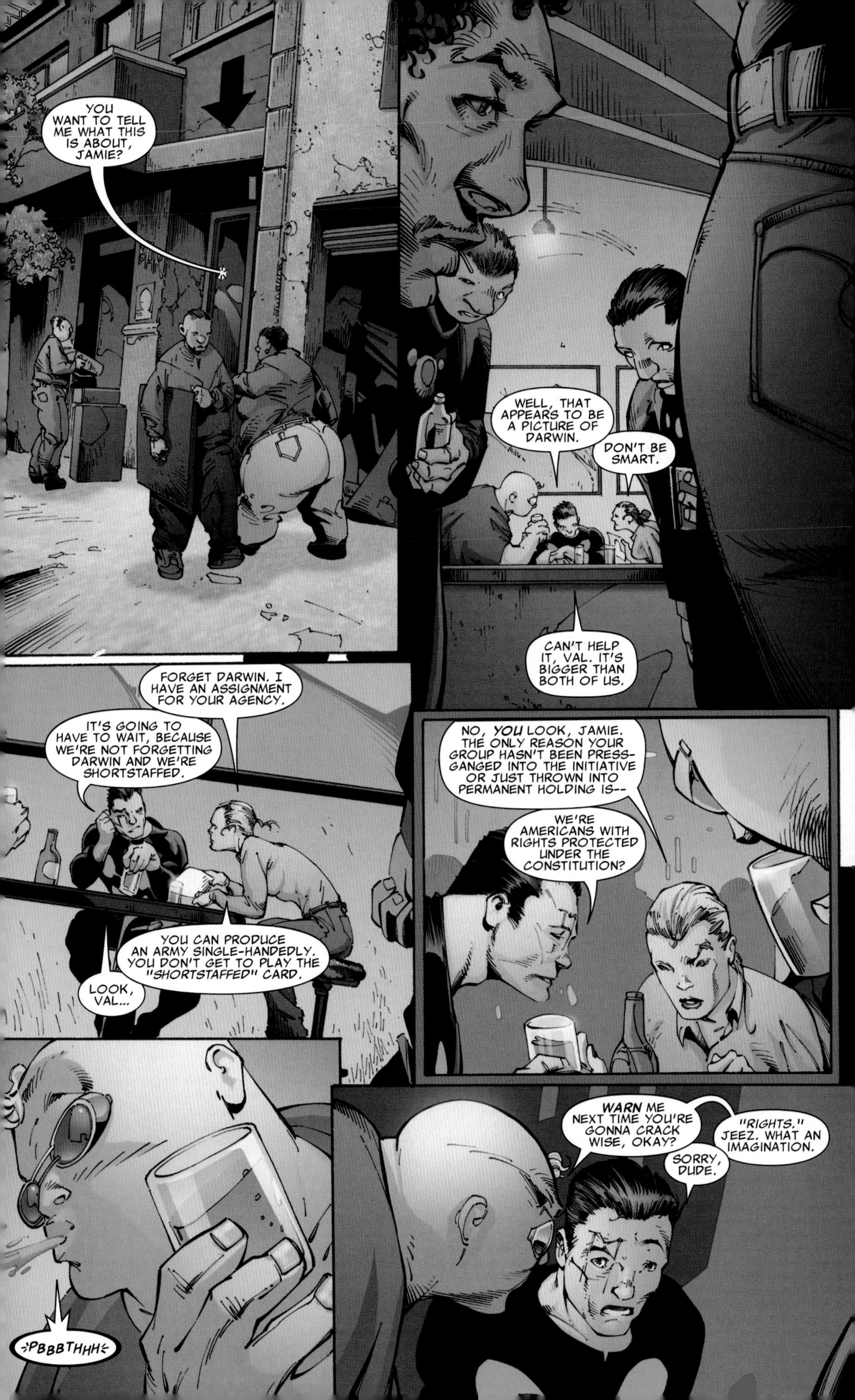

YOU WANT TO TELL ME WHAT THIS IS ABOUT, JAMIE?
WELL, THAT APPEARS TO BE A PICTURE OF DARWIN.
DON'T BE SMART.
CAN'T HELP IT, VAL. IT'S BIGGER THAN BOTH OF US.
FORGET DARWIN. I HAVE AN ASSIGNMENT FOR YOUR AGENCY.
IT'S GOING TO HAVE TO WAIT, BECAUSE WE'RE NOT FORGETTING DARWIN AND WE'RE SHORTSTAFFED.
YOU CAN PRODUCE AN ARMY SINGLE-HANDEDLY. YOU DON'T GET TO PLAY THE "SHORTSTAFFED" CARD.
LOOK, VAL...
NO, YOU LOOK, JAMIE. THE ONLY REASON YOUR GROUP HASN'T BEEN PRESS-GANGED INTO THE INITIATIVE OR JUST THROWN INTO PERMANENT HOLDING IS--
WE'RE AMERICANS WITH RIGHTS PROTECTED UNDER THE CONSTITUTION?
PBBBTHHH
WARN ME NEXT TIME YOU'RE GONNA CRACK WISE, OKAY?
SORRY, DUDE.
"RIGHTS." JEEZ. WHAT AN IMAGINATION.

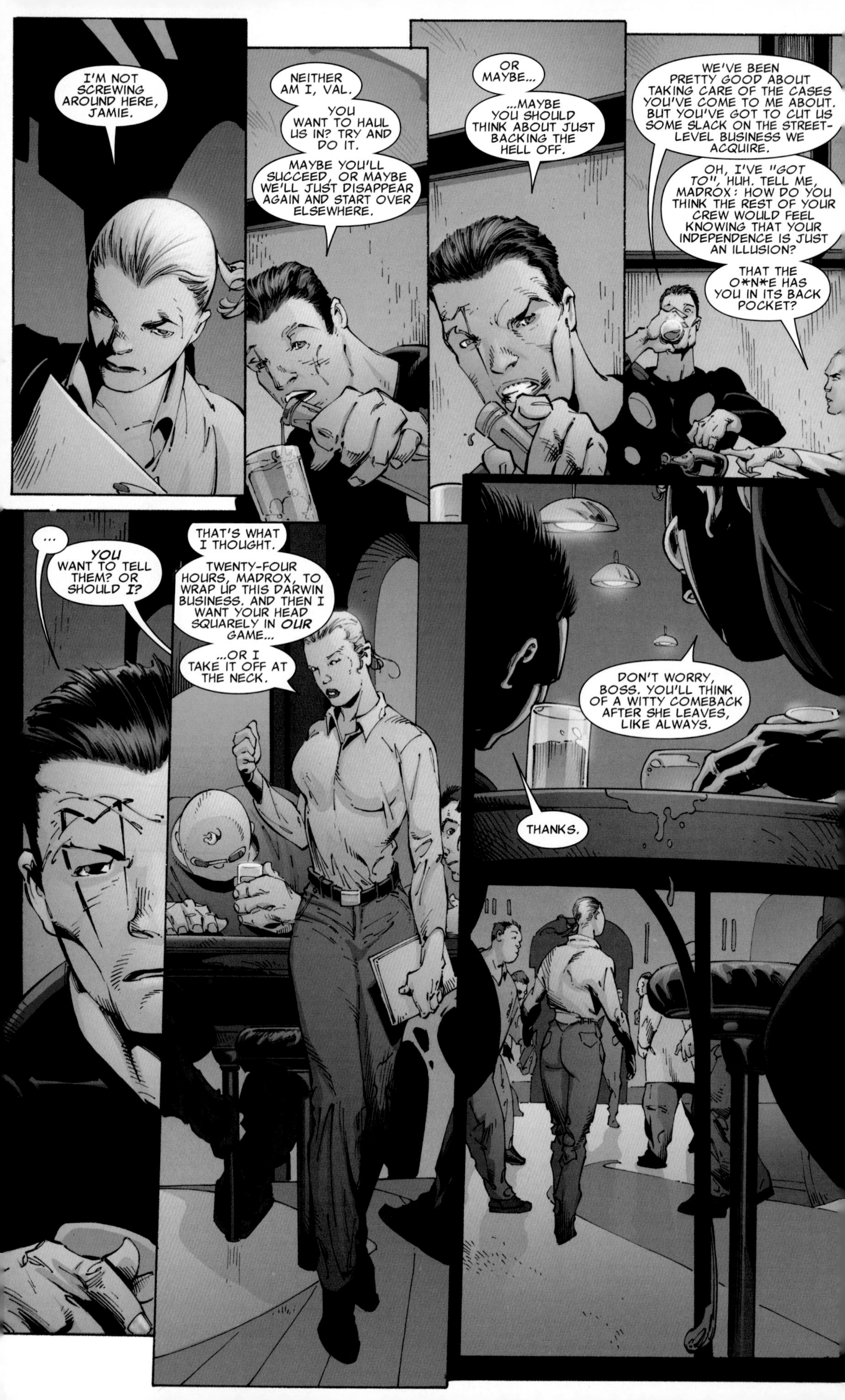
I'M NOT SCREWING AROUND HERE, JAMIE.
NEITHER AM I, VAL.
YOU WANT TO HAUL US IN? TRY AND DO IT.
MAYBE YOU'LL SUCCEED, OR MAYBE WE'LL JUST DISAPPEAR AGAIN AND START OVER ELSEWHERE.
OR MAYBE...
...MAYBE YOU SHOULD THINK ABOUT JUST BACKING THE HELL OFF.
WE'VE BEEN PRETTY GOOD ABOUT TAKING CARE OF THE CASES YOU'VE COME TO ME ABOUT. BUT YOU'VE GOT TO CUT US SOME SLACK ON THE STREET-LEVEL BUSINESS WE ACQUIRE.
OH, I'VE "GOT TO", HUH. TELL ME, MADROX: HOW DO YOU THINK THE REST OF YOUR CREW WOULD FEEL KNOWING THAT YOUR INDEPENDENCE IS JUST AN ILLUSION?
THAT THE O*N*E HAS YOU IN ITS BACK POCKET?
...
YOU WANT TO TELL THEM? OR SHOULD I?
THAT'S WHAT I THOUGHT.
TWENTY-FOUR HOURS, MADROX, TO WRAP UP THIS DARWIN BUSINESS. AND THEN I WANT YOUR HEAD SQUARELY IN OUR GAME...
...OR I TAKE IT OFF AT THE NECK.
DON'T WORRY, BOSS. YOU'LL THINK OF A WITTY COMEBACK AFTER SHE LEAVES, LIKE ALWAYS.
THANKS.

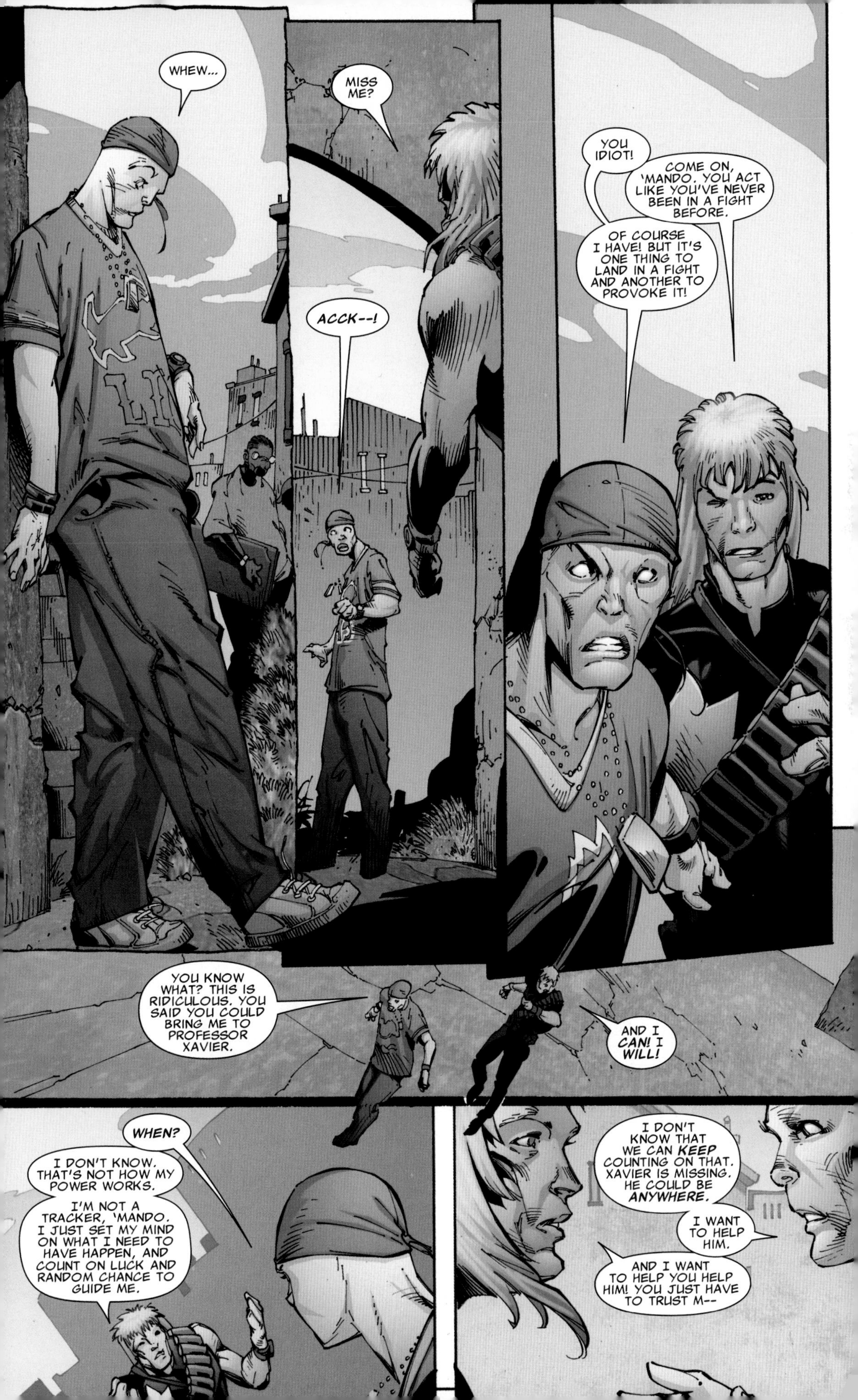
WHEW...
MISS ME?
ACCK--!
YOU IDIOT!
COME ON, 'MANDO. YOU ACT LIKE YOU'VE NEVER BEEN IN A FIGHT BEFORE.
OF COURSE I HAVE! BUT IT'S ONE THING TO LAND IN A FIGHT AND ANOTHER TO PROVOKE IT!
YOU KNOW WHAT? THIS IS RIDICULOUS. YOU SAID YOU COULD BRING ME TO PROFESSOR XAVIER.
AND I CAN! I WILL!
WHEN?
I DON'T KNOW. THAT'S NOT HOW MY POWER WORKS.
I'M NOT A TRACKER, 'MANDO. I JUST SET MY MIND ON WHAT I NEED TO HAVE HAPPEN, AND COUNT ON LUCK AND RANDOM CHANCE TO GUIDE ME.
I DON'T KNOW THAT WE CAN KEEP COUNTING ON THAT. XAVIER IS MISSING. HE COULD BE ANYWHERE.
I WANT TO HELP HIM.
AND I WANT TO HELP YOU HELP HIM! YOU JUST HAVE TO TRUST M--

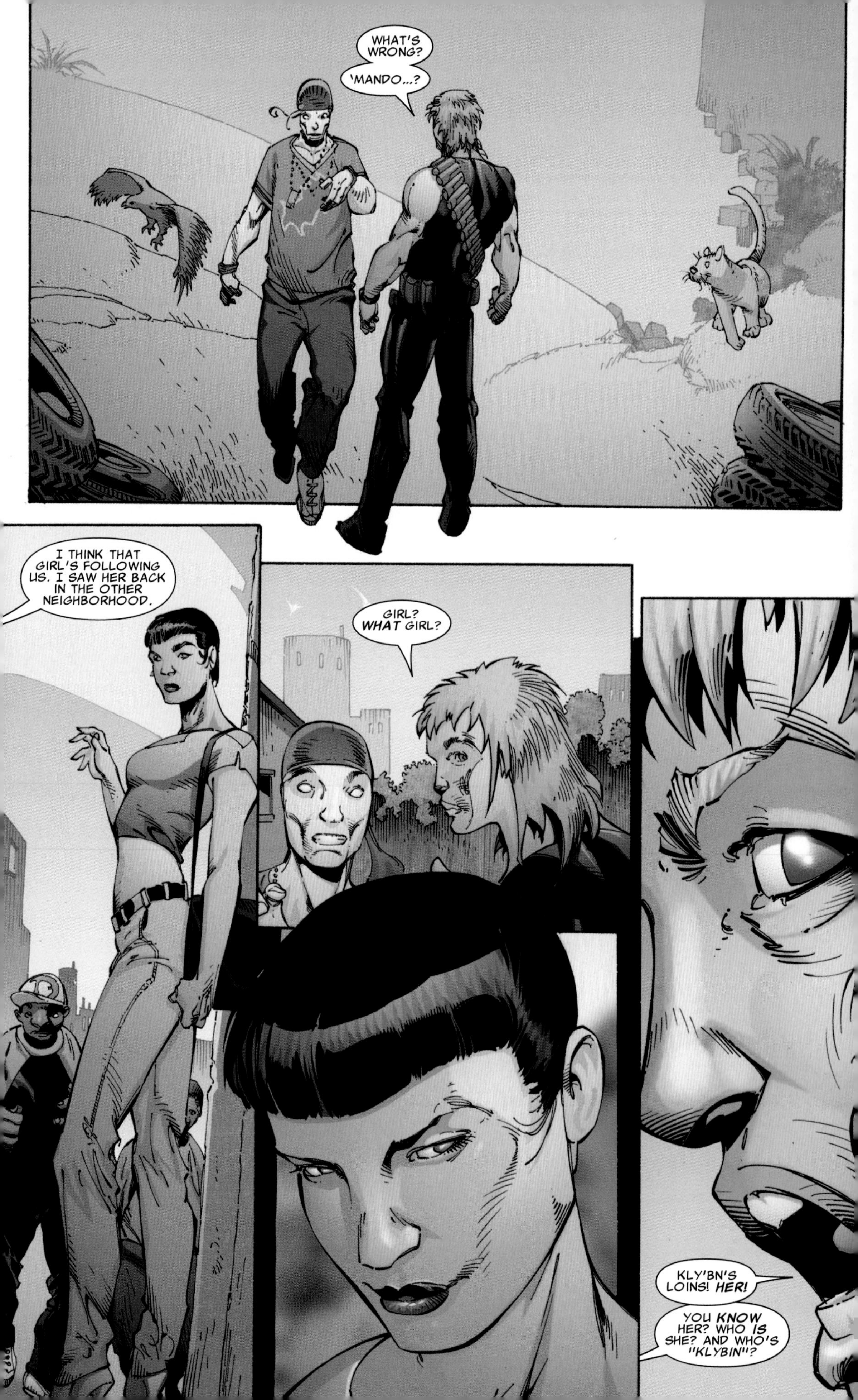
WHAT'S WRONG?
'MANDO...?
I THINK THAT GIRL'S FOLLOWING US. I SAW HER BACK IN THE OTHER NEIGHBORHOOD.
GIRL? WHAT GIRL?
KLY'BN'S LOINS! HER!
YOU KNOW HER? WHO IS SHE? AND WHO'S "KLYBIN"?

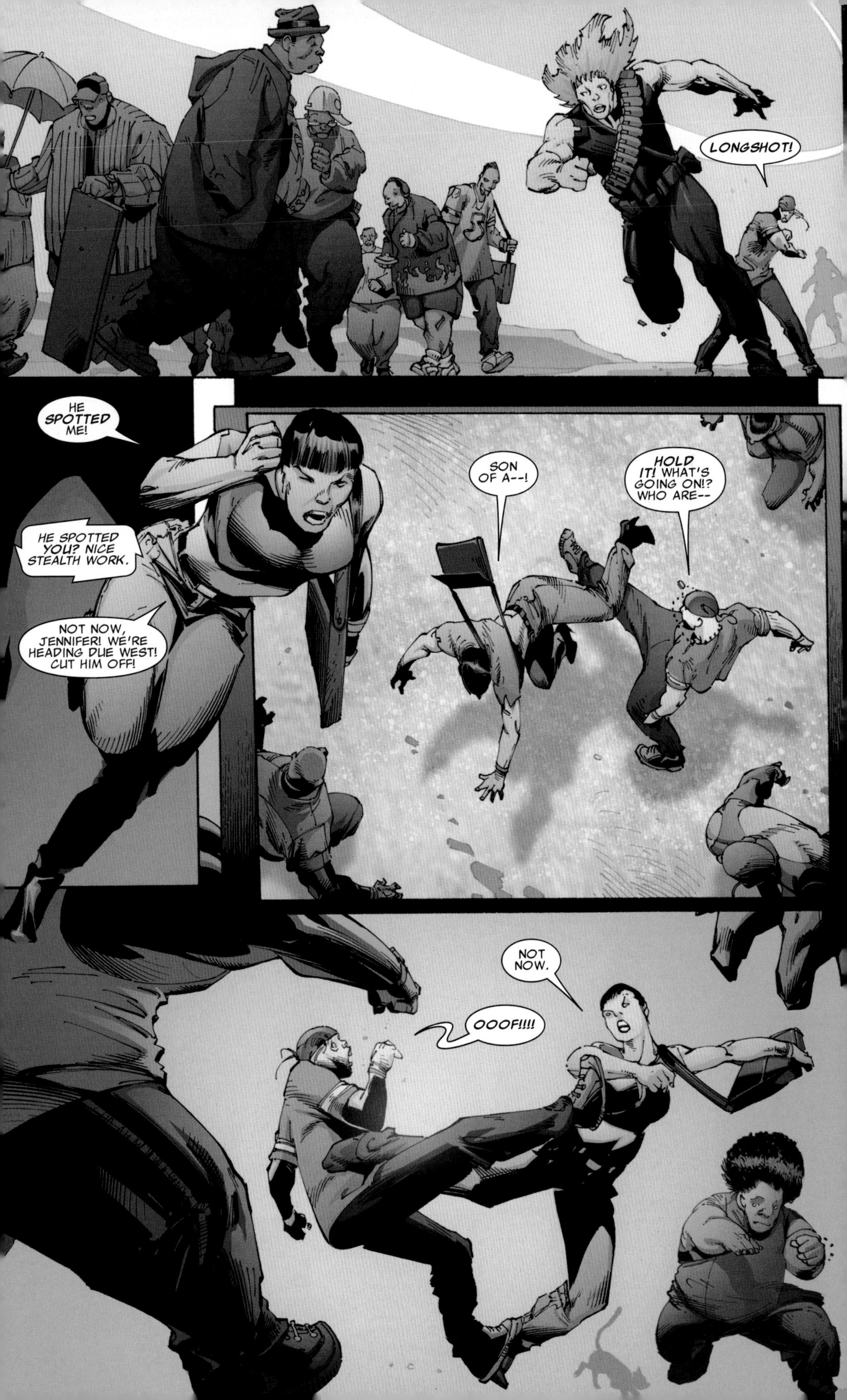
LONGSHOT!
HE SPOTTED ME!
HE SPOTTED YOU? NICE STEALTH WORK.
NOT NOW, JENNIFER! WE'RE HEADING DUE WEST! CUT HIM OFF!
SON OF A--!
HOLD IT! WHAT'S GOING ON!? WHO ARE--
NOT NOW.
OOOF!!!!

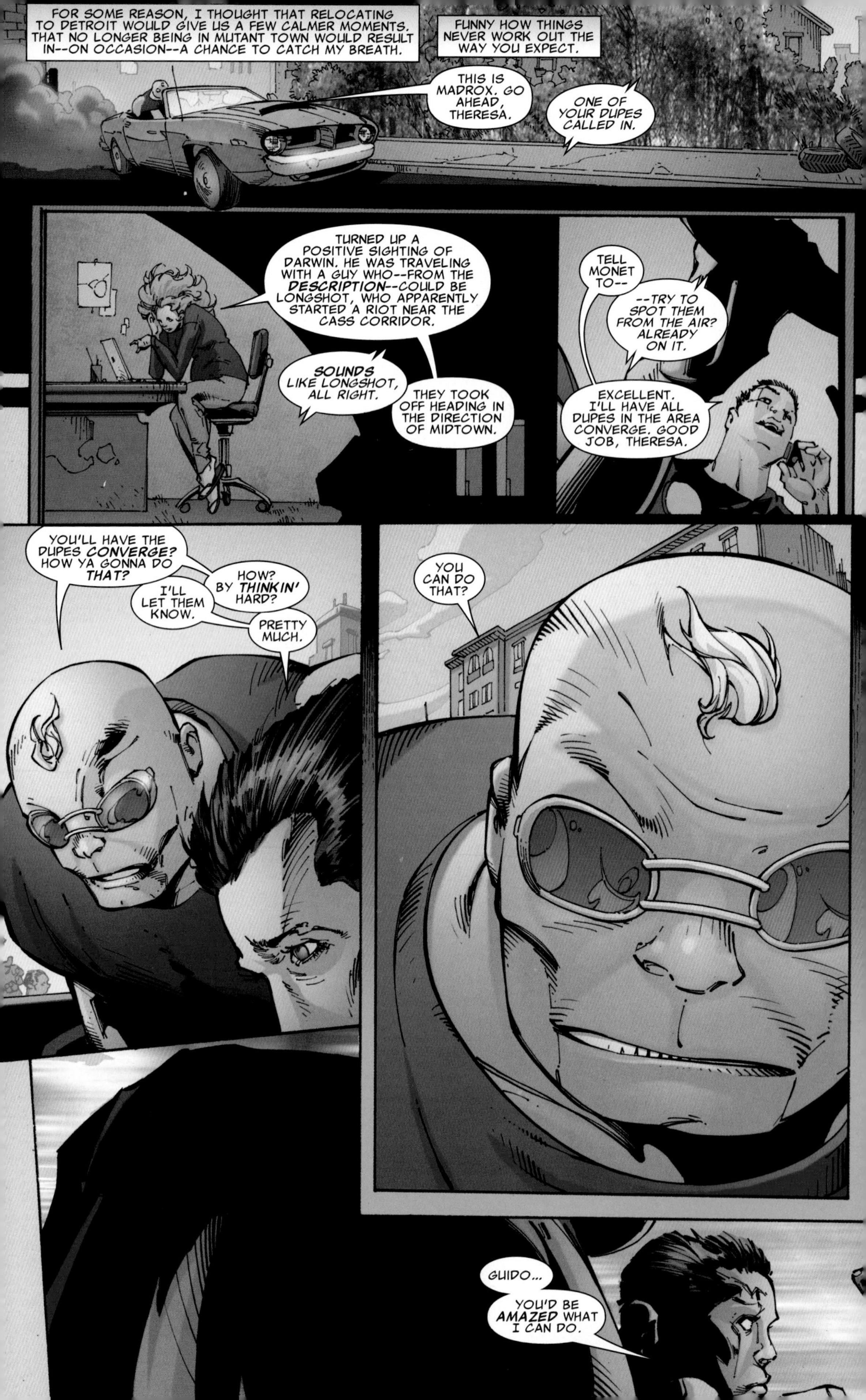
FOR SOME REASON, I THOUGHT THAT RELOCATING TO DETROIT WOULD GIVE US A FEW CALMER MOMENTS. THAT NO LONGER BEING IN MUTANT TOWN WOULD RESULT IN--ON OCCASION--A CHANCE TO CATCH MY BREATH.
FUNNY HOW THINGS NEVER WORK OUT THE WAY YOU EXPECT.
THIS IS MADROX. GO AHEAD, THERESA.
ONE OF YOUR DUPES CALLED IN.
TURNED UP A POSITIVE SIGHTING OF DARWIN. HE WAS TRAVELING WITH A GUY WHO--FROM THE DESCRIPTION--COULD BE LONGSHOT, WHO APPARENTLY STARTED A RIOT NEAR THE CASS CORRIDOR.
SOUNDS LIKE LONGSHOT, ALL RIGHT.
THEY TOOK OFF HEADING IN THE DIRECTION OF MIDTOWN.
TELL MONET TO--
--TRY TO SPOT THEM FROM THE AIR? ALREADY ON IT.
EXCELLENT. I'LL HAVE ALL DUPES IN THE AREA CONVERGE. GOOD JOB, THERESA.
YOU'LL HAVE THE DUPES CONVERGE? HOW YA GONNA DO THAT?
HOW? BY THINKIN' HARD?
I'LL LET THEM KNOW.
PRETTY MUCH.
YOU CAN DO THAT?
GUIDO...
YOU'D BE AMAZED WHAT I CAN DO.

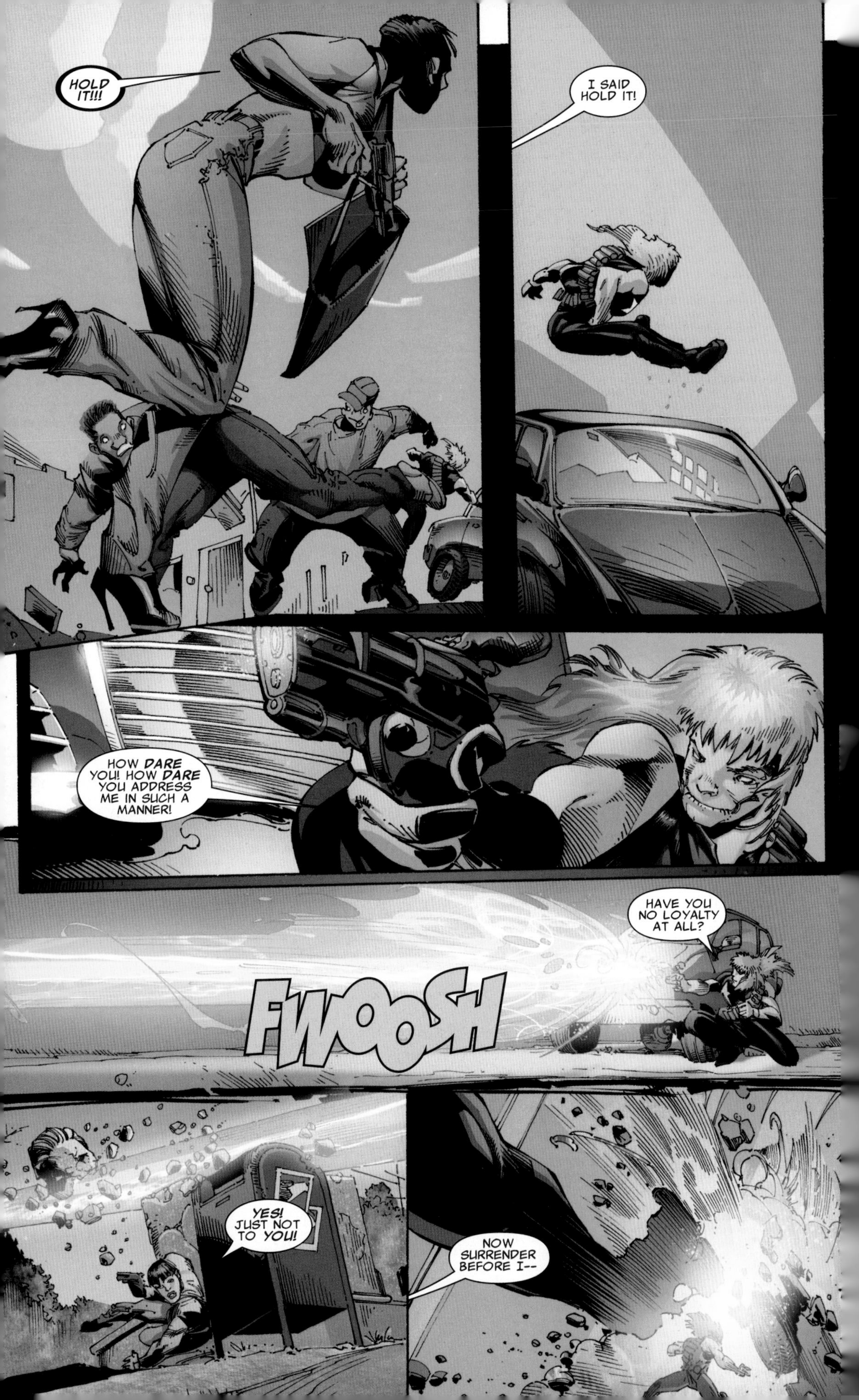
HOLD IT!!!
I SAID HOLD IT!
HOW DARE YOU! HOW DARE YOU ADDRESS ME IN SUCH A MANNER!
HAVE YOU NO LOYALTY AT ALL?
FWOOSH
YES! JUST NOT TO YOU!
NOW SURRENDER BEFORE I--

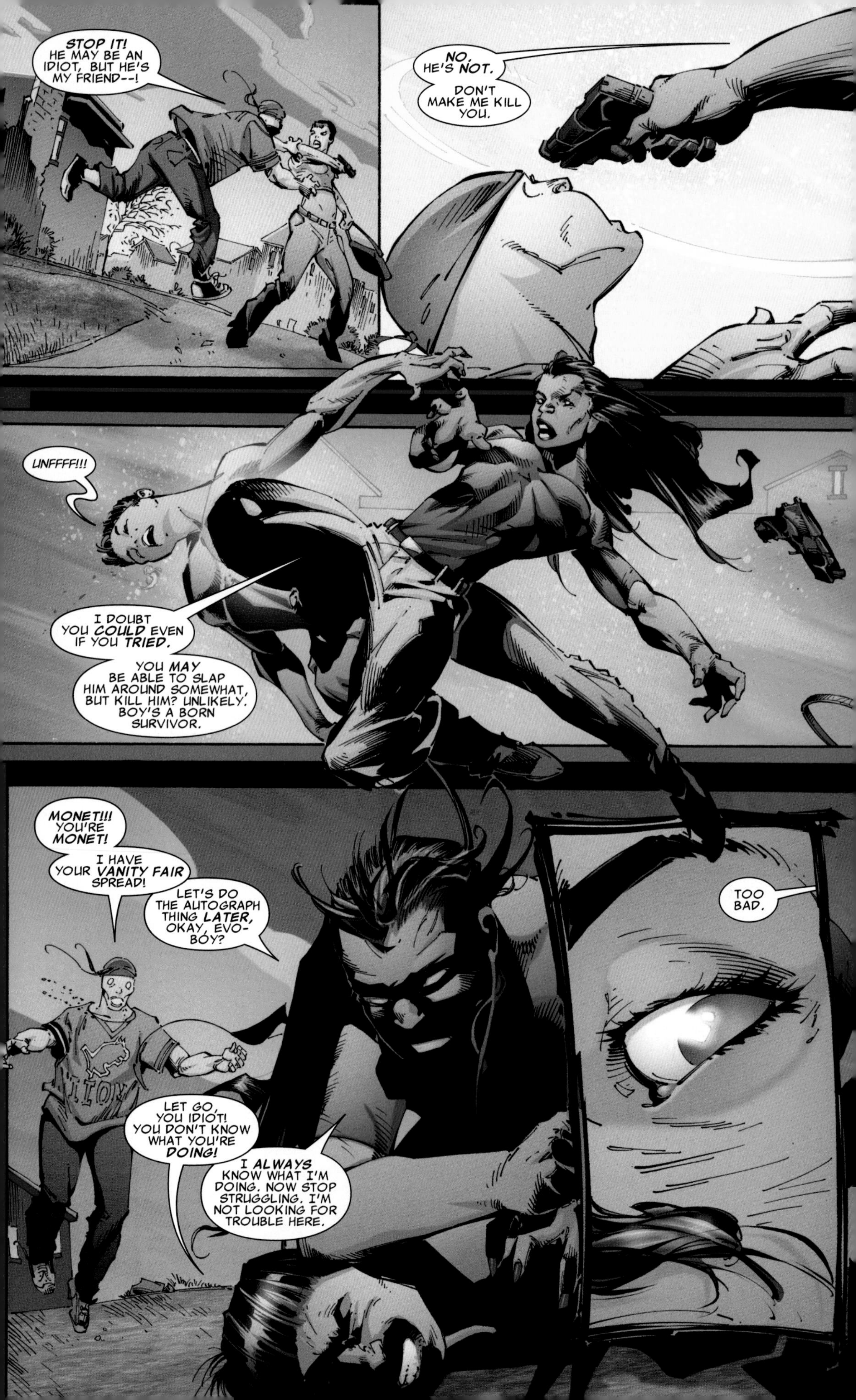
STOP IT! HE MAY BE AN IDIOT, BUT HE'S MY FRIEND--!
NO, HE'S NOT.
DON'T MAKE ME KILL YOU.
UNFFFF!!!
I DOUBT YOU COULD EVEN IF YOU TRIED.
YOU MAY BE ABLE TO SLAP HIM AROUND SOMEWHAT, BUT KILL HIM? UNLIKELY. BOY'S A BORN SURVIVOR.
MONET!!! YOU'RE MONET!
I HAVE YOUR VANITY FAIR SPREAD!
LET'S DO THE AUTOGRAPH THING LATER, OKAY, EVO-BOY?
TOO BAD.
LET GO, YOU IDIOT! YOU DON'T KNOW WHAT YOU'RE DOING!
I ALWAYS KNOW WHAT I'M DOING. NOW STOP STRUGGLING. I'M NOT LOOKING FOR TROUBLE HERE.

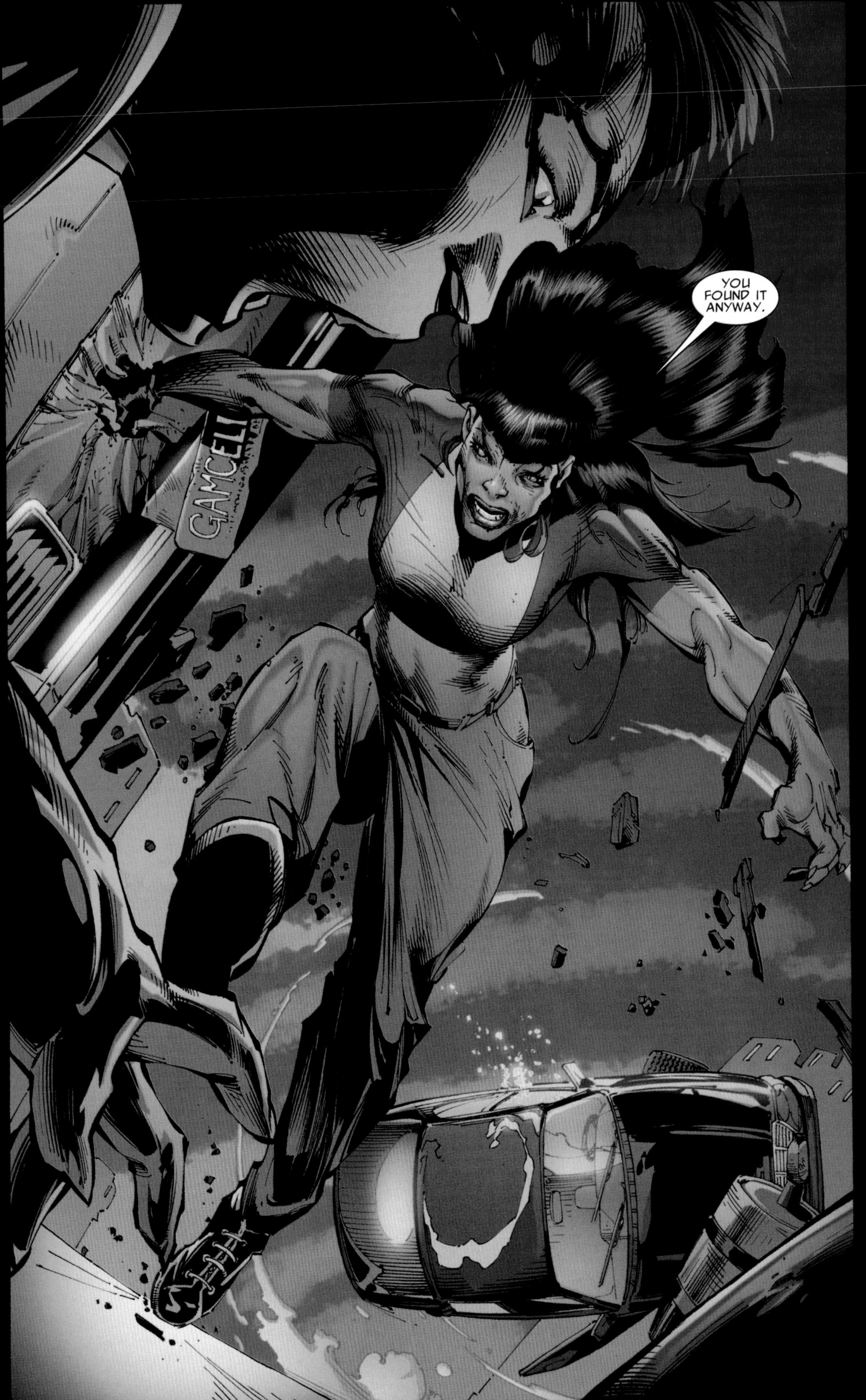
YOU FOUND IT ANYWAY.
GAMCELLI

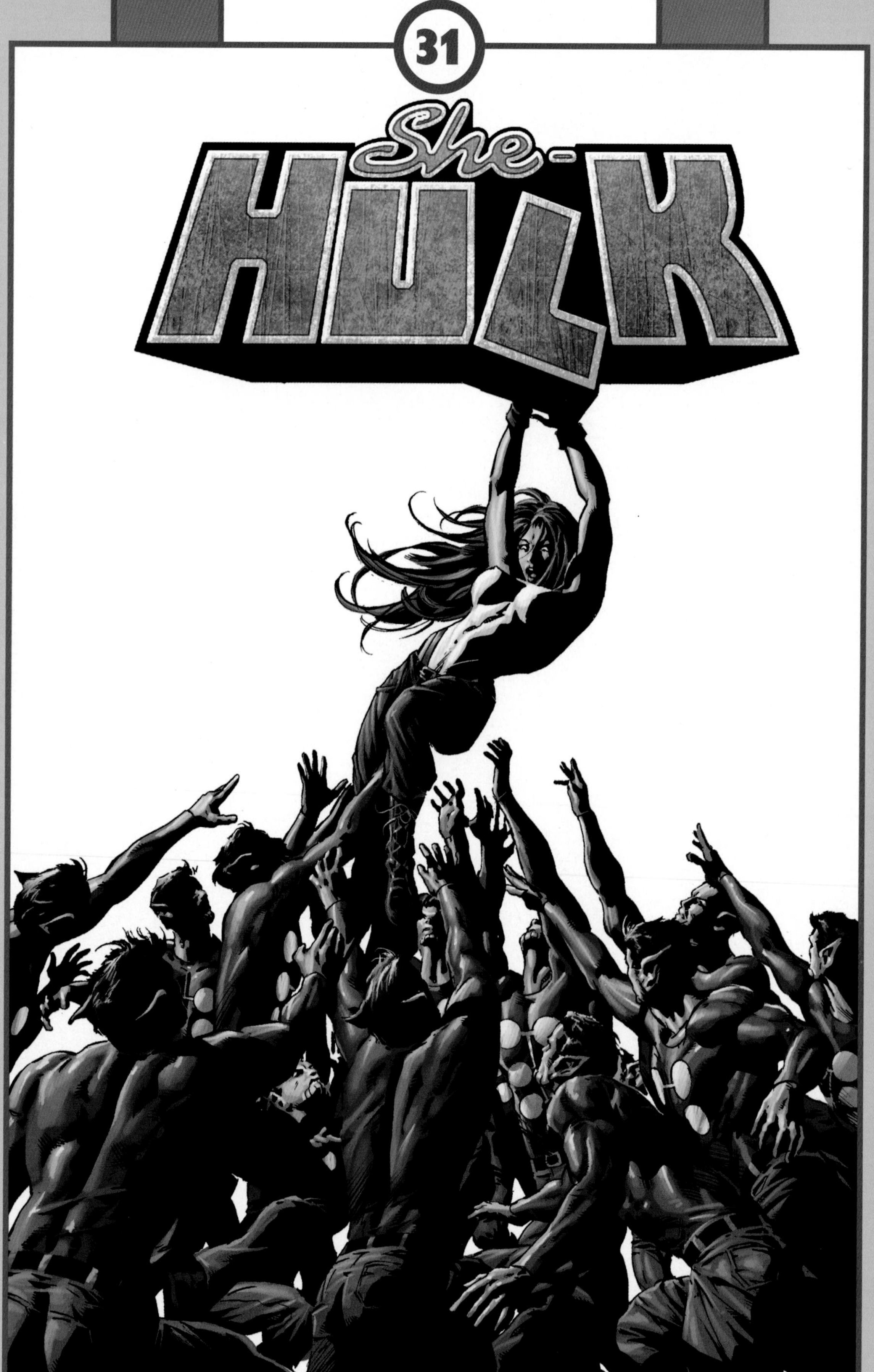
31
She-Hulk

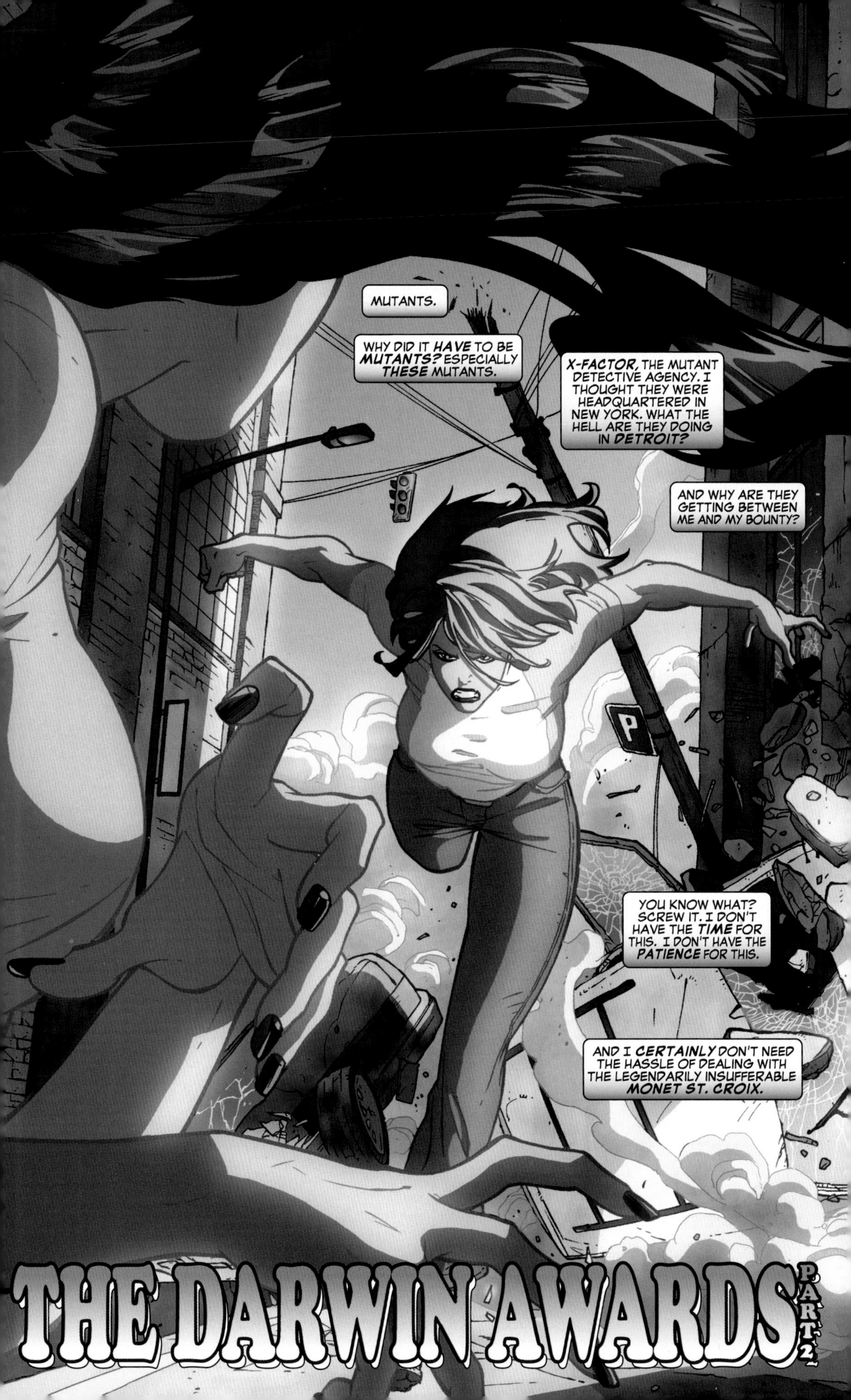
MUTANTS.
WHY DID IT HAVE TO BE MUTANTS? ESPECIALLY THESE MUTANTS.
X-FACTOR, THE MUTANT DETECTIVE AGENCY. I THOUGHT THEY WERE HEADQUARTERED IN NEW YORK. WHAT THE HELL ARE THEY DOING IN DETROIT?
AND WHY ARE THEY GETTING BETWEEN ME AND MY BOUNTY?
P
YOU KNOW WHAT? SCREW IT. I DON'T HAVE THE TIME FOR THIS. I DON'T HAVE THE PATIENCE FOR THIS.
AND I CERTAINLY DON'T NEED THE HASSLE OF DEALING WITH THE LEGENDARILY INSUFFERABLE MONET ST. CROIX.
THE DARWIN AWARDS PART 2

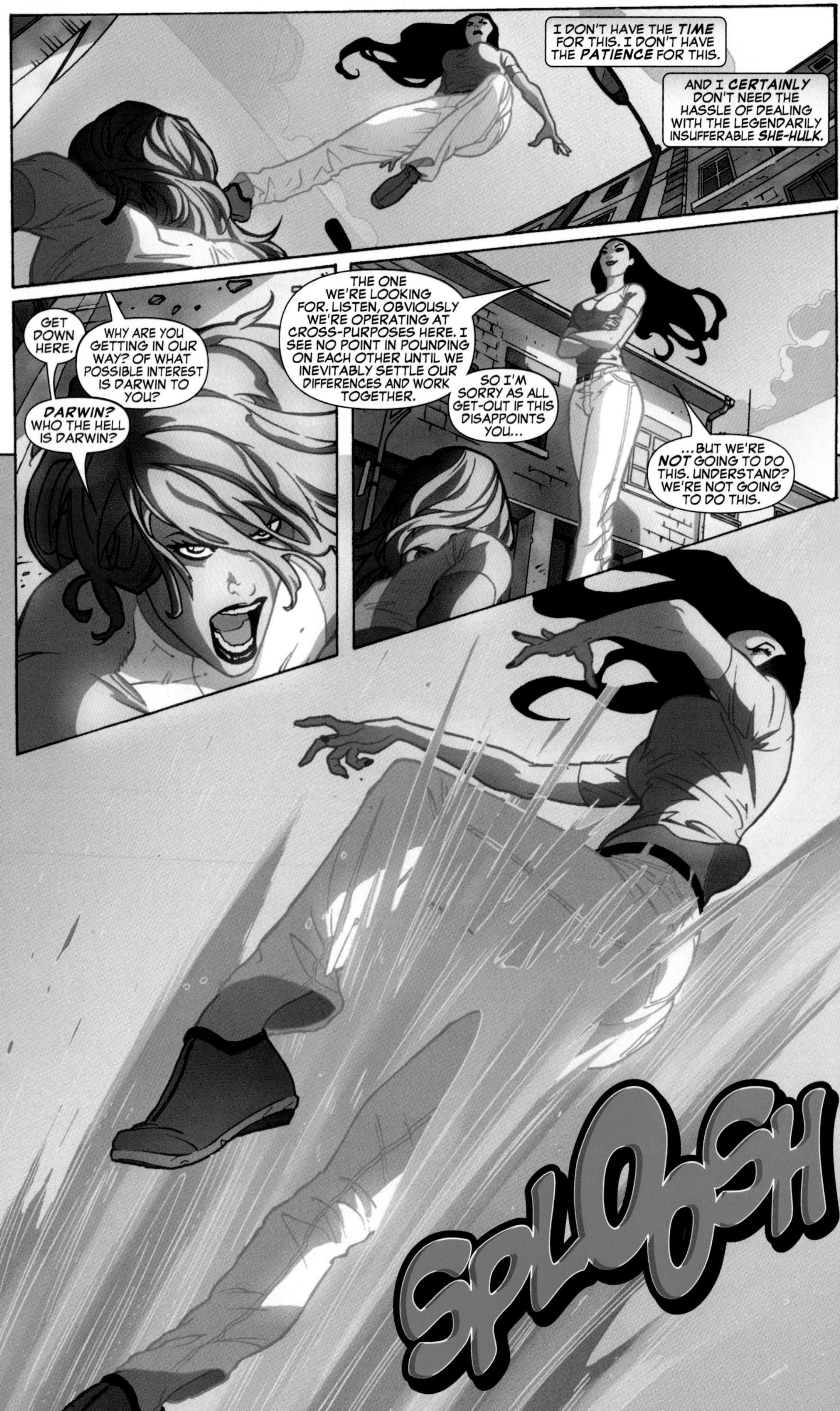
I DON'T HAVE THE *TIME* FOR THIS. I DON'T HAVE THE *PATIENCE* FOR THIS.
AND I *CERTAINLY* DON'T NEED THE HASSLE OF DEALING WITH THE LEGENDARILY INSUFFERABLE *SHE-HULK.*
GET DOWN HERE.
WHY ARE YOU GETTING IN OUR WAY? OF WHAT POSSIBLE INTEREST IS DARWIN TO YOU?
DARWIN? WHO THE HELL IS DARWIN?
THE ONE WE'RE LOOKING FOR. LISTEN, OBVIOUSLY WE'RE OPERATING AT CROSS-PURPOSES HERE. I SEE NO POINT IN POUNDING ON EACH OTHER UNTIL WE INEVITABLY SETTLE OUR DIFFERENCES AND WORK TOGETHER.
SO I'M SORRY AS ALL GET-OUT IF THIS DISAPPOINTS YOU...
...BUT WE'RE *NOT* GOING TO DO THIS. UNDERSTAND? WE'RE NOT GOING TO DO THIS.
SPLOOOSH

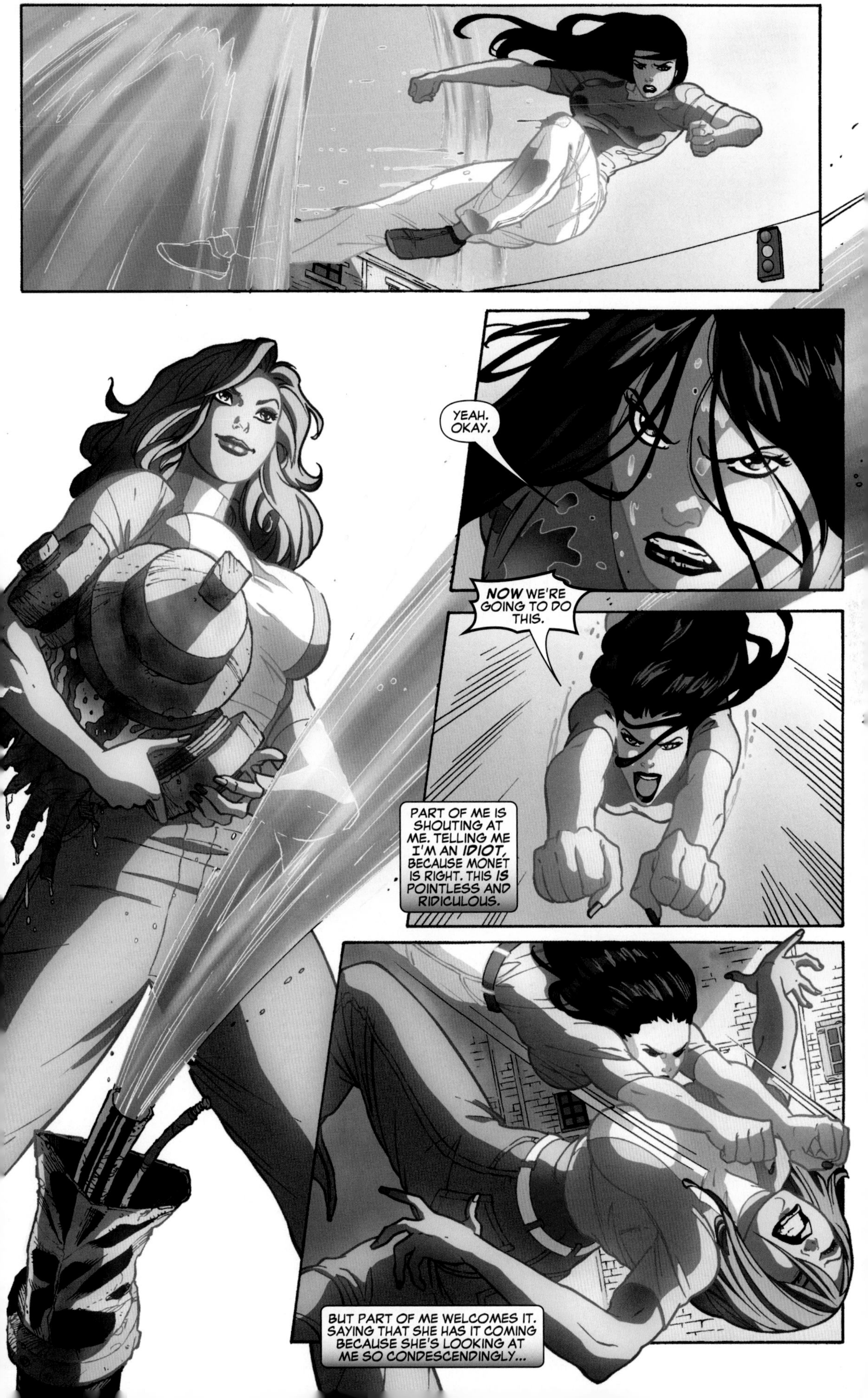
YEAH. OKAY.
NOW WE'RE GOING TO DO THIS.
PART OF ME IS SHOUTING AT ME. TELLING ME I'M AN IDIOT, BECAUSE MONET IS RIGHT. THIS IS POINTLESS AND RIDICULOUS.
BUT PART OF ME WELCOMES IT. SAYING THAT SHE HAS IT COMING BECAUSE SHE'S LOOKING AT ME SO CONDESCENDINGLY...

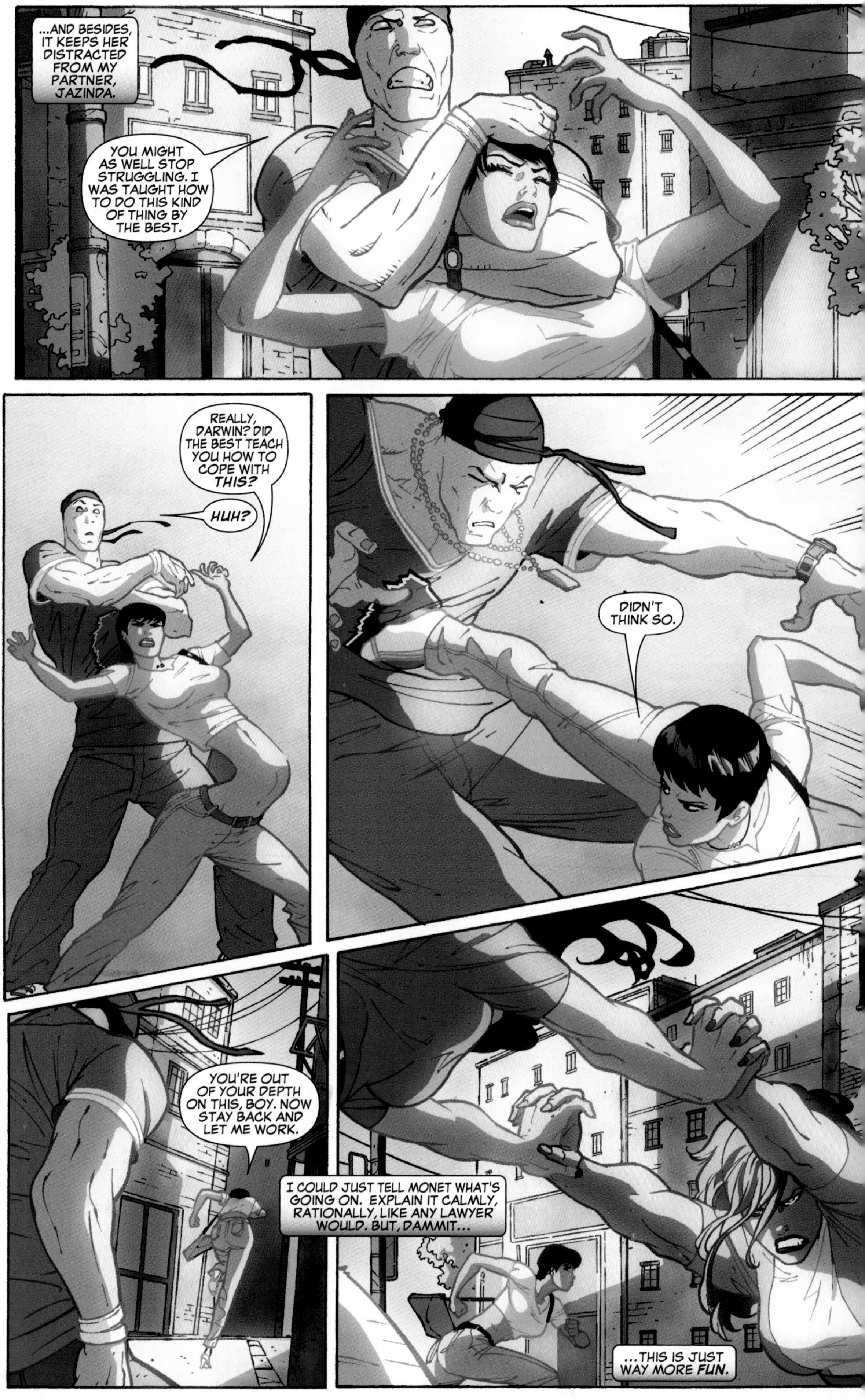
...AND BESIDES, IT KEEPS HER DISTRACTED FROM MY PARTNER, JAZINDA.
YOU MIGHT AS WELL STOP STRUGGLING. I WAS TAUGHT HOW TO DO THIS KIND OF THING BY THE BEST.
REALLY, DARWIN? DID THE BEST TEACH YOU HOW TO COPE WITH THIS?
HUH?
DIDN'T THINK SO.
YOU'RE OUT OF YOUR DEPTH ON THIS, BOY. NOW STAY BACK AND LET ME WORK.
I COULD JUST TELL MONET WHAT'S GOING ON. EXPLAIN IT CALMLY, RATIONALLY, LIKE ANY LAWYER WOULD. BUT, DAMMIT...
...THIS IS JUST WAY MORE FUN.

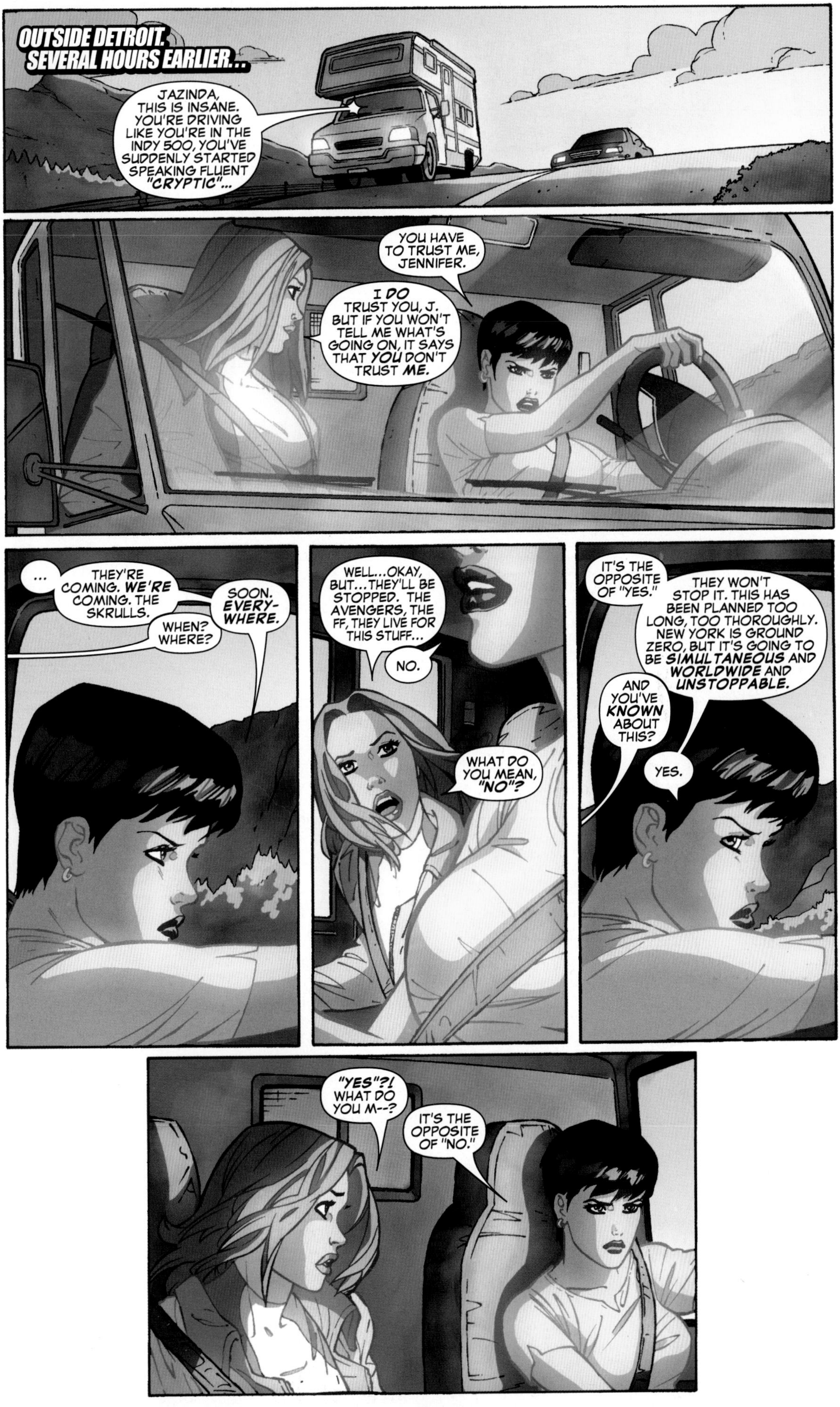
OUTSIDE DETROIT. SEVERAL HOURS EARLIER...
JAZINDA, THIS IS INSANE. YOU'RE DRIVING LIKE YOU'RE IN THE INDY 500, YOU'VE SUDDENLY STARTED SPEAKING FLUENT "CRYPTIC"...
YOU HAVE TO TRUST ME, JENNIFER.
I DO TRUST YOU, J. BUT IF YOU WON'T TELL ME WHAT'S GOING ON, IT SAYS THAT YOU DON'T TRUST ME.
...
THEY'RE COMING. WE'RE COMING. THE SKRULLS.
WHEN? WHERE?
SOON. EVERY-WHERE.
WELL...OKAY, BUT...THEY'LL BE STOPPED. THE AVENGERS, THE FF, THEY LIVE FOR THIS STUFF...
NO.
WHAT DO YOU MEAN, "NO"?
IT'S THE OPPOSITE OF "YES."
THEY WON'T STOP IT. THIS HAS BEEN PLANNED TOO LONG, TOO THOROUGHLY. NEW YORK IS GROUND ZERO, BUT IT'S GOING TO BE SIMULTANEOUS AND WORLDWIDE AND UNSTOPPABLE.
AND YOU'VE KNOWN ABOUT THIS?
YES.
"YES"?! WHAT DO YOU M--?
IT'S THE OPPOSITE OF "NO."

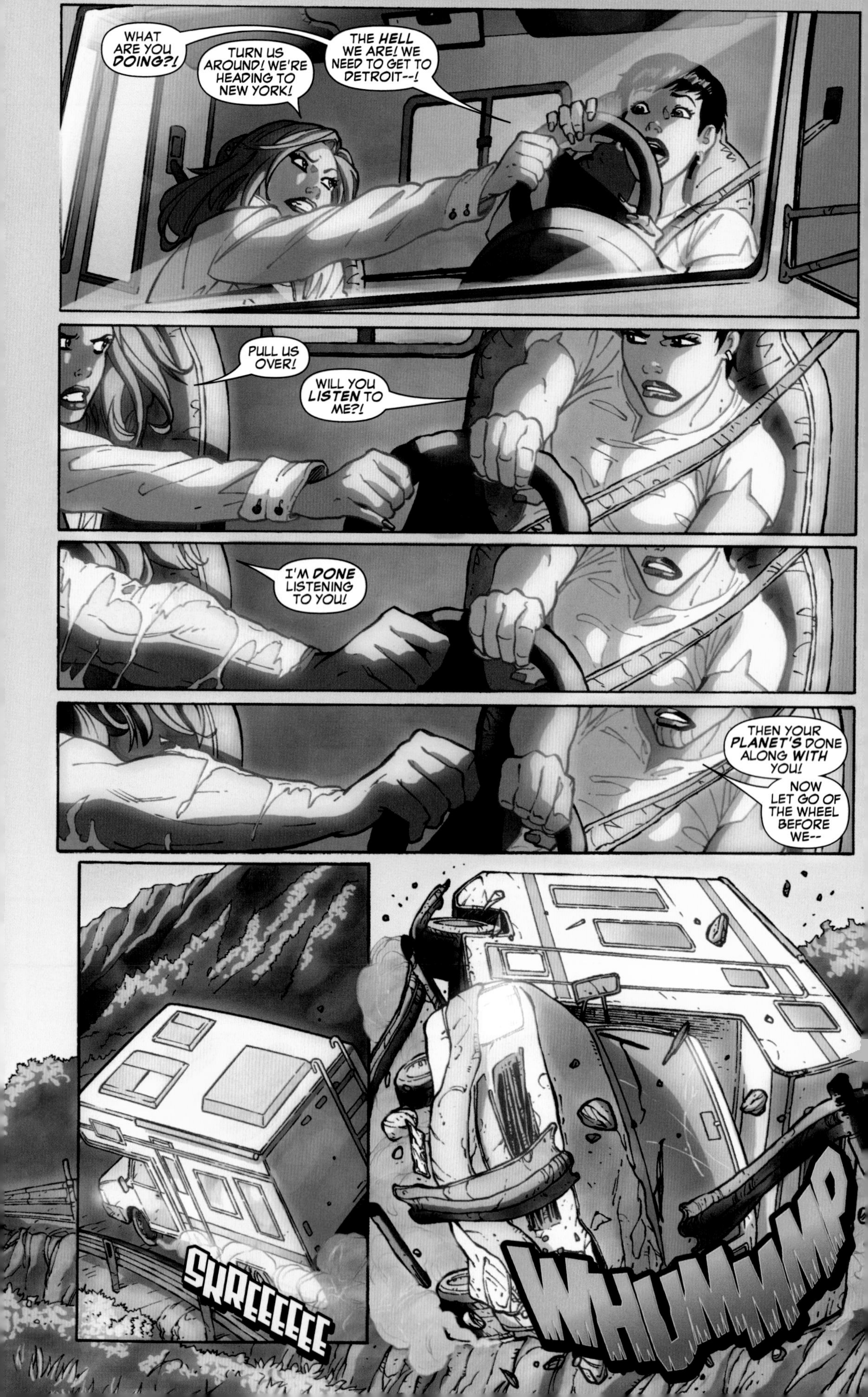
WHAT ARE YOU DOING?!
TURN US AROUND! WE'RE HEADING TO NEW YORK!
THE HELL WE ARE! WE NEED TO GET TO DETROIT--!
PULL US OVER!
WILL YOU LISTEN TO ME?!
I'M DONE LISTENING TO YOU!
THEN YOUR PLANET'S DONE ALONG WITH YOU!
NOW LET GO OF THE WHEEL BEFORE WE--
SKREEEEEEE
WHUMMMP

TERRIFIC.
I HOPE YOU'RE HAPPY, JENNI--

OOOOOOOF!

HOW DARE YOU!

YOU ACT LIKE MY *FRIEND* AND THEN YOU *KEEP* THIS FROM ME!

I *AM* YOUR FRIEND, YOU IDIOT.

YEAH? OKAY, HERE'S A COUPLE OF GUIDELINES TO BEING A FRIEND...

ONE: FRIENDS DON'T LET OTHER FRIENDS DRIVE DRUNK.

TWO: FRIENDS GIVE YOU A HEADS UP WHEN *ALIENS* ARE ABOUT TO TURN YOUR PLANET INTO A REAL-LIFE VERSION OF "SPACE INVADERS"!

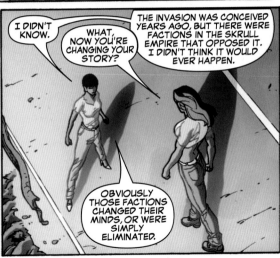

I DIDN'T KNOW.

WHAT, NOW YOU'RE CHANGING YOUR STORY?

THE INVASION WAS CONCEIVED YEARS AGO, BUT THERE WERE FACTIONS IN THE SKRULL EMPIRE THAT OPPOSED IT. I DIDN'T THINK IT WOULD EVER HAPPEN.

OBVIOUSLY THOSE FACTIONS CHANGED THEIR MINDS, OR WERE SIMPLY ELIMINATED.

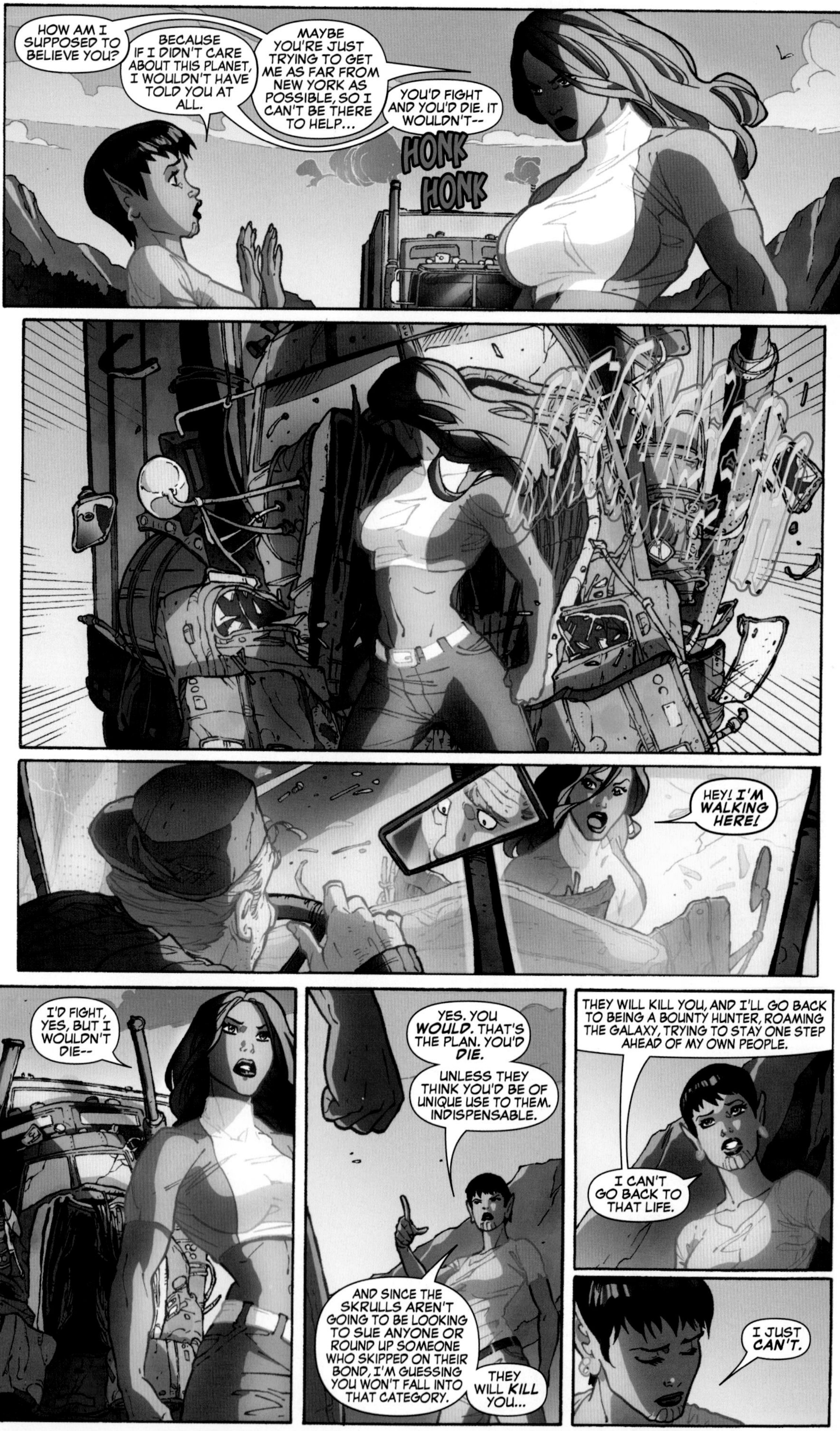
HOW AM I SUPPOSED TO BELIEVE YOU?
BECAUSE IF I DIDN'T CARE ABOUT THIS PLANET, I WOULDN'T HAVE TOLD YOU AT ALL.
MAYBE YOU'RE JUST TRYING TO GET ME AS FAR FROM NEW YORK AS POSSIBLE, SO I CAN'T BE THERE TO HELP...
YOU'D FIGHT AND YOU'D DIE. IT WOULDN'T--
HONK
HONK
HEY! I'M WALKING HERE!
I'D FIGHT, YES, BUT I WOULDN'T DIE--
YES. YOU WOULD. THAT'S THE PLAN. YOU'D DIE.
UNLESS THEY THINK YOU'D BE OF UNIQUE USE TO THEM. INDISPENSABLE.
AND SINCE THE SKRULLS AREN'T GOING TO BE LOOKING TO SUE ANYONE OR ROUND UP SOMEONE WHO SKIPPED ON THEIR BOND, I'M GUESSING YOU WON'T FALL INTO THAT CATEGORY.
THEY WILL KILL YOU...
THEY WILL KILL YOU, AND I'LL GO BACK TO BEING A BOUNTY HUNTER, ROAMING THE GALAXY, TRYING TO STAY ONE STEP AHEAD OF MY OWN PEOPLE.
I CAN'T GO BACK TO THAT LIFE.
I JUST CAN'T.

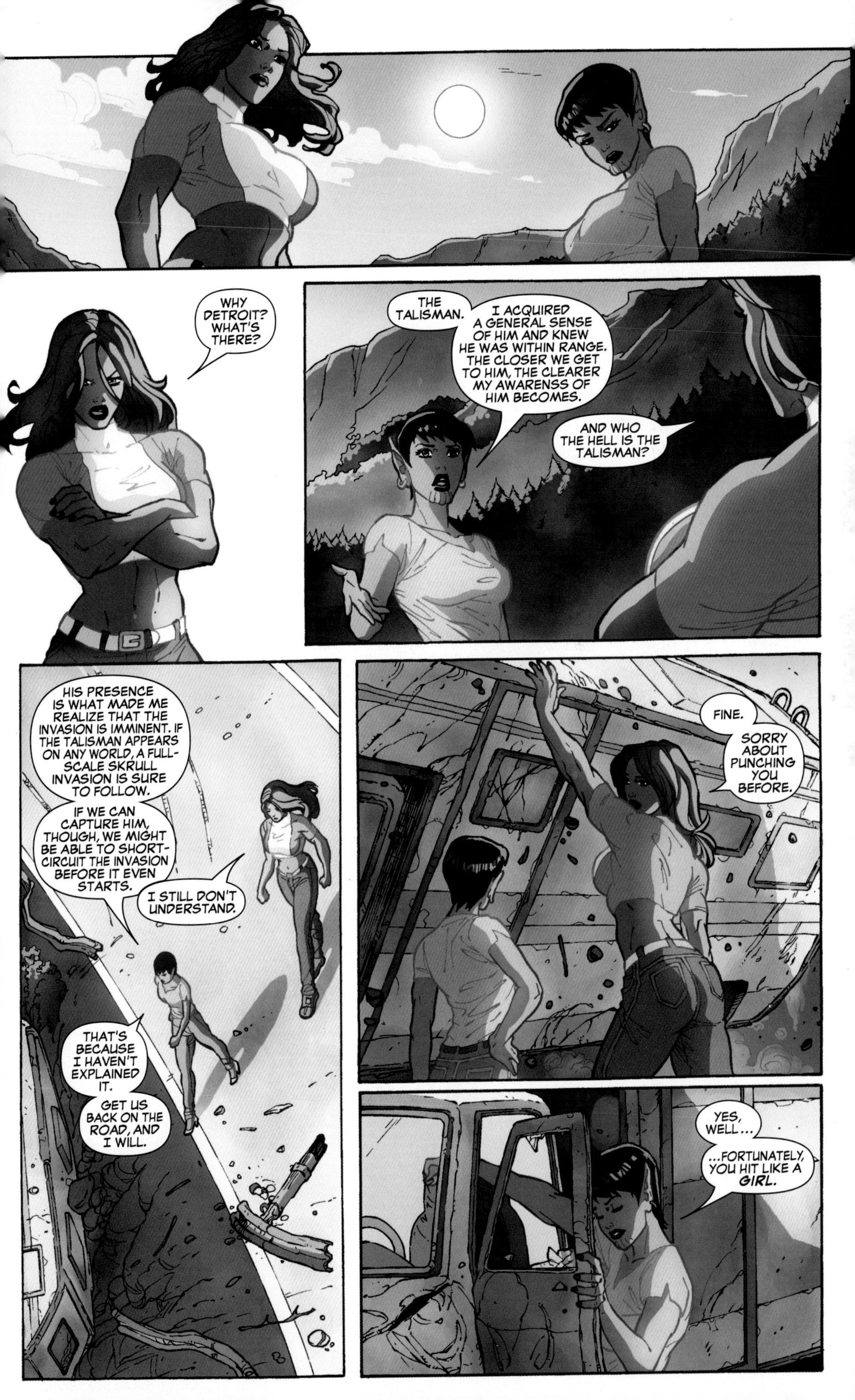
WHY DETROIT? WHAT'S THERE?
THE TALISMAN.
I ACQUIRED A GENERAL SENSE OF HIM AND KNEW HE WAS WITHIN RANGE. THE CLOSER WE GET TO HIM, THE CLEARER MY AWARENSS OF HIM BECOMES.
AND WHO THE HELL IS THE TALISMAN?
HIS PRESENCE IS WHAT MADE ME REALIZE THAT THE INVASION IS IMMINENT. IF THE TALISMAN APPEARS ON ANY WORLD, A FULL-SCALE SKRULL INVASION IS SURE TO FOLLOW.
IF WE CAN CAPTURE HIM, THOUGH, WE MIGHT BE ABLE TO SHORT-CIRCUIT THE INVASION BEFORE IT EVEN STARTS.
I STILL DON'T UNDERSTAND.
THAT'S BECAUSE I HAVEN'T EXPLAINED IT.
GET US BACK ON THE ROAD, AND I WILL.
FINE.
SORRY ABOUT PUNCHING YOU BEFORE.
YES, WELL...
...FORTUNATELY, YOU HIT LIKE A GIRL.

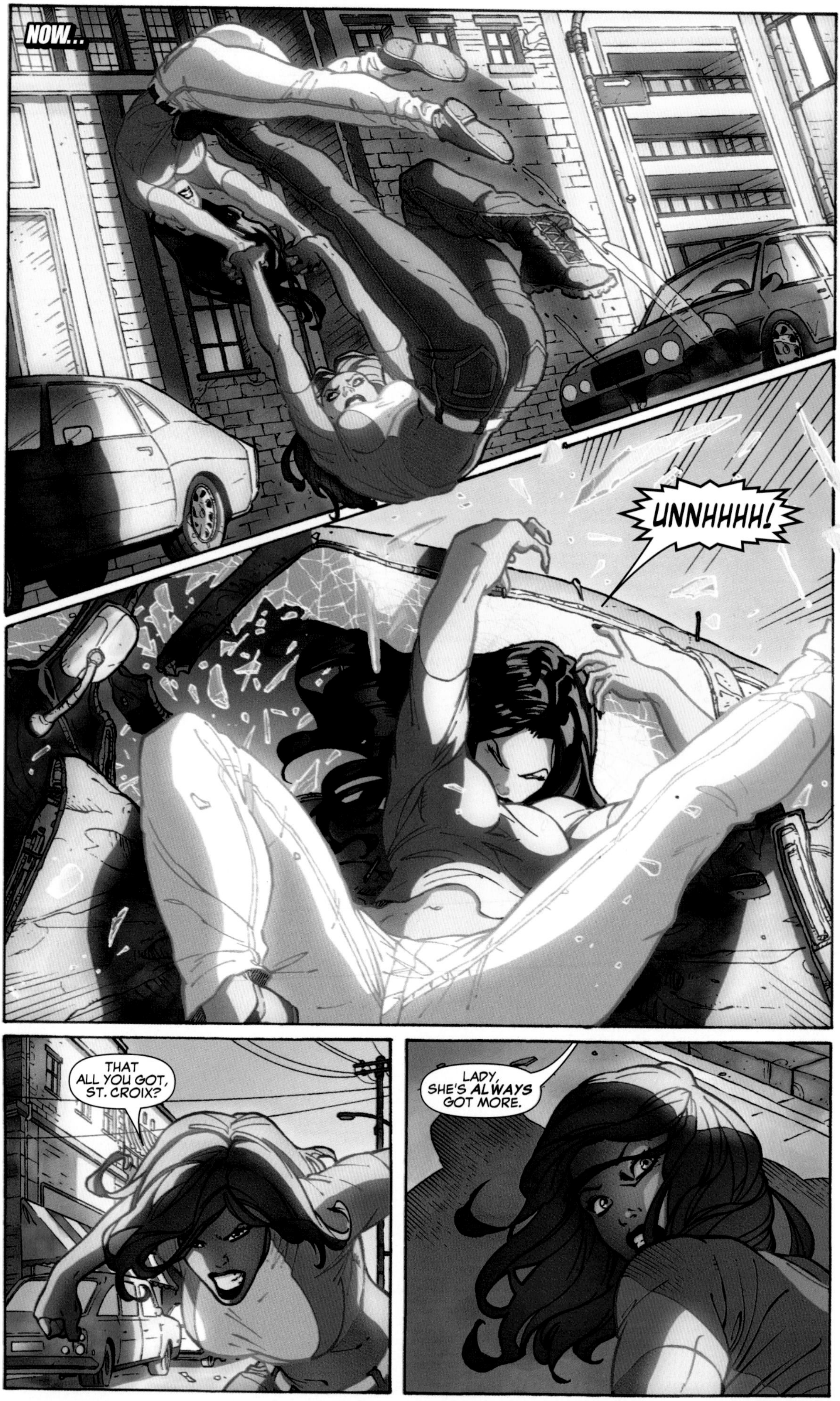
NOW...
UNNHHHH!
THAT ALL YOU GOT, ST. CROIX?
LADY, SHE'S ALWAYS GOT MORE.

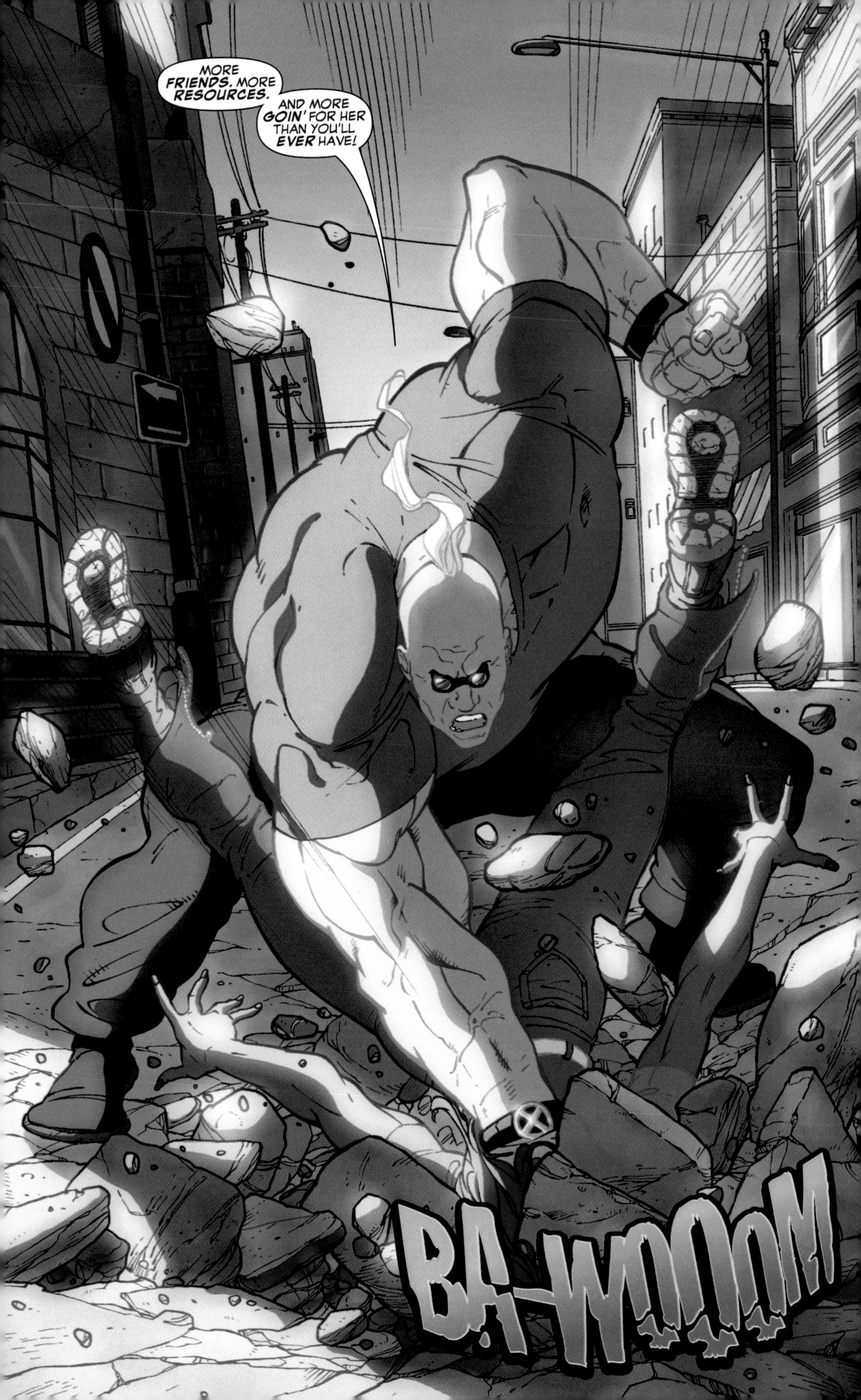
MORE FRIENDS. MORE RESOURCES.
AND MORE GOIN' FOR HER THAN YOU'LL EVER HAVE!
BA-WOOOM

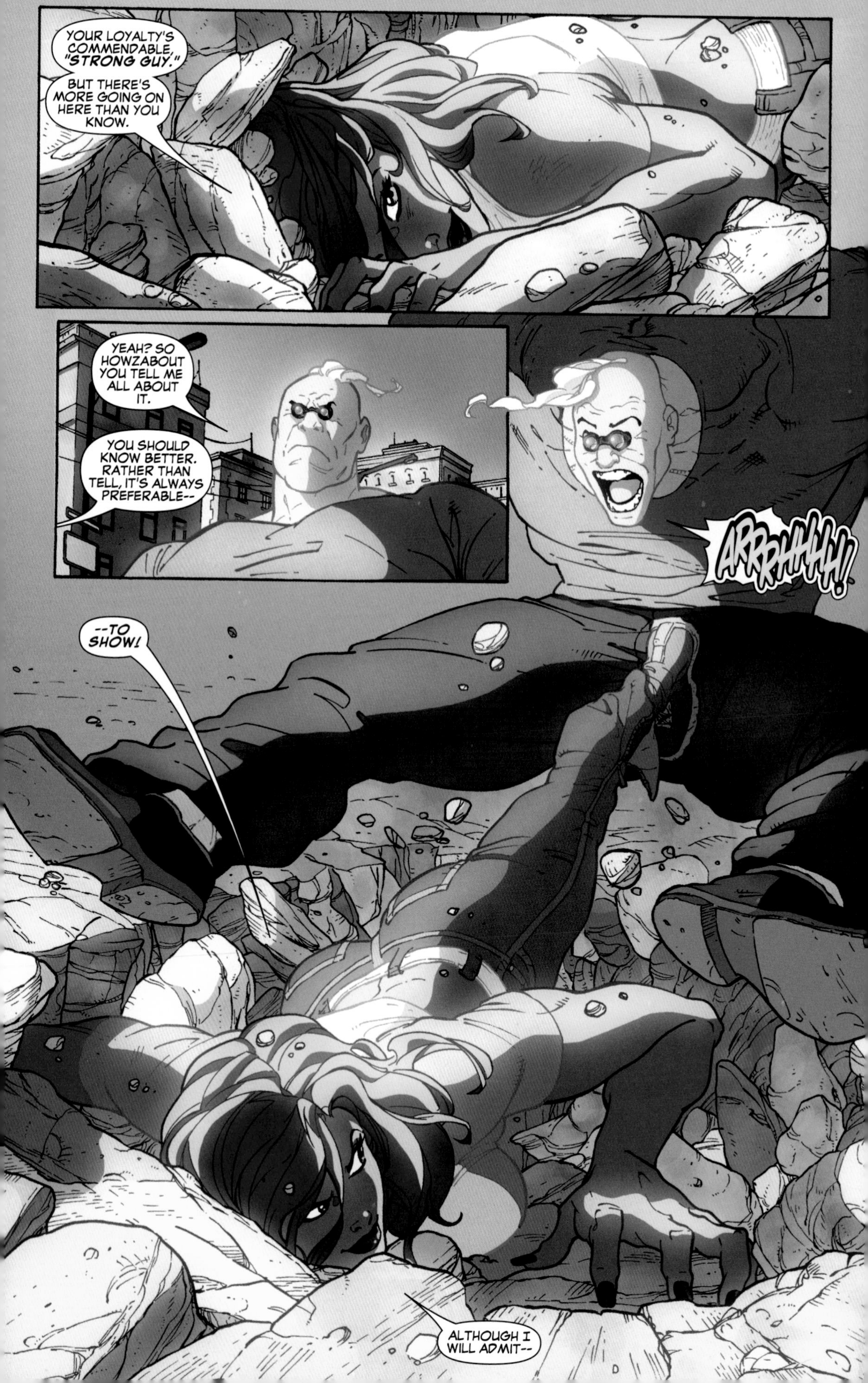
YOUR LOYALTY'S COMMENDABLE, "STRONG GUY."
BUT THERE'S MORE GOING ON HERE THAN YOU KNOW.
YEAH? SO HOWZABOUT YOU TELL ME ALL ABOUT IT.
YOU SHOULD KNOW BETTER. RATHER THAN TELL, IT'S ALWAYS PREFERABLE--
ARRRHHHH!
--TO SHOW!
ALTHOUGH I WILL ADMIT--

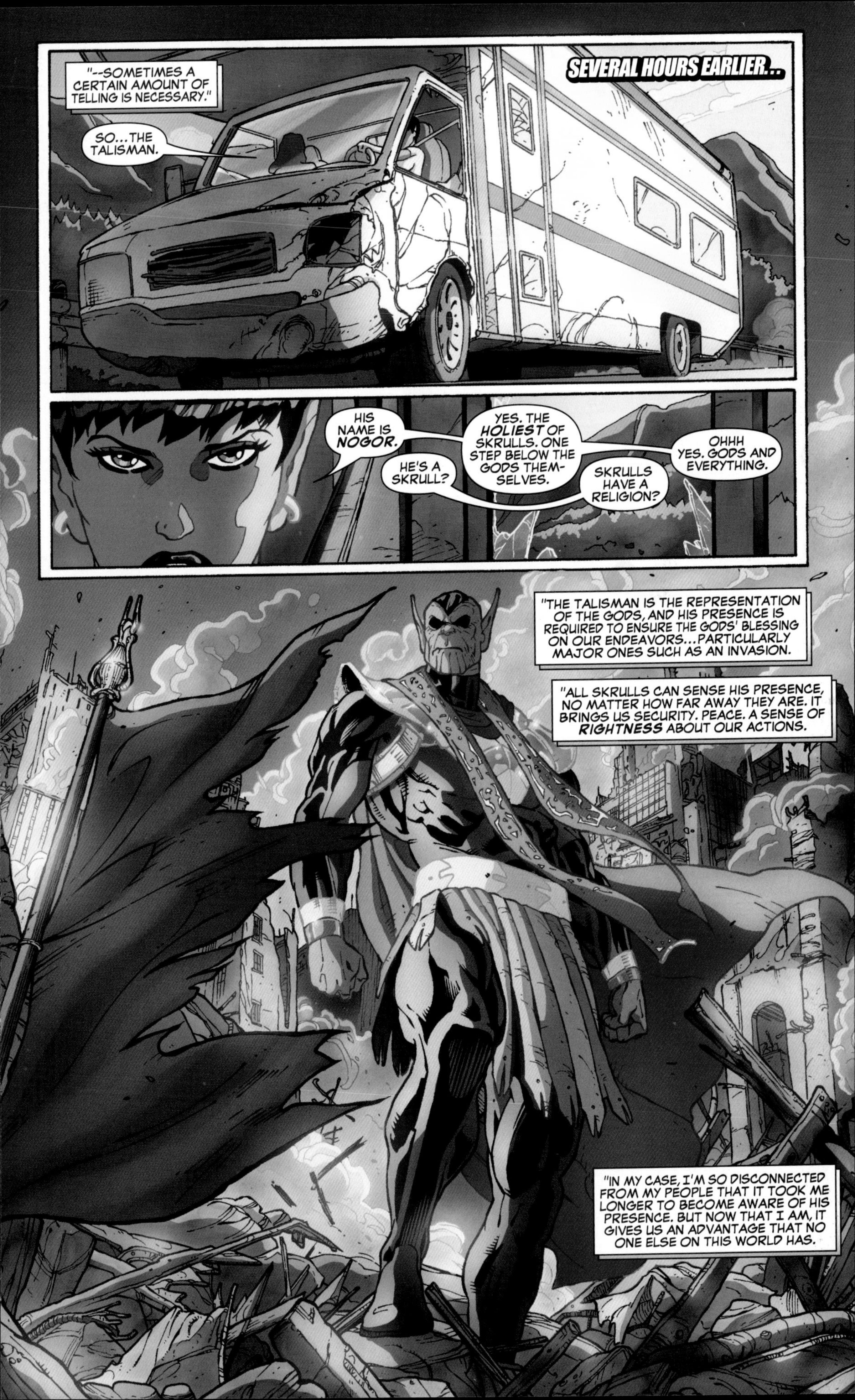
"--SOMETIMES A CERTAIN AMOUNT OF TELLING IS NECESSARY."
SEVERAL HOURS EARLIER...
SO...THE TALISMAN.
HIS NAME IS NOGOR.
HE'S A SKRULL?
YES. THE HOLIEST OF SKRULLS. ONE STEP BELOW THE GODS THEMSELVES.
SKRULLS HAVE A RELIGION?
OHHH YES. GODS AND EVERYTHING.
"THE TALISMAN IS THE REPRESENTATION OF THE GODS, AND HIS PRESENCE IS REQUIRED TO ENSURE THE GODS' BLESSING ON OUR ENDEAVORS...PARTICULARLY MAJOR ONES SUCH AS AN INVASION.
"ALL SKRULLS CAN SENSE HIS PRESENCE, NO MATTER HOW FAR AWAY THEY ARE. IT BRINGS US SECURITY. PEACE. A SENSE OF RIGHTNESS ABOUT OUR ACTIONS.
"IN MY CASE, I'M SO DISCONNECTED FROM MY PEOPLE THAT IT TOOK ME LONGER TO BECOME AWARE OF HIS PRESENCE. BUT NOW THAT I AM, IT GIVES US AN ADVANTAGE THAT NO ONE ELSE ON THIS WORLD HAS.

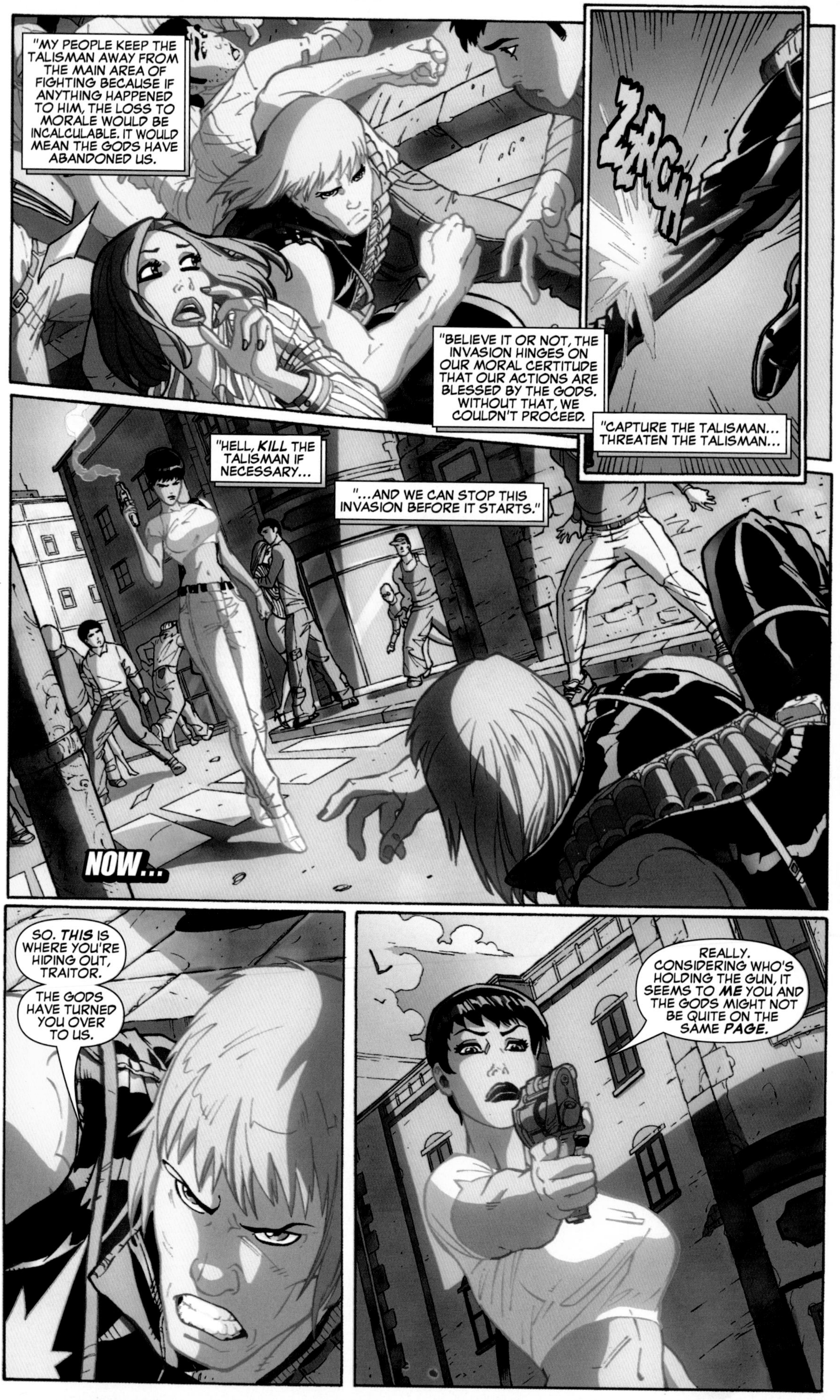
"MY PEOPLE KEEP THE TALISMAN AWAY FROM THE MAIN AREA OF FIGHTING BECAUSE IF ANYTHING HAPPENED TO HIM, THE LOSS TO MORALE WOULD BE INCALCULABLE. IT WOULD MEAN THE GODS HAVE ABANDONED US.
ZZRCH
"BELIEVE IT OR NOT, THE INVASION HINGES ON OUR MORAL CERTITUDE THAT OUR ACTIONS ARE BLESSED BY THE GODS. WITHOUT THAT, WE COULDN'T PROCEED.
"CAPTURE THE TALISMAN... THREATEN THE TALISMAN...
"HELL, KILL THE TALISMAN IF NECESSARY...
"...AND WE CAN STOP THIS INVASION BEFORE IT STARTS."
NOW...
SO. THIS IS WHERE YOU'RE HIDING OUT, TRAITOR.
THE GODS HAVE TURNED YOU OVER TO US.
REALLY. CONSIDERING WHO'S HOLDING THE GUN, IT SEEMS TO ME YOU AND THE GODS MIGHT NOT BE QUITE ON THE SAME PAGE.

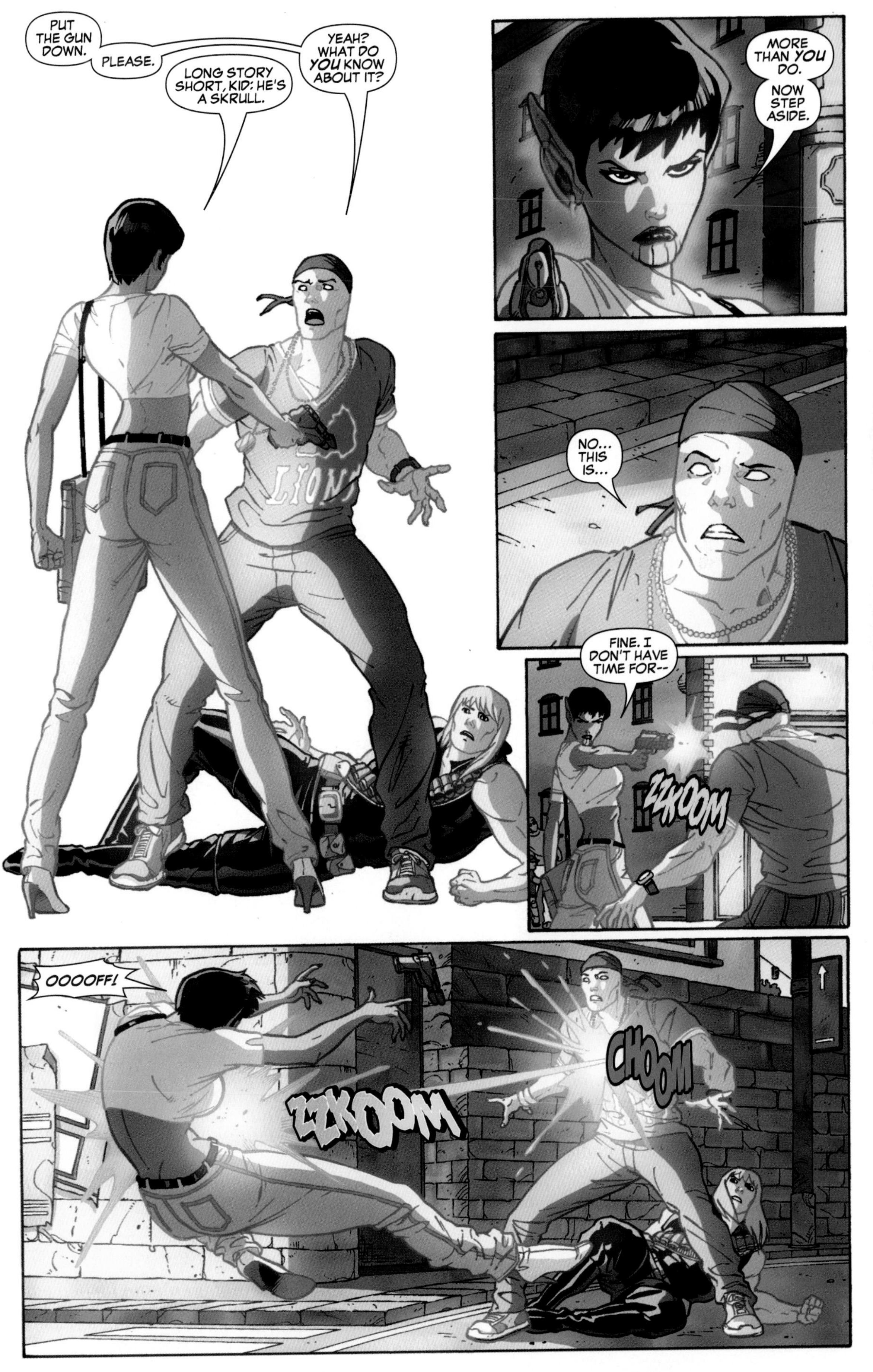
PUT THE GUN DOWN.
PLEASE.
YEAH? WHAT DO YOU KNOW ABOUT IT?
LONG STORY SHORT, KID: HE'S A SKRULL.
LIONS
MORE THAN YOU DO.
NOW STEP ASIDE.
NO... THIS IS...
FINE. I DON'T HAVE TIME FOR--
ZZKOOM
OOOOFF!
CHOOM
ZZKOOM

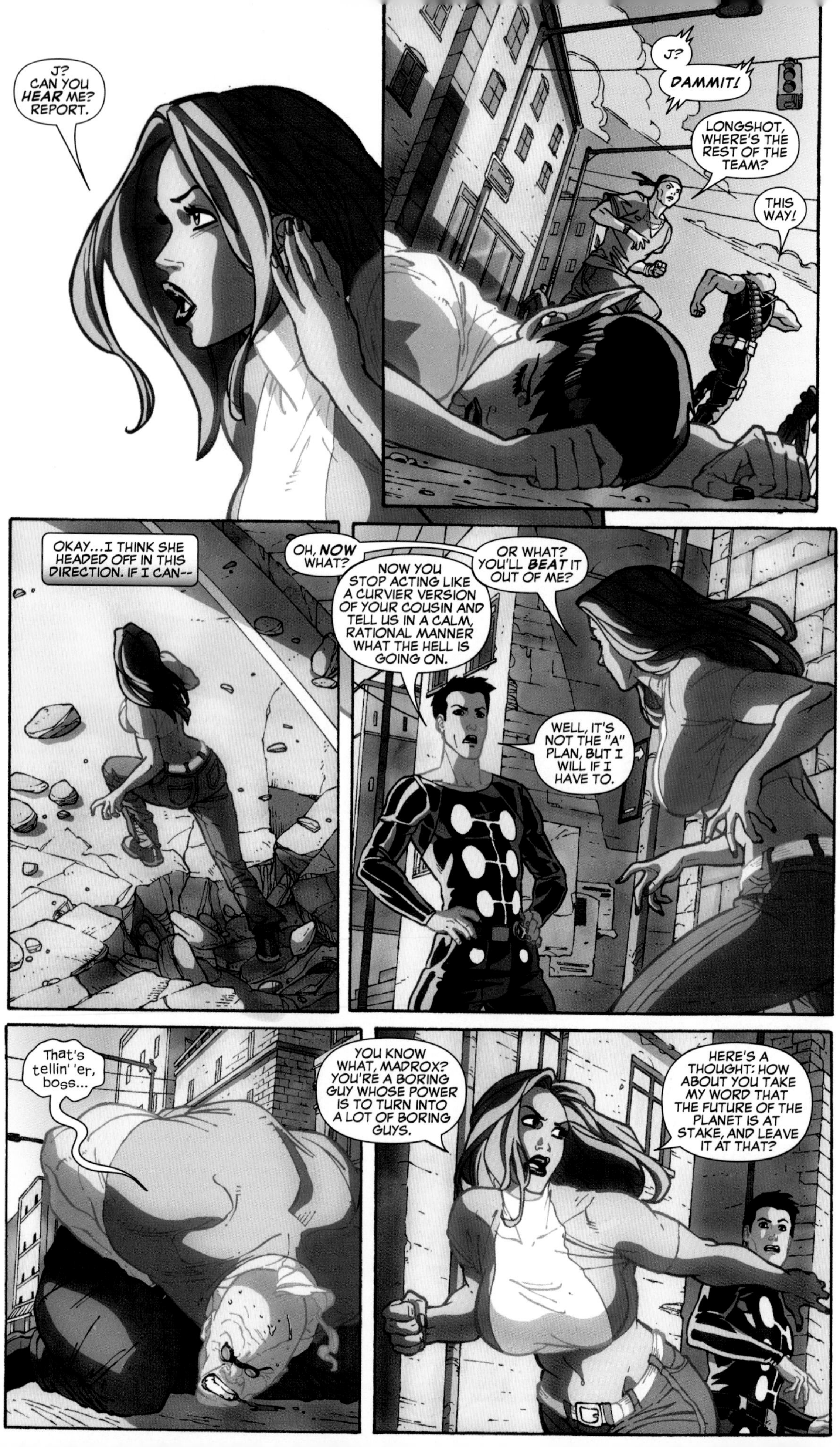
J? CAN YOU HEAR ME? REPORT.
J?
DAMMIT!
LONGSHOT, WHERE'S THE REST OF THE TEAM?
THIS WAY!
OKAY...I THINK SHE HEADED OFF IN THIS DIRECTION. IF I CAN--
OH, NOW WHAT?
NOW YOU STOP ACTING LIKE A CURVIER VERSION OF YOUR COUSIN AND TELL US IN A CALM, RATIONAL MANNER WHAT THE HELL IS GOING ON.
OR WHAT? YOU'LL BEAT IT OUT OF ME?
WELL, IT'S NOT THE "A" PLAN, BUT I WILL IF I HAVE TO.
That's tellin' 'er, boss...
YOU KNOW WHAT, MADROX? YOU'RE A BORING GUY WHOSE POWER IS TO TURN INTO A LOT OF BORING GUYS.
HERE'S A THOUGHT: HOW ABOUT YOU TAKE MY WORD THAT THE FUTURE OF THE PLANET IS AT STAKE, AND LEAVE IT AT THAT?

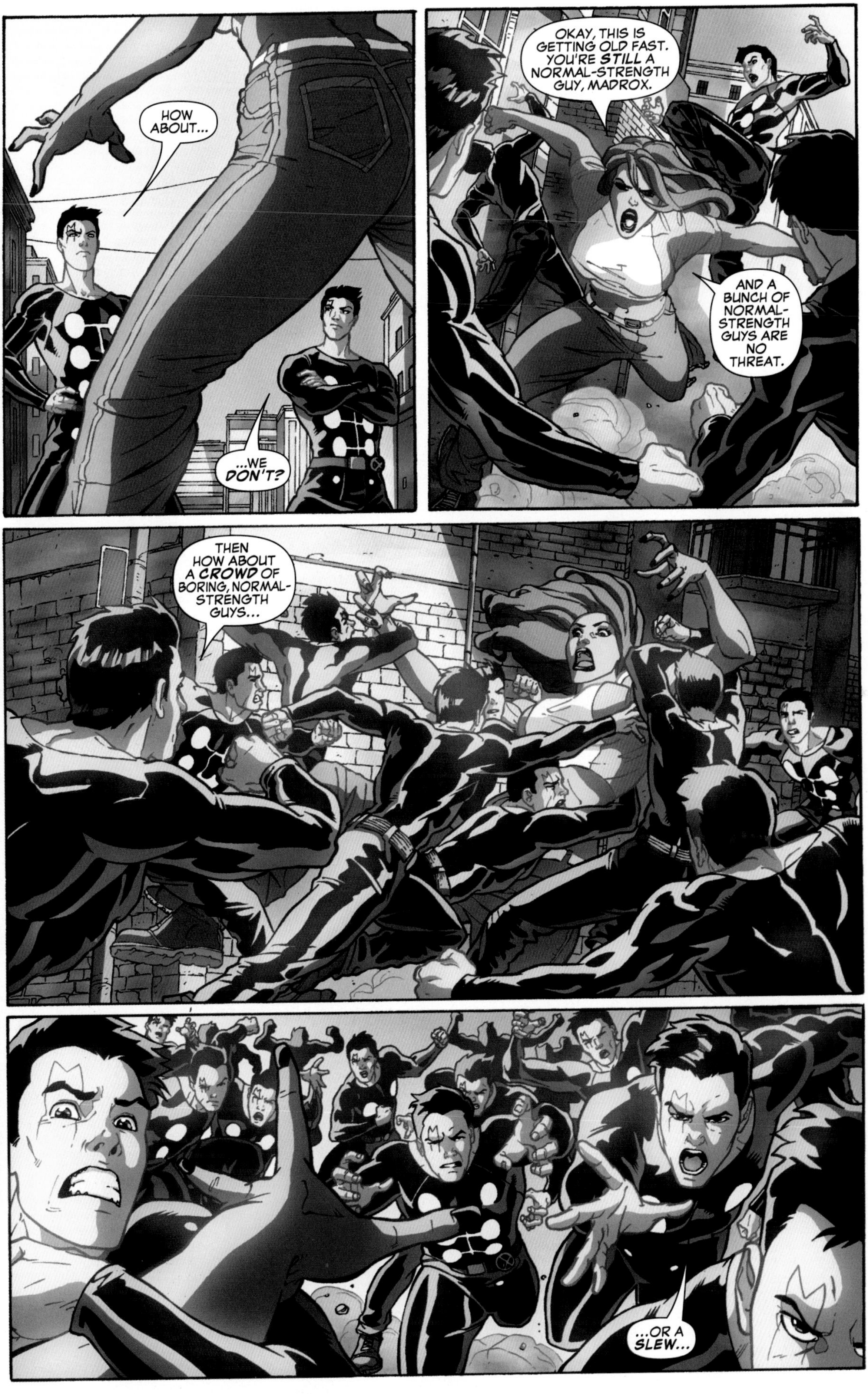
HOW ABOUT...
...WE DON'T?
OKAY, THIS IS GETTING OLD FAST. YOU'RE STILL A NORMAL-STRENGTH GUY, MADROX.
AND A BUNCH OF NORMAL-STRENGTH GUYS ARE NO THREAT.
THEN HOW ABOUT A CROWD OF BORING, NORMAL-STRENGTH GUYS...
...OR A SLEW...

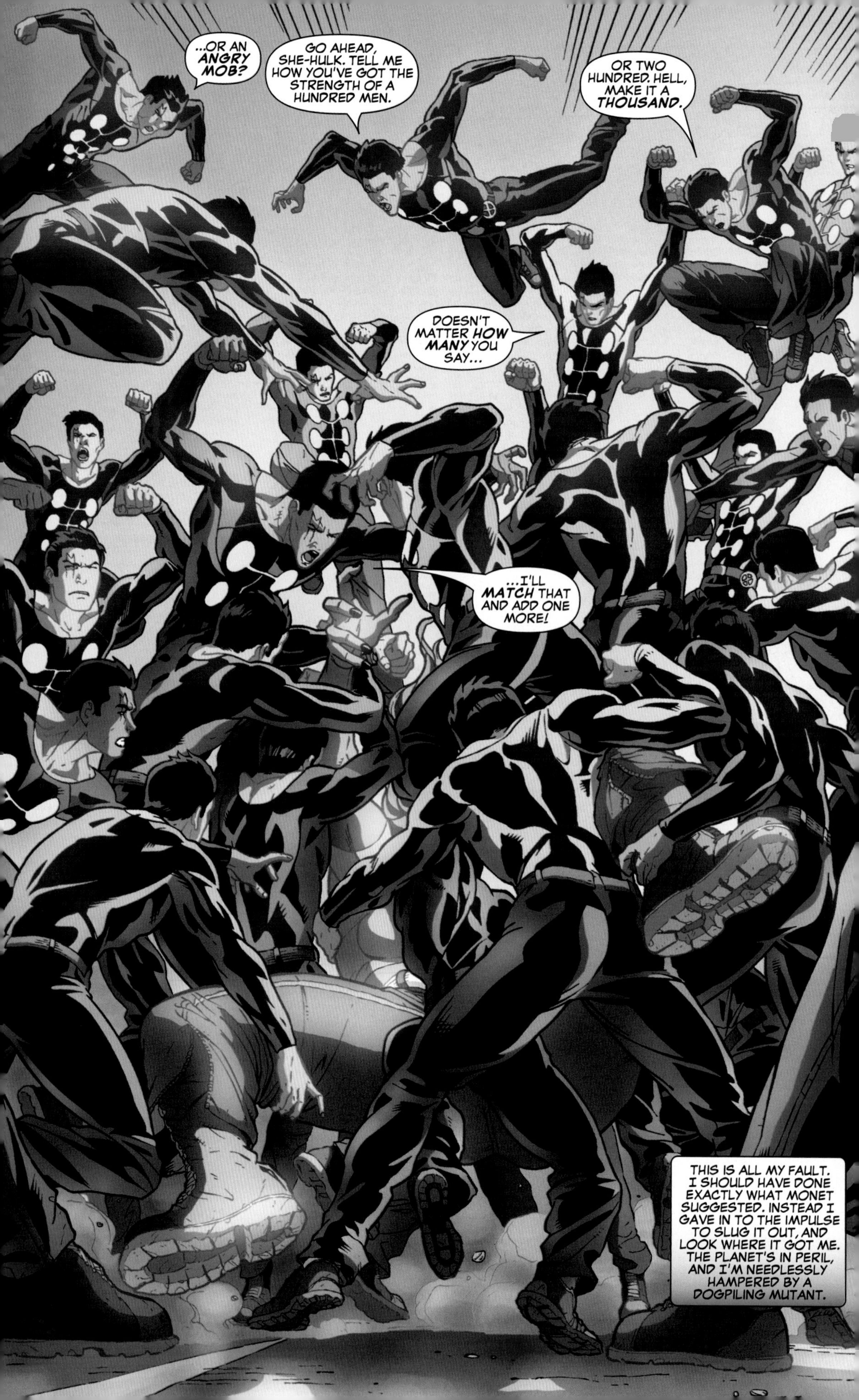
...OR AN ANGRY MOB?
GO AHEAD, SHE-HULK. TELL ME HOW YOU'VE GOT THE STRENGTH OF A HUNDRED MEN.
OR TWO HUNDRED. HELL, MAKE IT A THOUSAND.
DOESN'T MATTER HOW MANY YOU SAY...
...I'LL MATCH THAT AND ADD ONE MORE!
THIS IS ALL MY FAULT. I SHOULD HAVE DONE EXACTLY WHAT MONET SUGGESTED. INSTEAD I GAVE IN TO THE IMPULSE TO SLUG IT OUT, AND LOOK WHERE IT GOT ME. THE PLANET'S IN PERIL, AND I'M NEEDLESSLY HAMPERED BY A DOGPILING MUTANT.

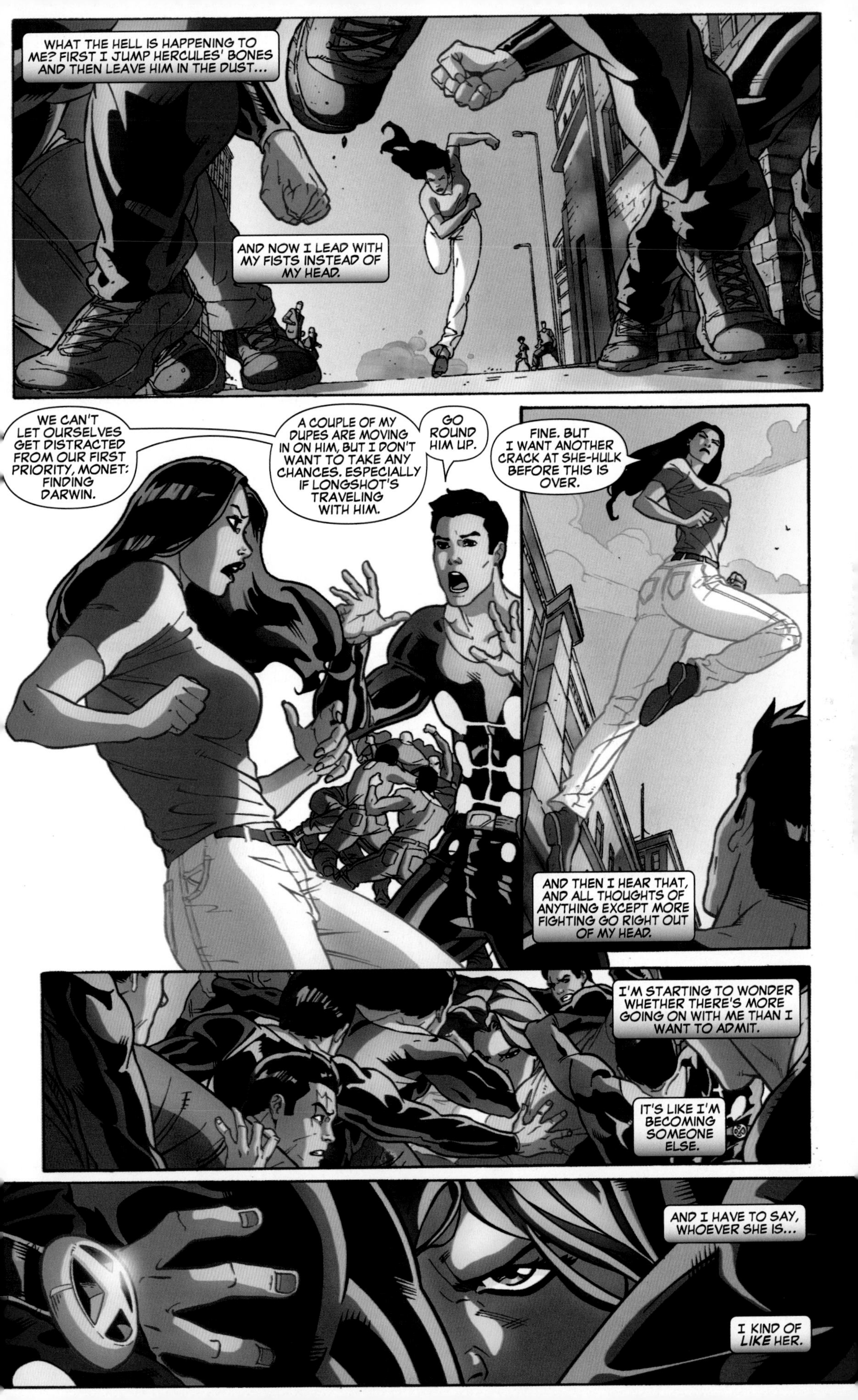
WHAT THE HELL IS HAPPENING TO ME? FIRST I JUMP HERCULES' BONES AND THEN LEAVE HIM IN THE DUST...
AND NOW I LEAD WITH MY FISTS INSTEAD OF MY HEAD.
WE CAN'T LET OURSELVES GET DISTRACTED FROM OUR FIRST PRIORITY, MONET: FINDING DARWIN.
A COUPLE OF MY DUPES ARE MOVING IN ON HIM, BUT I DON'T WANT TO TAKE ANY CHANCES. ESPECIALLY IF LONGSHOT'S TRAVELING WITH HIM.
GO ROUND HIM UP.
FINE. BUT I WANT ANOTHER CRACK AT SHE-HULK BEFORE THIS IS OVER.
AND THEN I HEAR THAT, AND ALL THOUGHTS OF ANYTHING EXCEPT MORE FIGHTING GO RIGHT OUT OF MY HEAD.
I'M STARTING TO WONDER WHETHER THERE'S MORE GOING ON WITH ME THAN I WANT TO ADMIT.
IT'S LIKE I'M BECOMING SOMEONE ELSE.
AND I HAVE TO SAY, WHOEVER SHE IS...
I KIND OF LIKE HER.

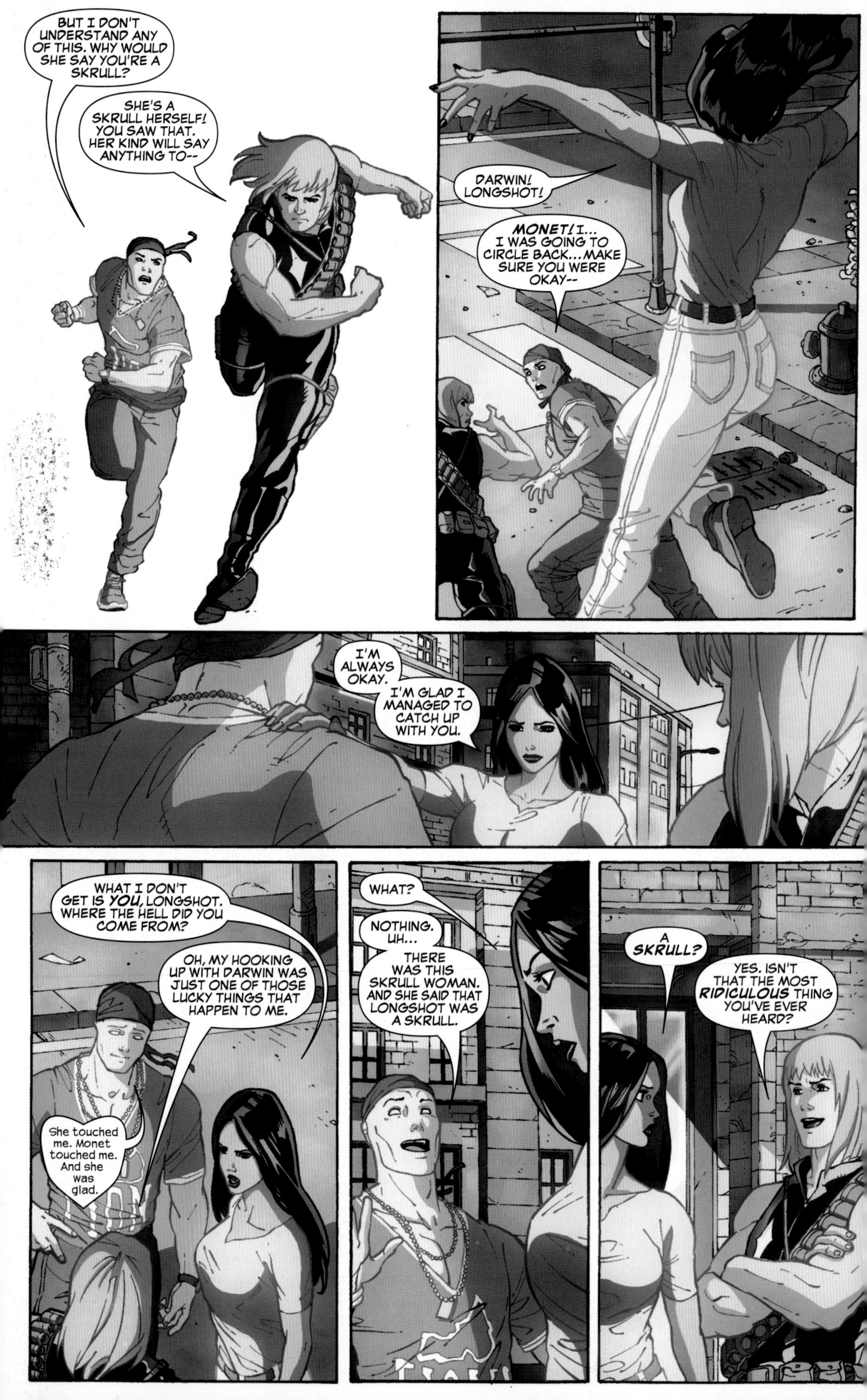

BUT I DON'T UNDERSTAND ANY OF THIS. WHY WOULD SHE SAY YOU'RE A SKRULL?
SHE'S A SKRULL HERSELF! YOU SAW THAT. HER KIND WILL SAY ANYTHING TO--
DARWIN! LONGSHOT!
MONET! I... I WAS GOING TO CIRCLE BACK... MAKE SURE YOU WERE OKAY--
I'M ALWAYS OKAY.
I'M GLAD I MANAGED TO CATCH UP WITH YOU.
WHAT I DON'T GET IS YOU, LONGSHOT. WHERE THE HELL DID YOU COME FROM?
OH, MY HOOKING UP WITH DARWIN WAS JUST ONE OF THOSE LUCKY THINGS THAT HAPPEN TO ME.
She touched me. Monet touched me. And she was glad.
WHAT?
NOTHING. UH...
THERE WAS THIS SKRULL WOMAN. AND SHE SAID THAT LONGSHOT WAS A SKRULL.
A SKRULL?
YES. ISN'T THAT THE MOST RIDICULOUS THING YOU'VE EVER HEARD?

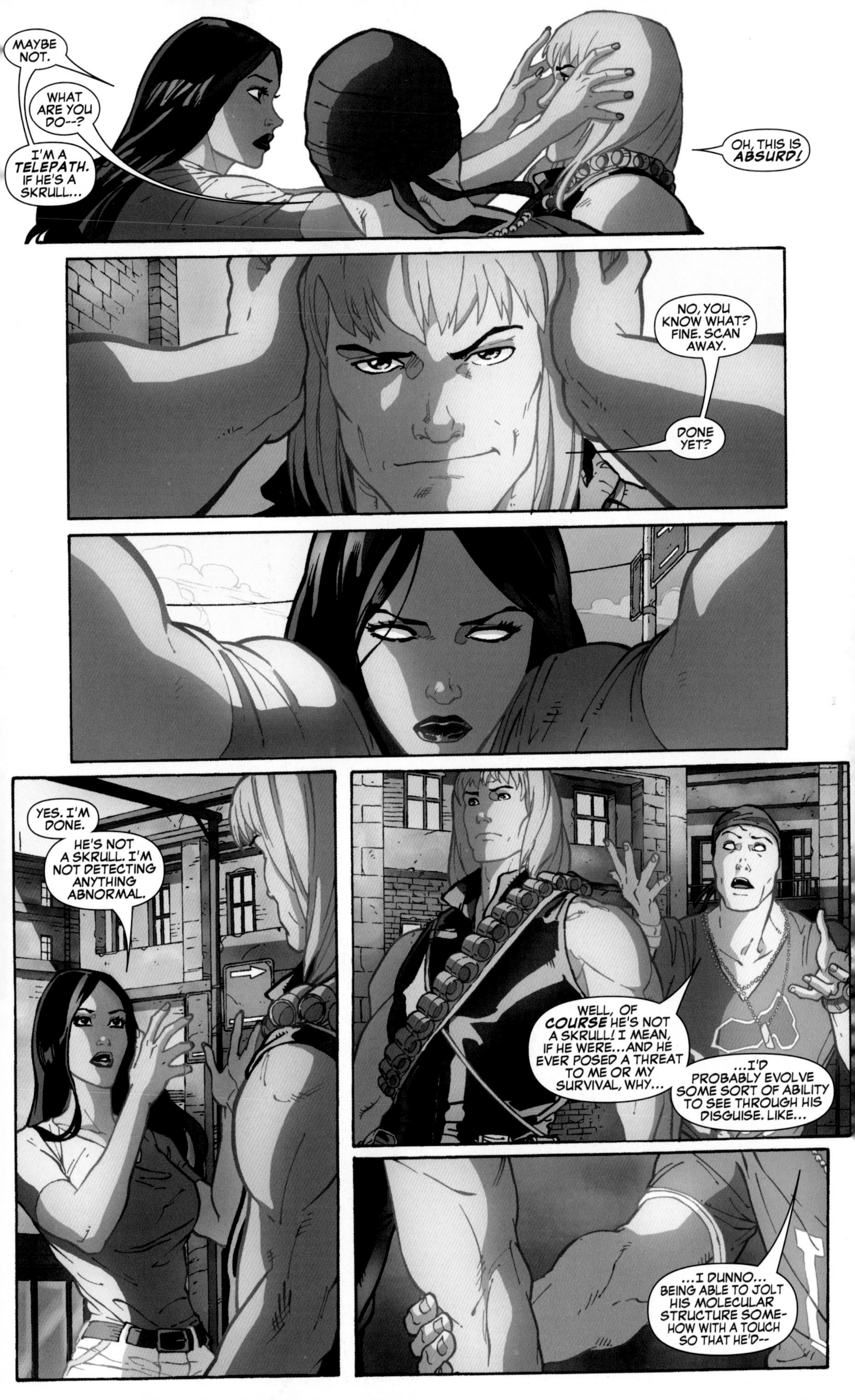
MAYBE NOT.
WHAT ARE YOU DO--?
I'M A **TELEPATH**. IF HE'S A SKRULL...
OH, THIS IS **ABSURD!**
NO, YOU KNOW WHAT? FINE. SCAN AWAY.
DONE YET?
YES. I'M DONE.
HE'S NOT A SKRULL. I'M NOT DETECTING ANYTHING ABNORMAL.
WELL, OF **COURSE** HE'S NOT A SKRULL! I MEAN, IF HE WERE...AND HE EVER POSED A THREAT TO ME OR MY SURVIVAL, WHY...
...I'D PROBABLY EVOLVE SOME SORT OF ABILITY TO SEE THROUGH HIS DISGUISE. LIKE...
...I DUNNO... BEING ABLE TO JOLT HIS MOLECULAR STRUCTURE SOME-HOW WITH A TOUCH SO THAT HE'D--

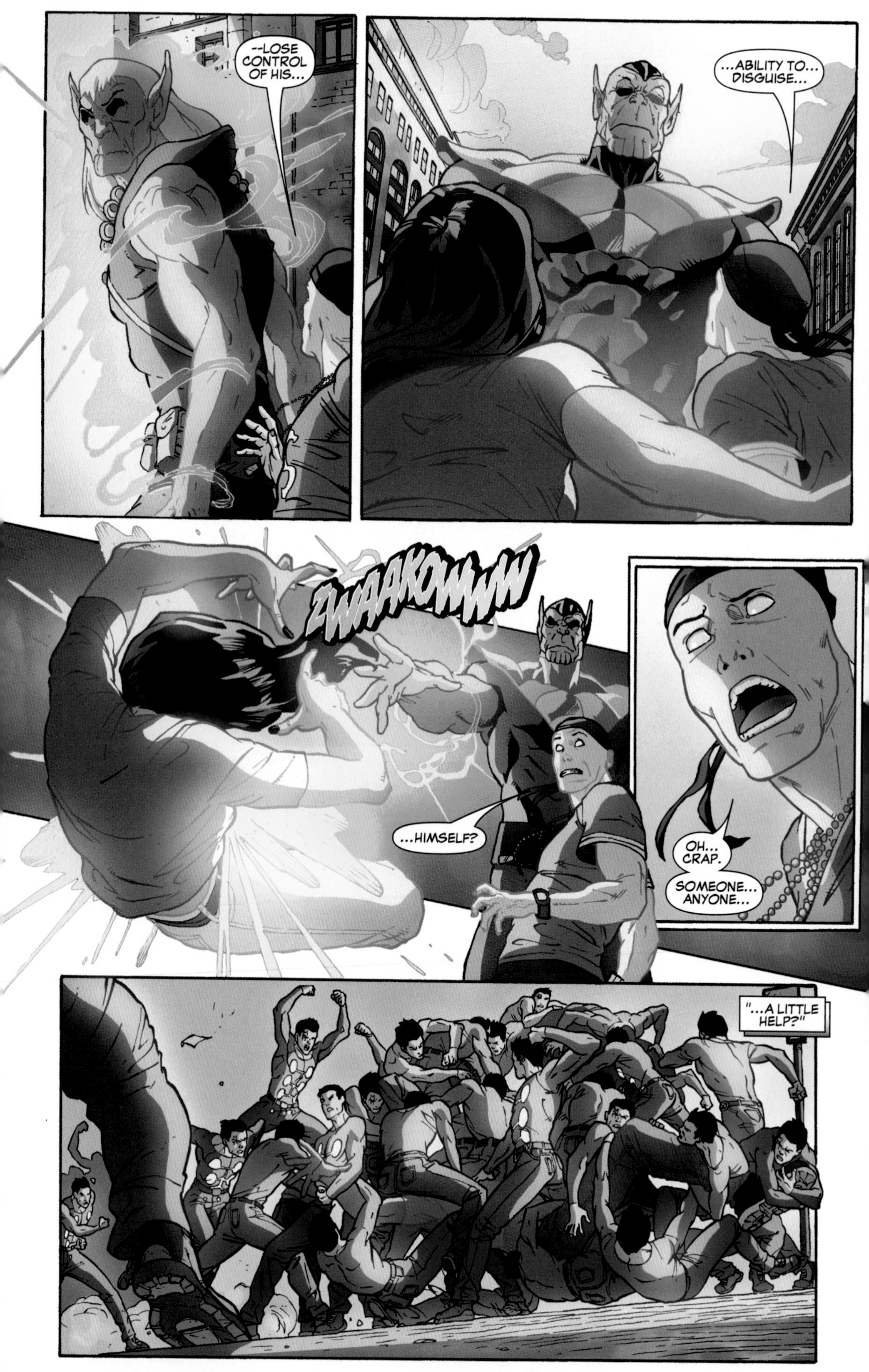
--LOSE CONTROL OF HIS...
...ABILITY TO... DISGUISE...
ZWAAKOWWW
...HIMSELF?
OH... CRAP.
SOMEONE... ANYONE...
"...A LITTLE HELP?"

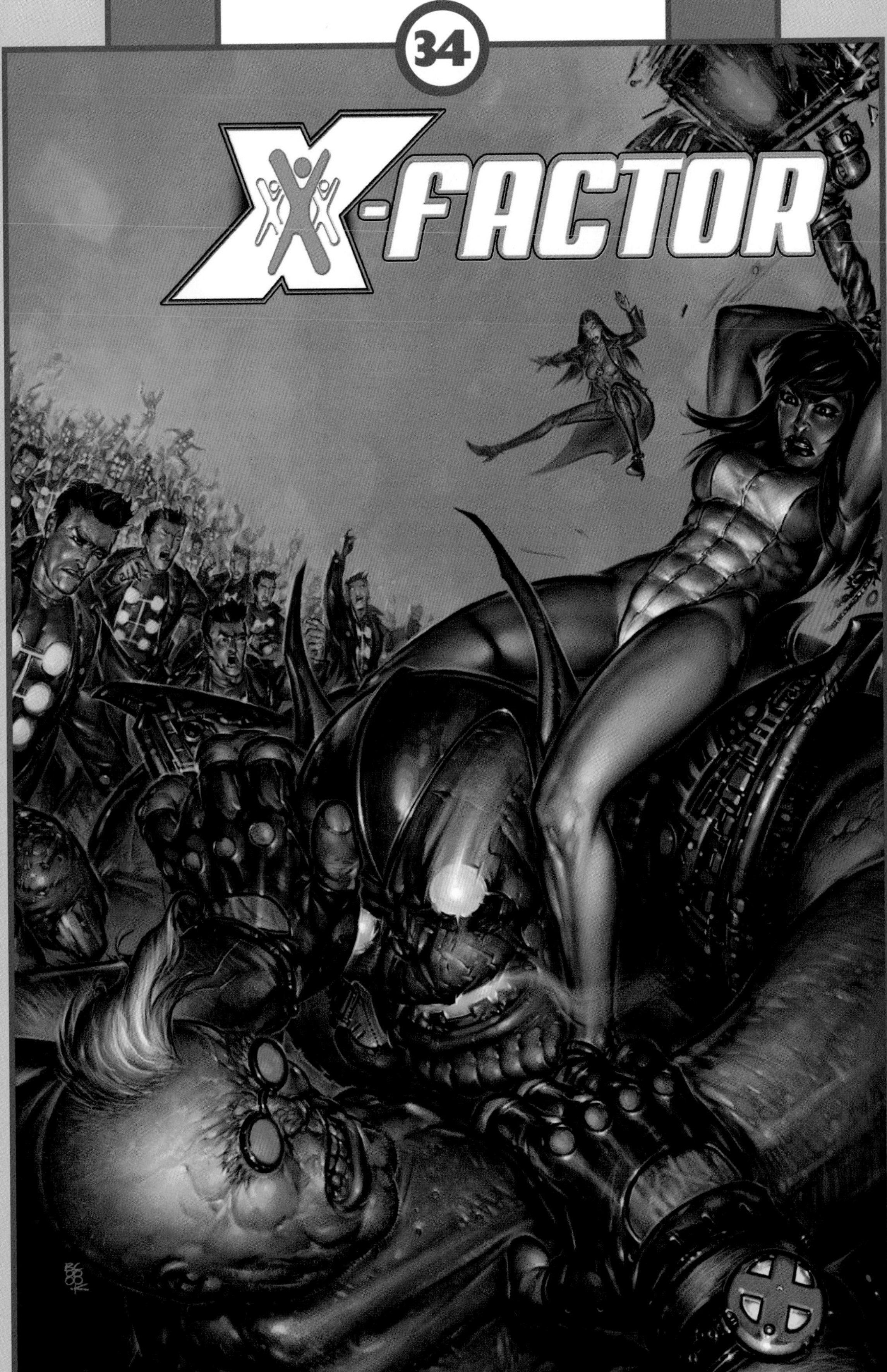
34
X-FACTOR

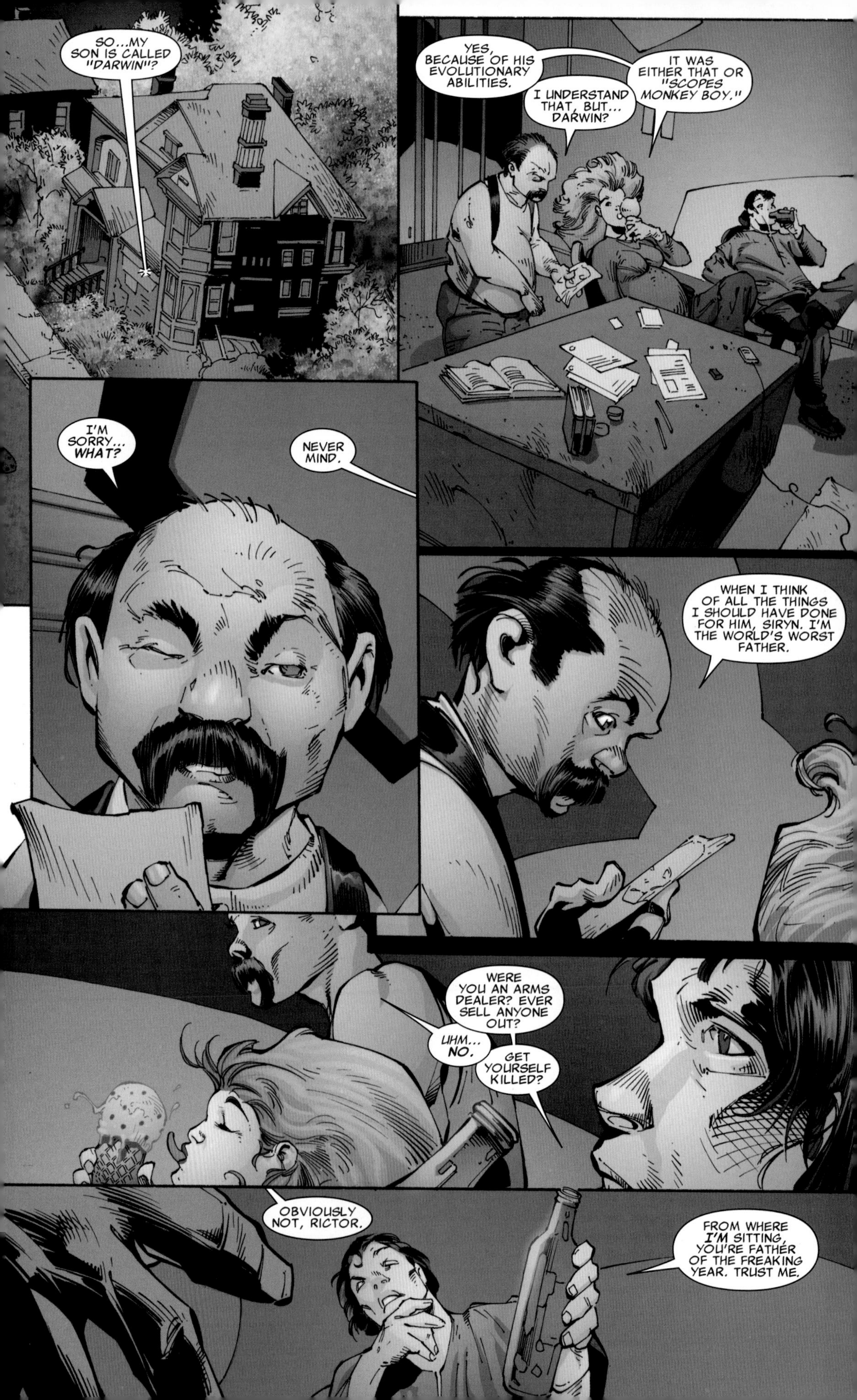
SO...MY SON IS CALLED "DARWIN"?
YES, BECAUSE OF HIS EVOLUTIONARY ABILITIES.
IT WAS EITHER THAT OR "SCOPES MONKEY BOY."
I UNDERSTAND THAT, BUT... DARWIN?
I'M SORRY... WHAT?
NEVER MIND.
WHEN I THINK OF ALL THE THINGS I SHOULD HAVE DONE FOR HIM, SIRYN. I'M THE WORLD'S WORST FATHER.
WERE YOU AN ARMS DEALER? EVER SELL ANYONE OUT?
UHM... NO.
GET YOURSELF KILLED?
OBVIOUSLY NOT, RICTOR.
FROM WHERE I'M SITTING, YOU'RE FATHER OF THE FREAKING YEAR. TRUST ME.

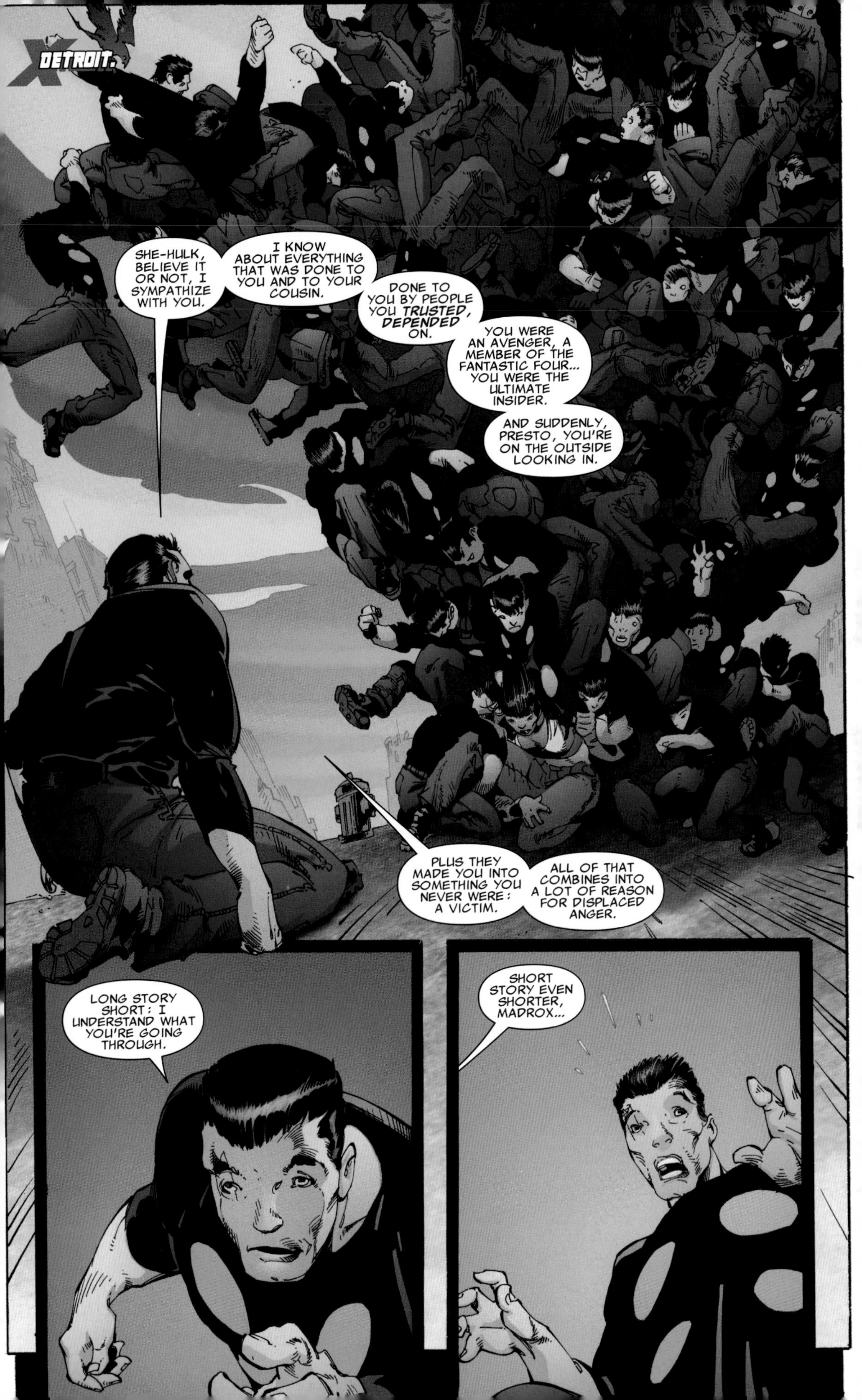
DETROIT.
SHE-HULK, BELIEVE IT OR NOT, I SYMPATHIZE WITH YOU.
I KNOW ABOUT EVERYTHING THAT WAS DONE TO YOU AND TO YOUR COUSIN.
DONE TO YOU BY PEOPLE YOU TRUSTED, DEPENDED ON.
YOU WERE AN AVENGER, A MEMBER OF THE FANTASTIC FOUR... YOU WERE THE ULTIMATE INSIDER.
AND SUDDENLY, PRESTO, YOU'RE ON THE OUTSIDE LOOKING IN.
PLUS THEY MADE YOU INTO SOMETHING YOU NEVER WERE: A VICTIM.
ALL OF THAT COMBINES INTO A LOT OF REASON FOR DISPLACED ANGER.
LONG STORY SHORT: I UNDERSTAND WHAT YOU'RE GOING THROUGH.
SHORT STORY EVEN SHORTER, MADROX...

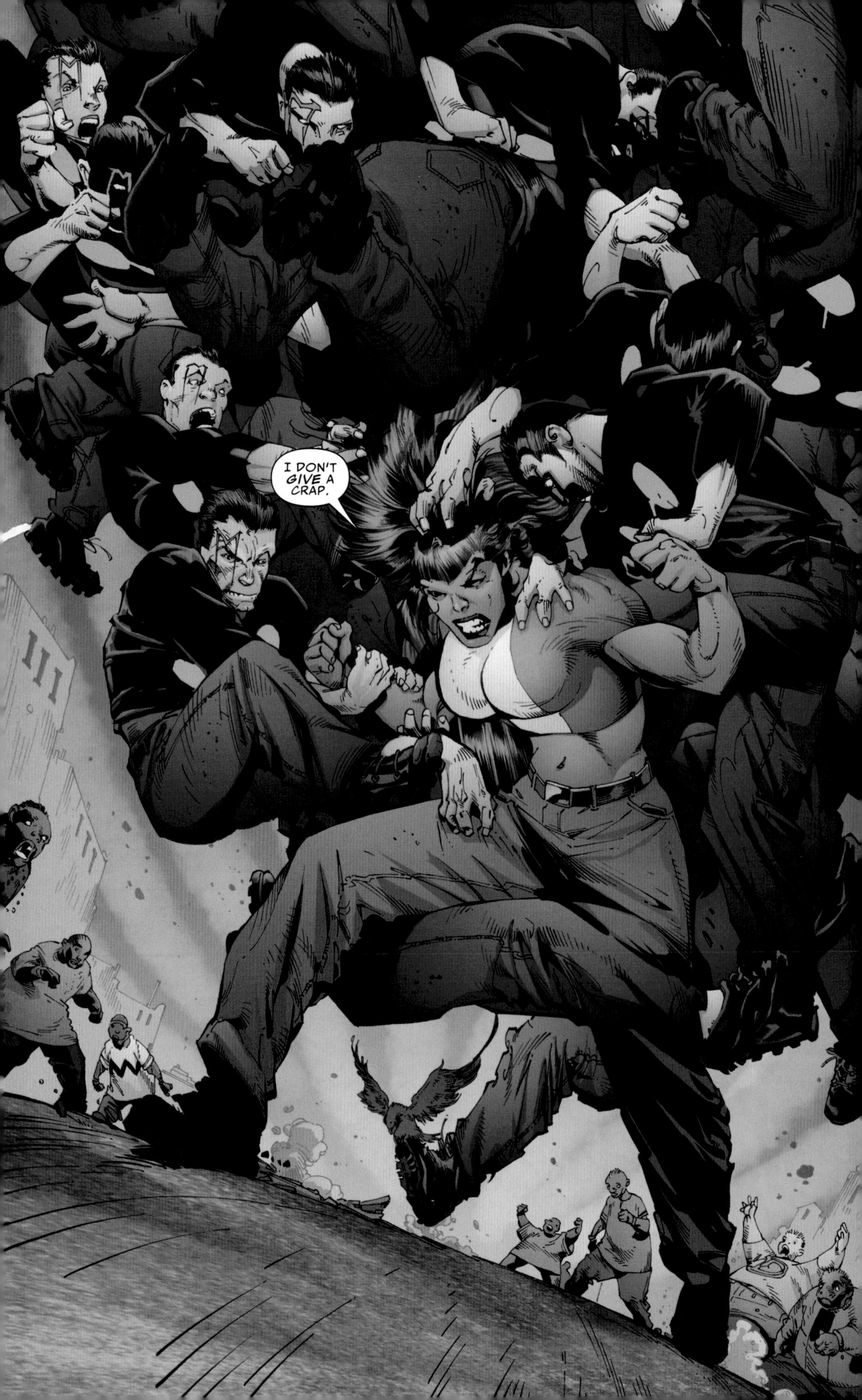
I DON'T GIVE A CRAP.

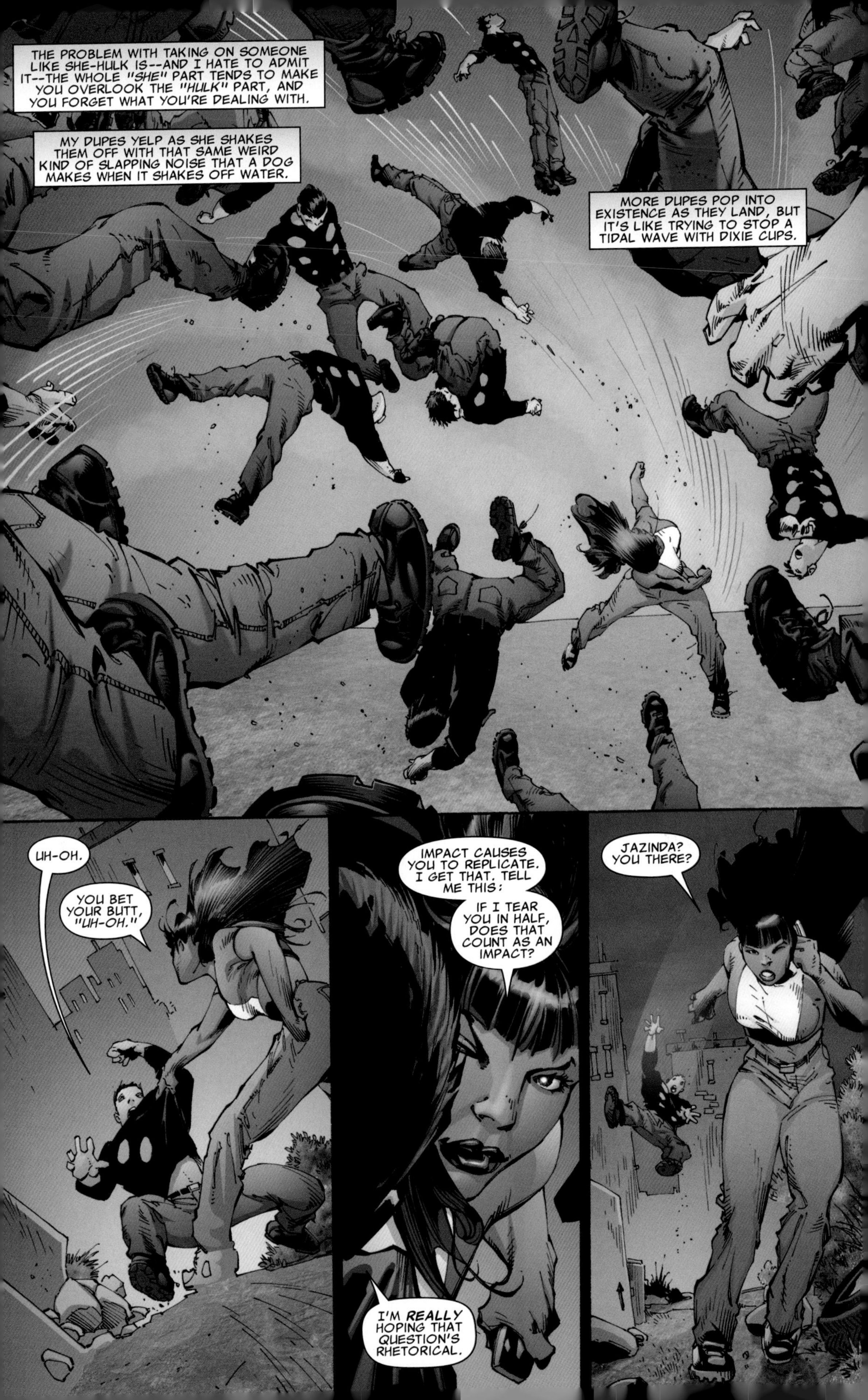
THE PROBLEM WITH TAKING ON SOMEONE LIKE SHE-HULK IS--AND I HATE TO ADMIT IT--THE WHOLE "SHE" PART TENDS TO MAKE YOU OVERLOOK THE "HULK" PART, AND YOU FORGET WHAT YOU'RE DEALING WITH.
MY DUPES YELP AS SHE SHAKES THEM OFF WITH THAT SAME WEIRD KIND OF SLAPPING NOISE THAT A DOG MAKES WHEN IT SHAKES OFF WATER.
MORE DUPES POP INTO EXISTENCE AS THEY LAND, BUT IT'S LIKE TRYING TO STOP A TIDAL WAVE WITH DIXIE CUPS.
UH-OH.
YOU BET YOUR BUTT, "UH-OH."
IMPACT CAUSES YOU TO REPLICATE. I GET THAT. TELL ME THIS:
IF I TEAR YOU IN HALF, DOES THAT COUNT AS AN IMPACT?
I'M REALLY HOPING THAT QUESTION'S RHETORICAL.
JAZINDA? YOU THERE?

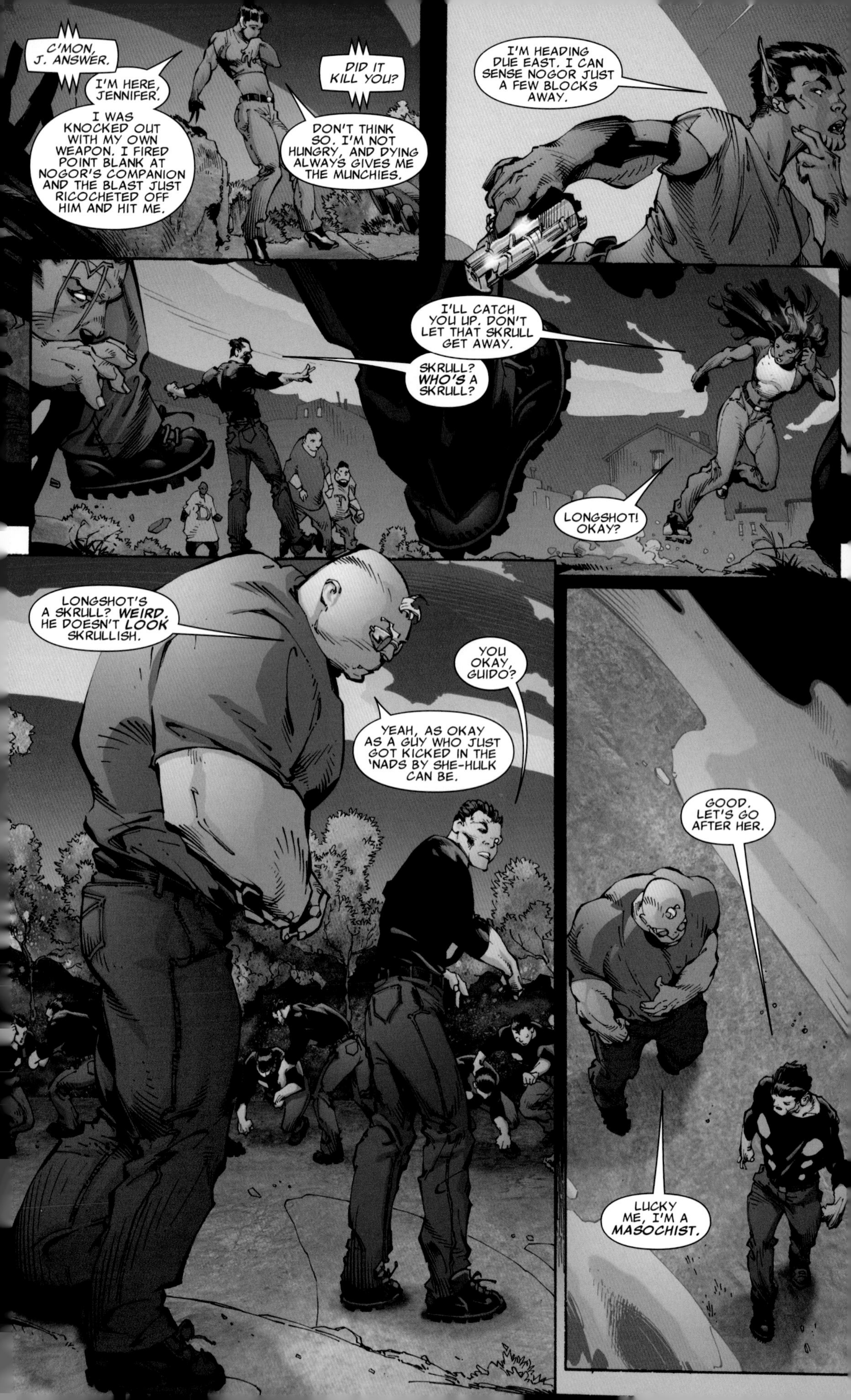
C'MON, J. ANSWER.
I'M HERE, JENNIFER.
I WAS KNOCKED OUT WITH MY OWN WEAPON. I FIRED POINT BLANK AT NOGOR'S COMPANION AND THE BLAST JUST RICOCHETED OFF HIM AND HIT ME.
DID IT KILL YOU?
DON'T THINK SO. I'M NOT HUNGRY, AND DYING ALWAYS GIVES ME THE MUNCHIES.
I'M HEADING DUE EAST. I CAN SENSE NOGOR JUST A FEW BLOCKS AWAY.
I'LL CATCH YOU UP. DON'T LET THAT SKRULL GET AWAY.
SKRULL? WHO'S A SKRULL?
LONGSHOT! OKAY?
LONGSHOT'S A SKRULL? WEIRD. HE DOESN'T LOOK SKRULLISH.
YOU OKAY, GUIDO?
YEAH, AS OKAY AS A GUY WHO JUST GOT KICKED IN THE 'NADS BY SHE-HULK CAN BE.
GOOD. LET'S GO AFTER HER.
LUCKY ME, I'M A MASOCHIST.

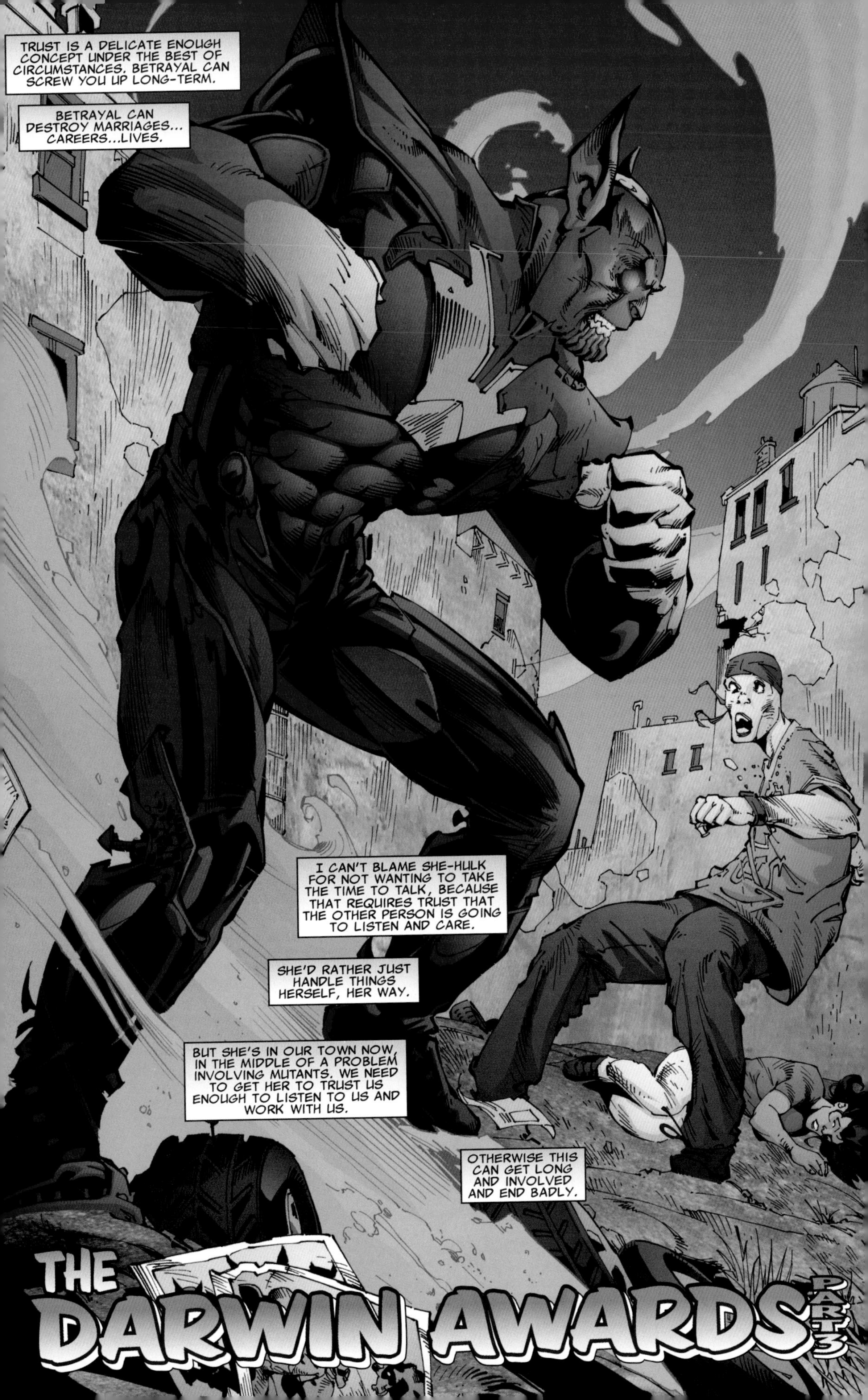
TRUST IS A DELICATE ENOUGH CONCEPT UNDER THE BEST OF CIRCUMSTANCES. BETRAYAL CAN SCREW YOU UP LONG-TERM.
BETRAYAL CAN DESTROY MARRIAGES... CAREERS...LIVES.
I CAN'T BLAME SHE-HULK FOR NOT WANTING TO TAKE THE TIME TO TALK, BECAUSE THAT REQUIRES TRUST THAT THE OTHER PERSON IS GOING TO LISTEN AND CARE.
SHE'D RATHER JUST HANDLE THINGS HERSELF, HER WAY.
BUT SHE'S IN OUR TOWN NOW, IN THE MIDDLE OF A PROBLEM INVOLVING MUTANTS. WE NEED TO GET HER TO TRUST US ENOUGH TO LISTEN TO US AND WORK WITH US.
OTHERWISE THIS CAN GET LONG AND INVOLVED AND END BADLY.
THE DARWIN AWARDS PART 3

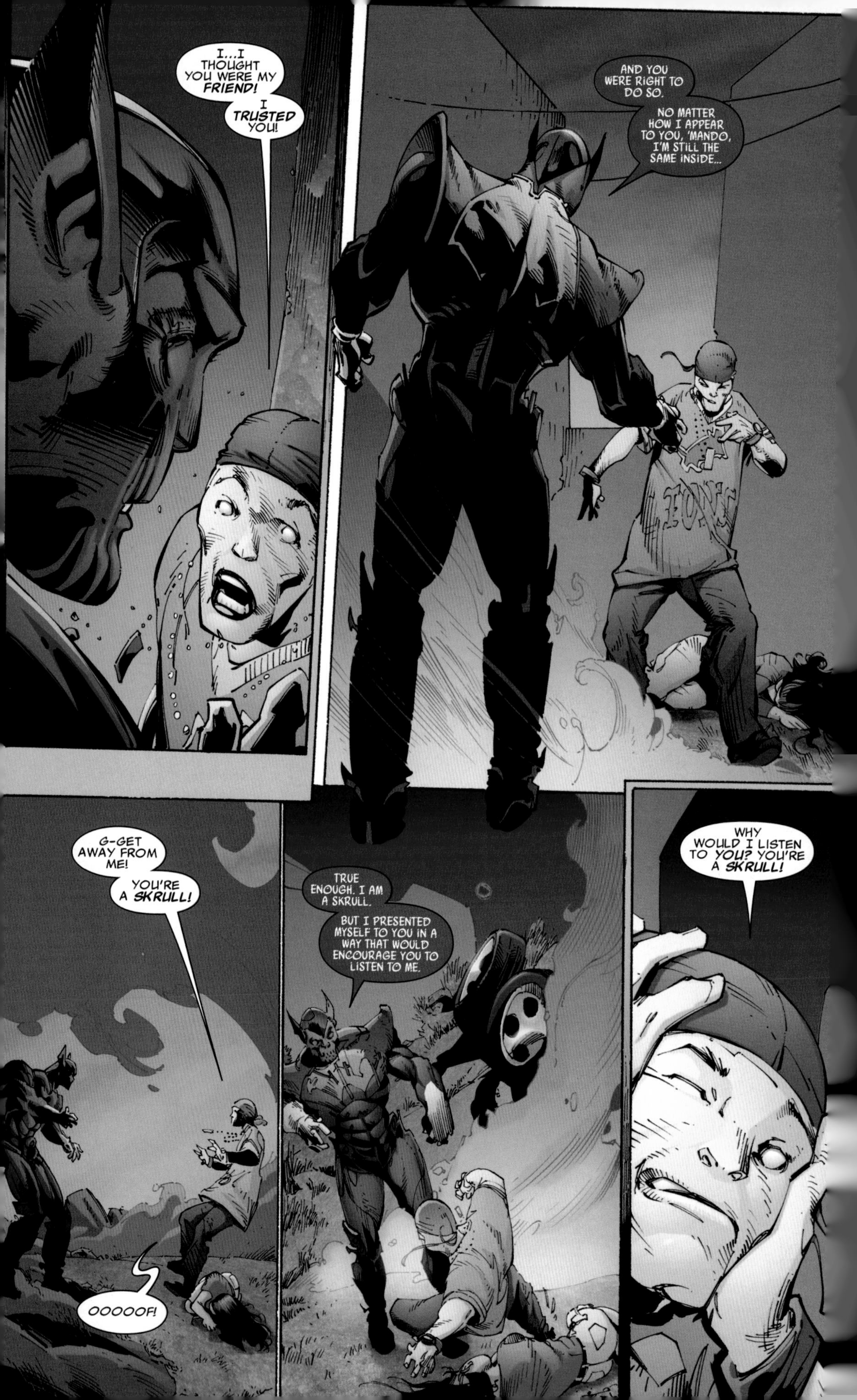
I...I THOUGHT YOU WERE MY *FRIEND!*
I *TRUSTED* YOU!
AND YOU WERE RIGHT TO DO SO.
NO MATTER HOW I APPEAR TO YOU, 'MANDO, I'M STILL THE SAME INSIDE...
G-GET AWAY FROM ME!
YOU'RE A *SKRULL!*
OOOOOF!
TRUE ENOUGH. I AM A SKRULL.
BUT I PRESENTED MYSELF TO YOU IN A WAY THAT WOULD ENCOURAGE YOU TO LISTEN TO ME.
WHY WOULD I LISTEN TO *YOU?* YOU'RE A *SKRULL!*

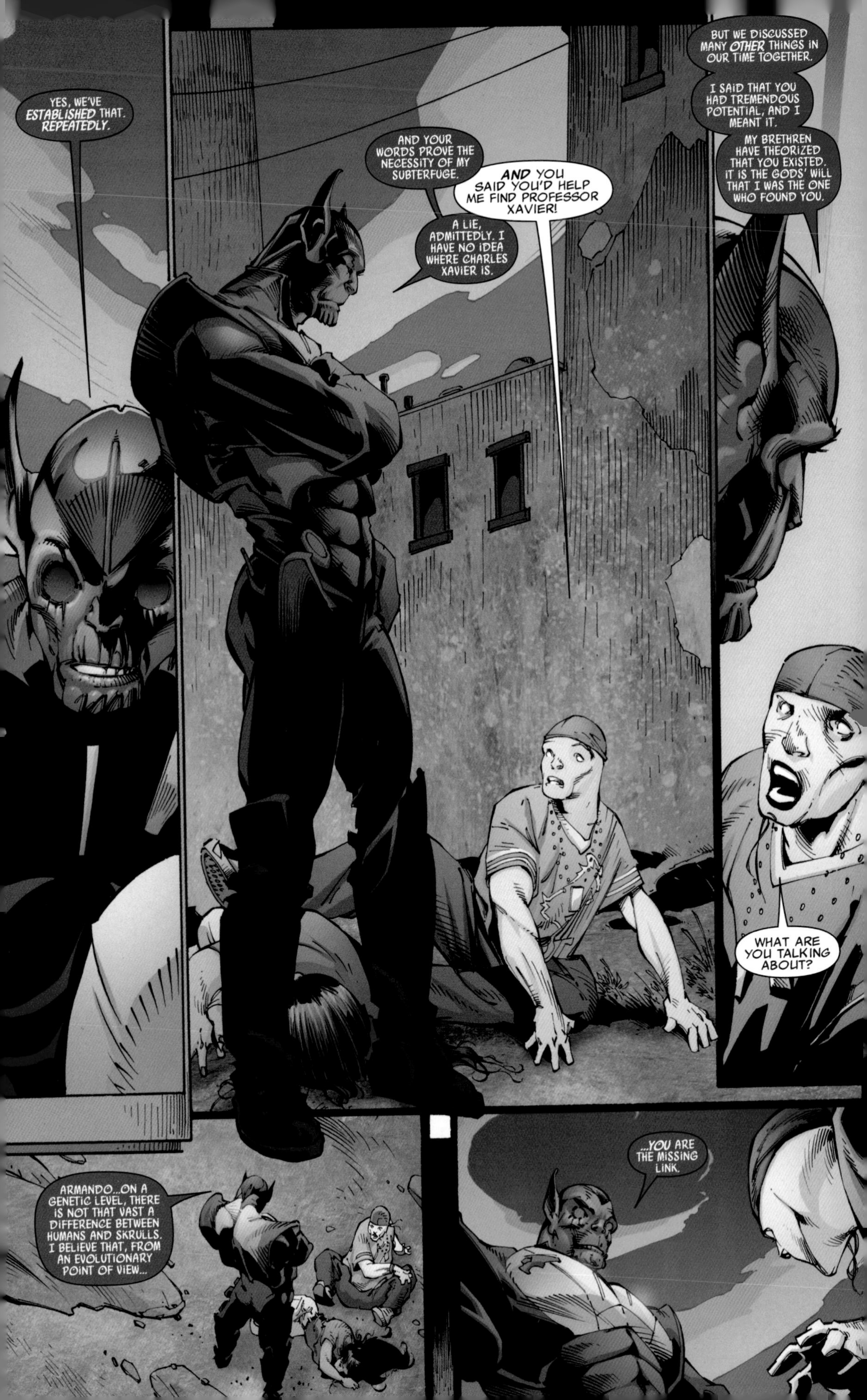
YES, WE'VE *ESTABLISHED* THAT. *REPEATEDLY.*
AND YOUR WORDS PROVE THE NECESSITY OF MY SUBTERFUGE.
AND YOU SAID YOU'D HELP ME FIND PROFESSOR XAVIER!
A LIE, ADMITTEDLY. I HAVE NO IDEA WHERE CHARLES XAVIER IS.
BUT WE DISCUSSED MANY *OTHER* THINGS IN OUR TIME TOGETHER.
I SAID THAT YOU HAD TREMENDOUS POTENTIAL, AND I MEANT IT.
MY BRETHREN HAVE THEORIZED THAT YOU EXISTED. IT IS THE GODS' WILL THAT I WAS THE ONE WHO FOUND YOU.
WHAT ARE YOU TALKING ABOUT?
ARMANDO...ON A GENETIC LEVEL, THERE IS NOT THAT VAST A DIFFERENCE BETWEEN HUMANS AND SKRULLS. I BELIEVE THAT, FROM AN EVOLUTIONARY POINT OF VIEW...
...*YOU* ARE THE MISSING LINK.

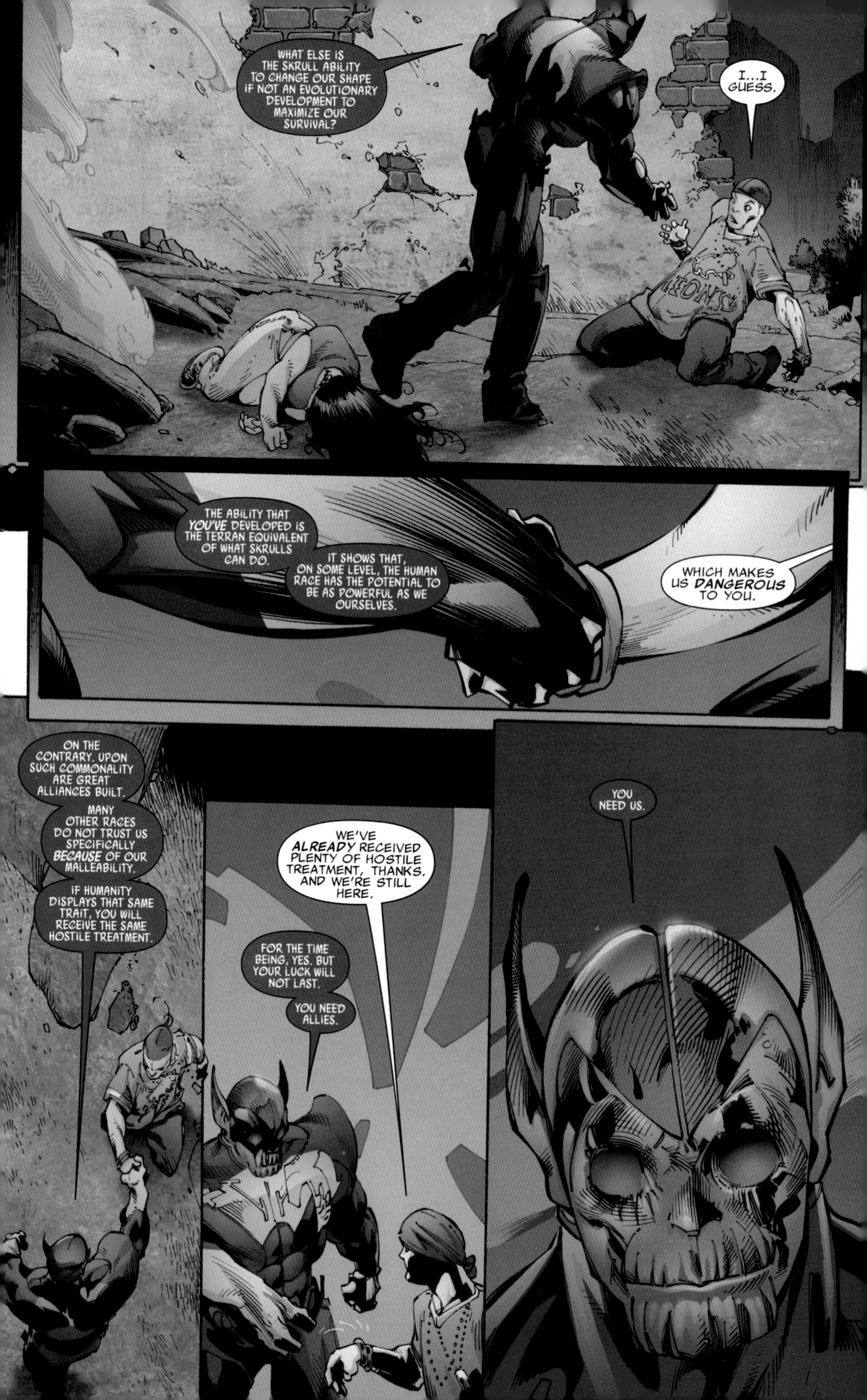
WHAT ELSE IS THE SKRULL ABILITY TO CHANGE OUR SHAPE IF NOT AN EVOLUTIONARY DEVELOPMENT TO MAXIMIZE OUR SURVIVAL?
I...I GUESS.
THE ABILITY THAT YOU'VE DEVELOPED IS THE TERRAN EQUIVALENT OF WHAT SKRULLS CAN DO.
IT SHOWS THAT, ON SOME LEVEL, THE HUMAN RACE HAS THE POTENTIAL TO BE AS POWERFUL AS WE OURSELVES.
WHICH MAKES US DANGEROUS TO YOU.
ON THE CONTRARY. UPON SUCH COMMONALITY ARE GREAT ALLIANCES BUILT.
MANY OTHER RACES DO NOT TRUST US SPECIFICALLY BECAUSE OF OUR MALLEABILITY.
IF HUMANITY DISPLAYS THAT SAME TRAIT, YOU WILL RECEIVE THE SAME HOSTILE TREATMENT.
WE'VE ALREADY RECEIVED PLENTY OF HOSTILE TREATMENT, THANKS. AND WE'RE STILL HERE.
FOR THE TIME BEING, YES. BUT YOUR LUCK WILL NOT LAST.
YOU NEED ALLIES.
YOU NEED US.

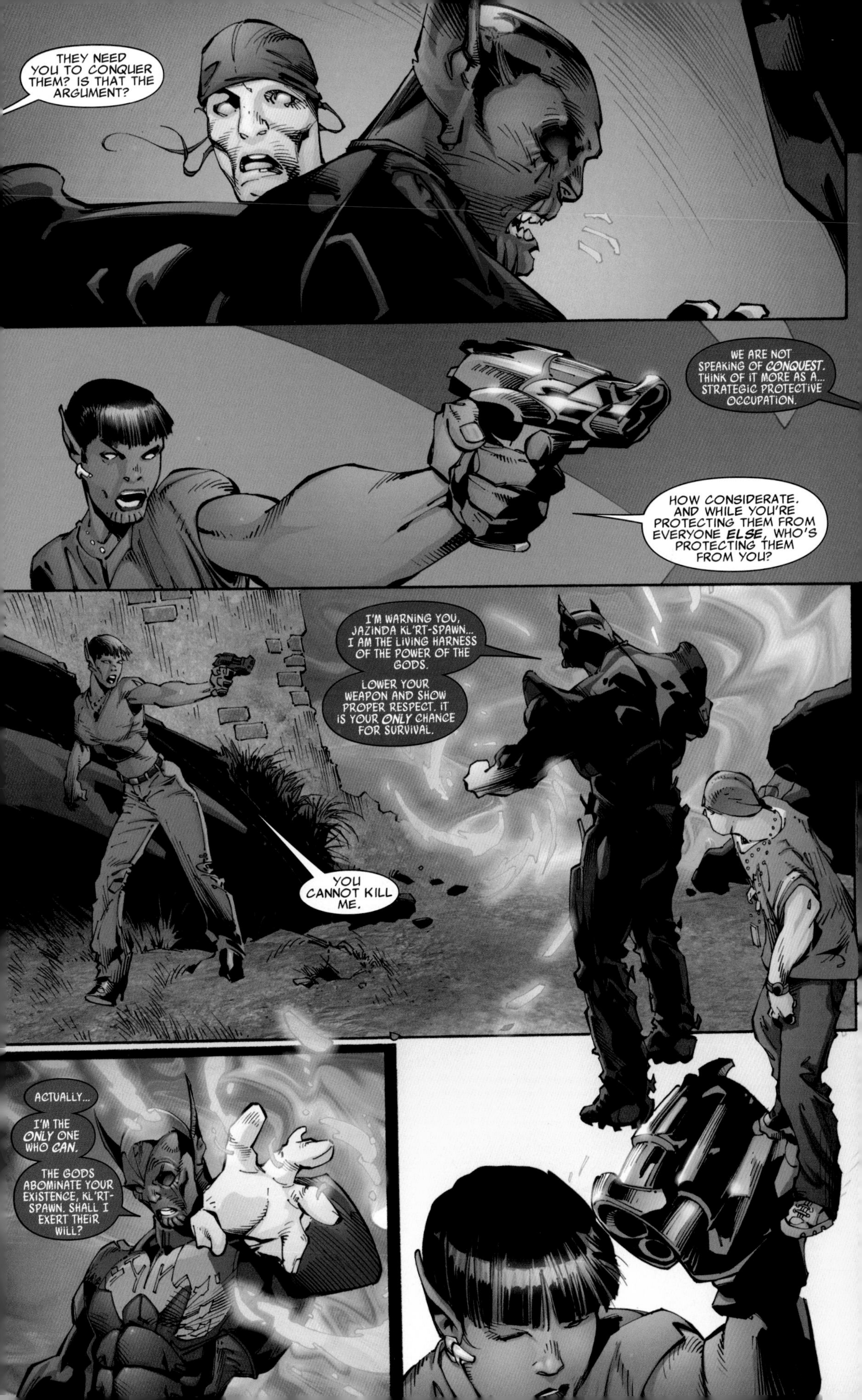
THEY NEED YOU TO CONQUER THEM? IS THAT THE ARGUMENT?
WE ARE NOT SPEAKING OF CONQUEST. THINK OF IT MORE AS A... STRATEGIC PROTECTIVE OCCUPATION.
HOW CONSIDERATE. AND WHILE YOU'RE PROTECTING THEM FROM EVERYONE ELSE, WHO'S PROTECTING THEM FROM YOU?
I'M WARNING YOU, JAZINDA KL'RT-SPAWN... I AM THE LIVING HARNESS OF THE POWER OF THE GODS.
LOWER YOUR WEAPON AND SHOW PROPER RESPECT. IT IS YOUR ONLY CHANCE FOR SURVIVAL.
YOU CANNOT KILL ME.
ACTUALLY...
I'M THE ONLY ONE WHO CAN.
THE GODS ABOMINATE YOUR EXISTENCE, KL'RT-SPAWN. SHALL I EXERT THEIR WILL?

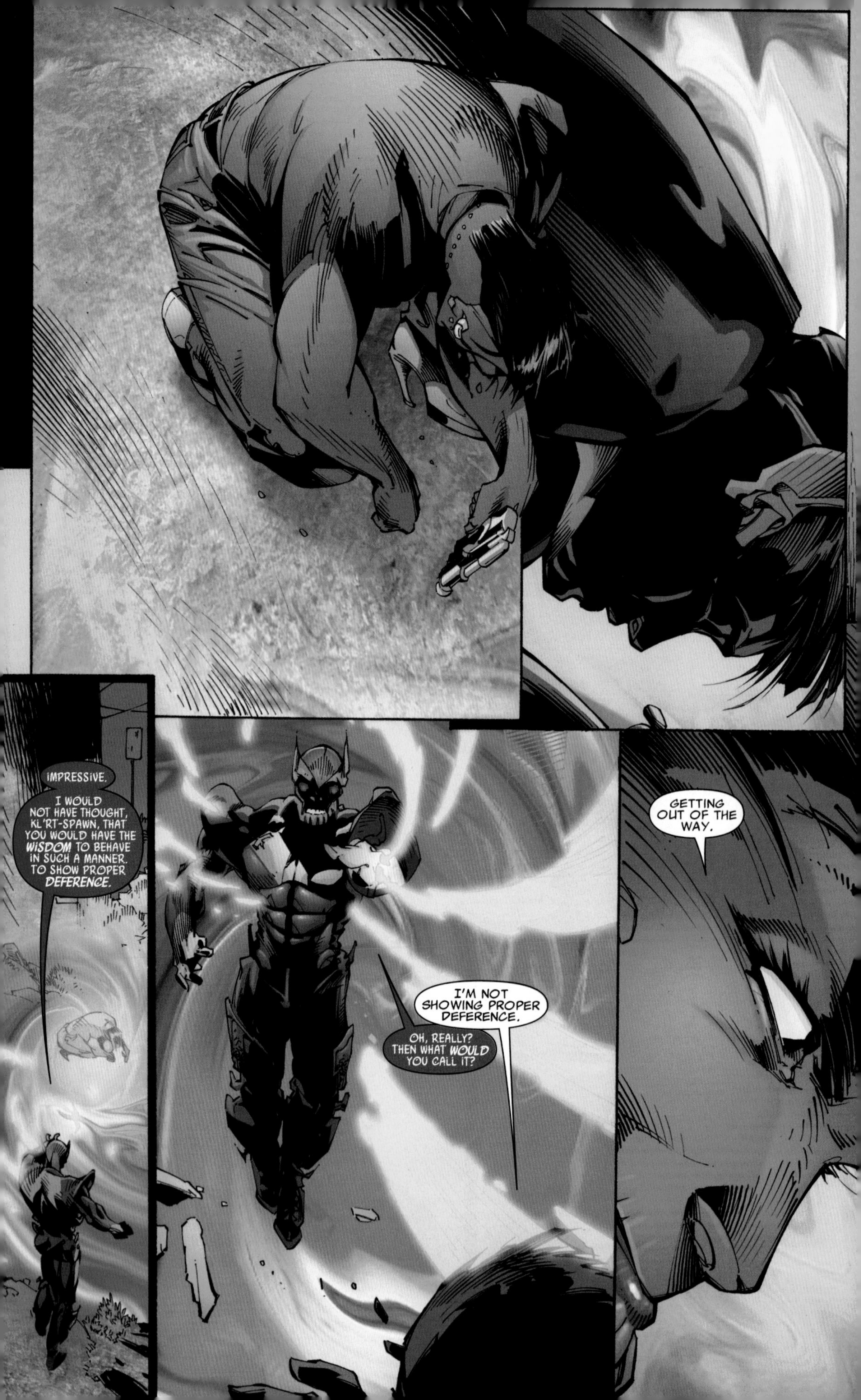
IMPRESSIVE.
I WOULD NOT HAVE THOUGHT, KL'RT-SPAWN, THAT YOU WOULD HAVE THE WISDOM TO BEHAVE IN SUCH A MANNER. TO SHOW PROPER DEFERENCE.
I'M NOT SHOWING PROPER DEFERENCE.
OH, REALLY? THEN WHAT WOULD YOU CALL IT?
GETTING OUT OF THE WAY.

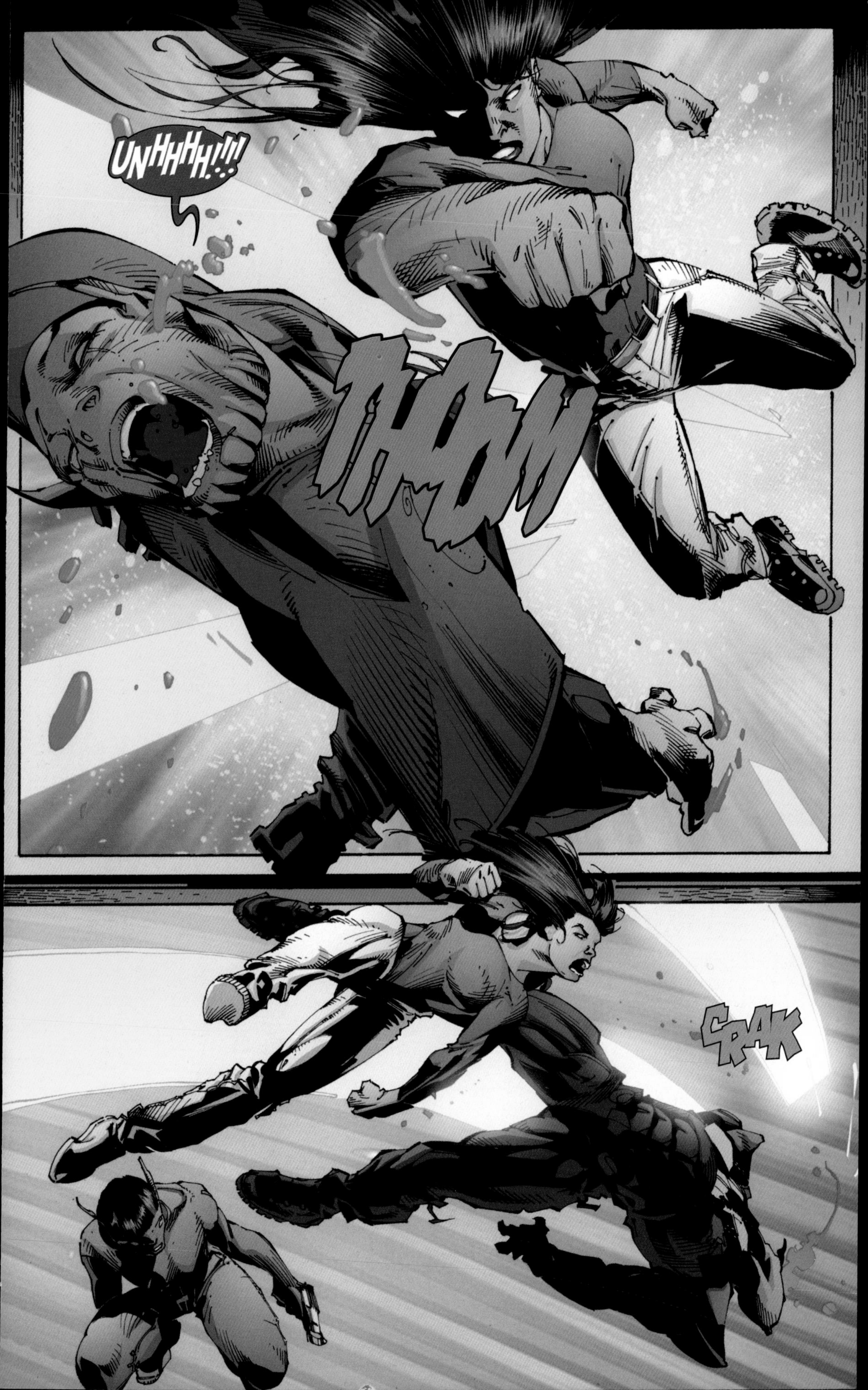
UNHHHH!!!!
THOOM
CRAK

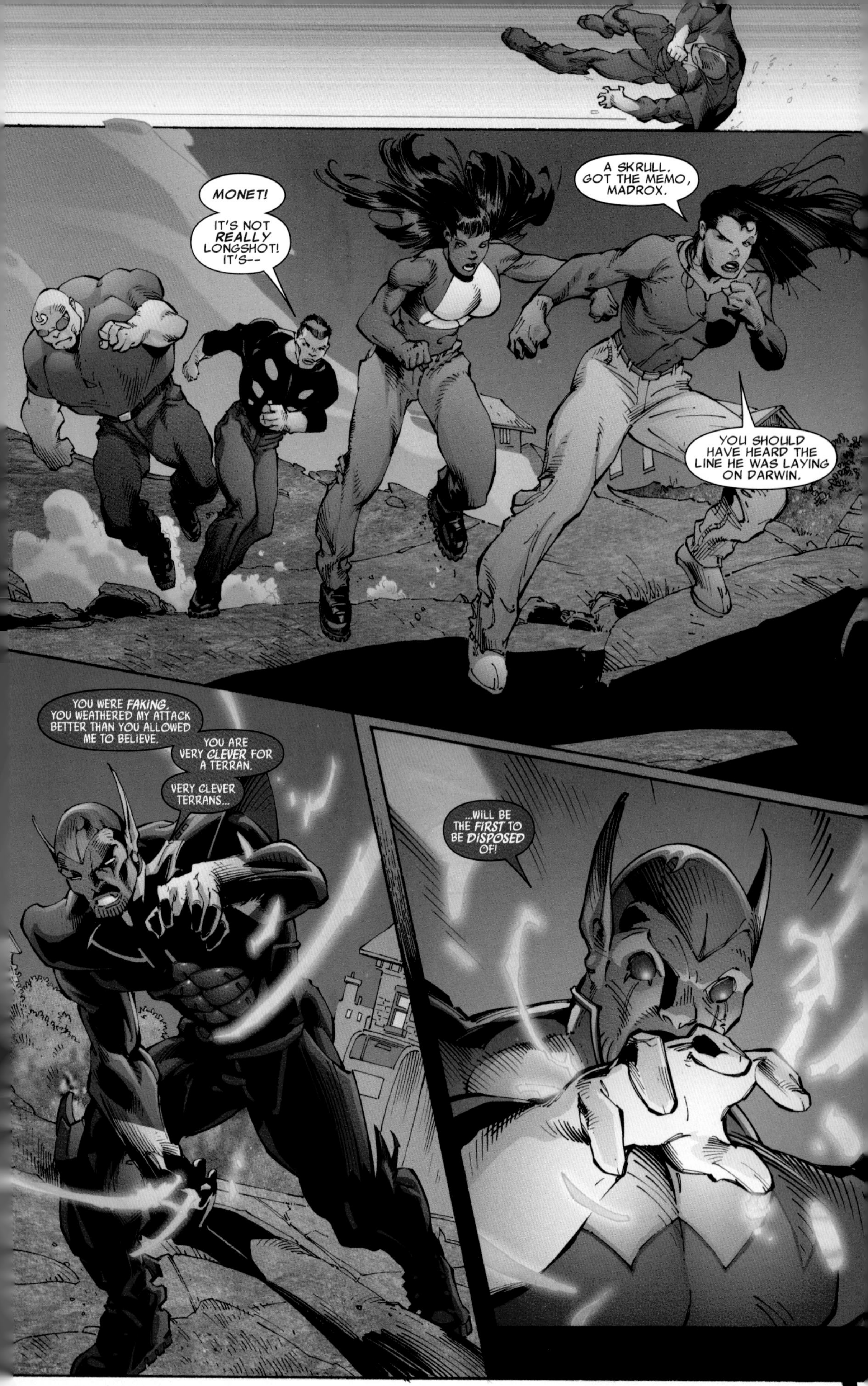
MONET!
IT'S NOT REALLY LONGSHOT! IT'S--
A SKRULL. GOT THE MEMO, MADROX.
YOU SHOULD HAVE HEARD THE LINE HE WAS LAYING ON DARWIN.
YOU WERE FAKING. YOU WEATHERED MY ATTACK BETTER THAN YOU ALLOWED ME TO BELIEVE.
YOU ARE VERY CLEVER FOR A TERRAN.
VERY CLEVER TERRANS...
...WILL BE THE FIRST TO BE DISPOSED OF!

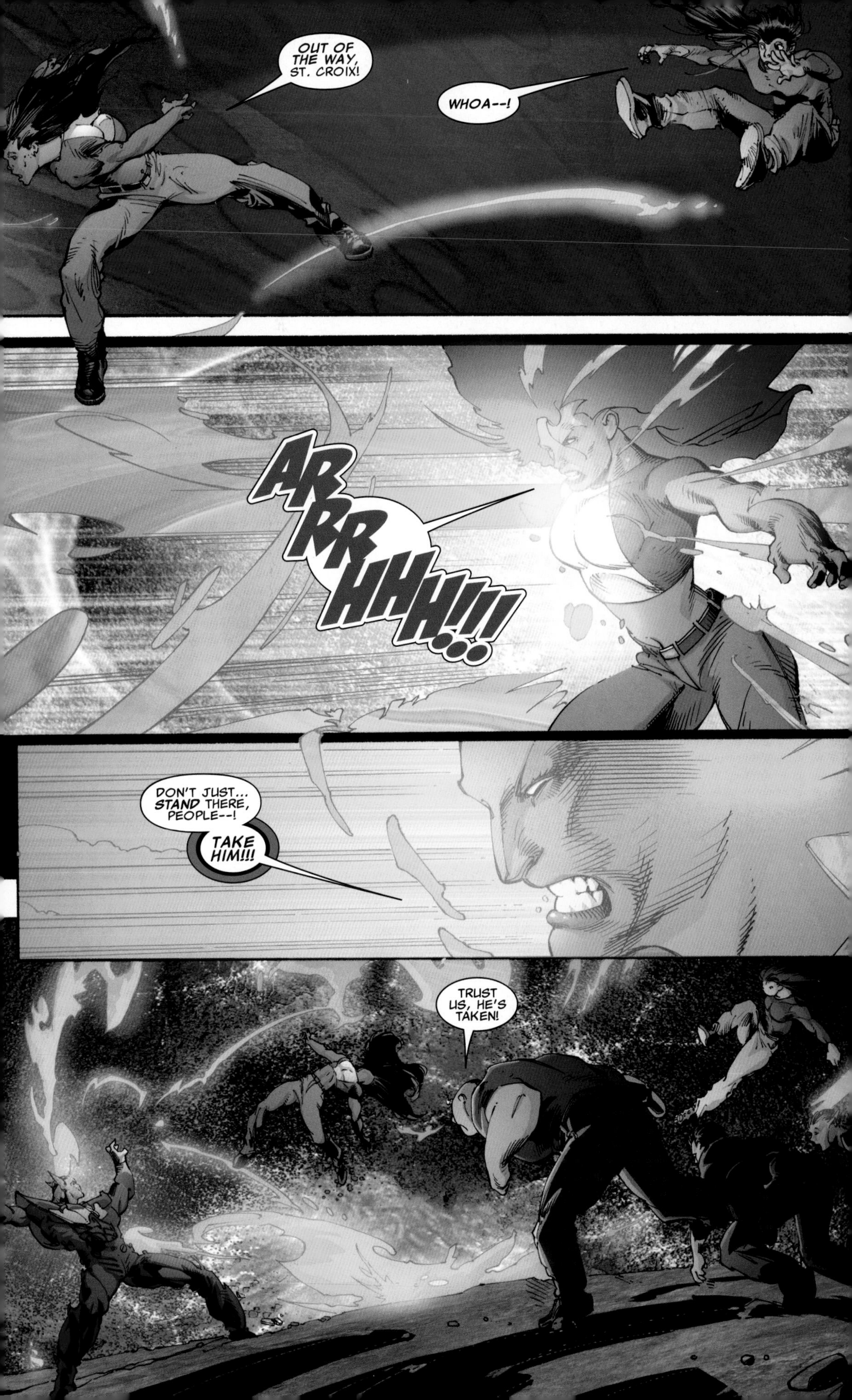
OUT OF THE WAY, ST. CROIX!
WHOA--!
ARRRHHH!!!...
DON'T JUST... STAND THERE, PEOPLE--!
TAKE HIM!!!
TRUST US, HE'S TAKEN!

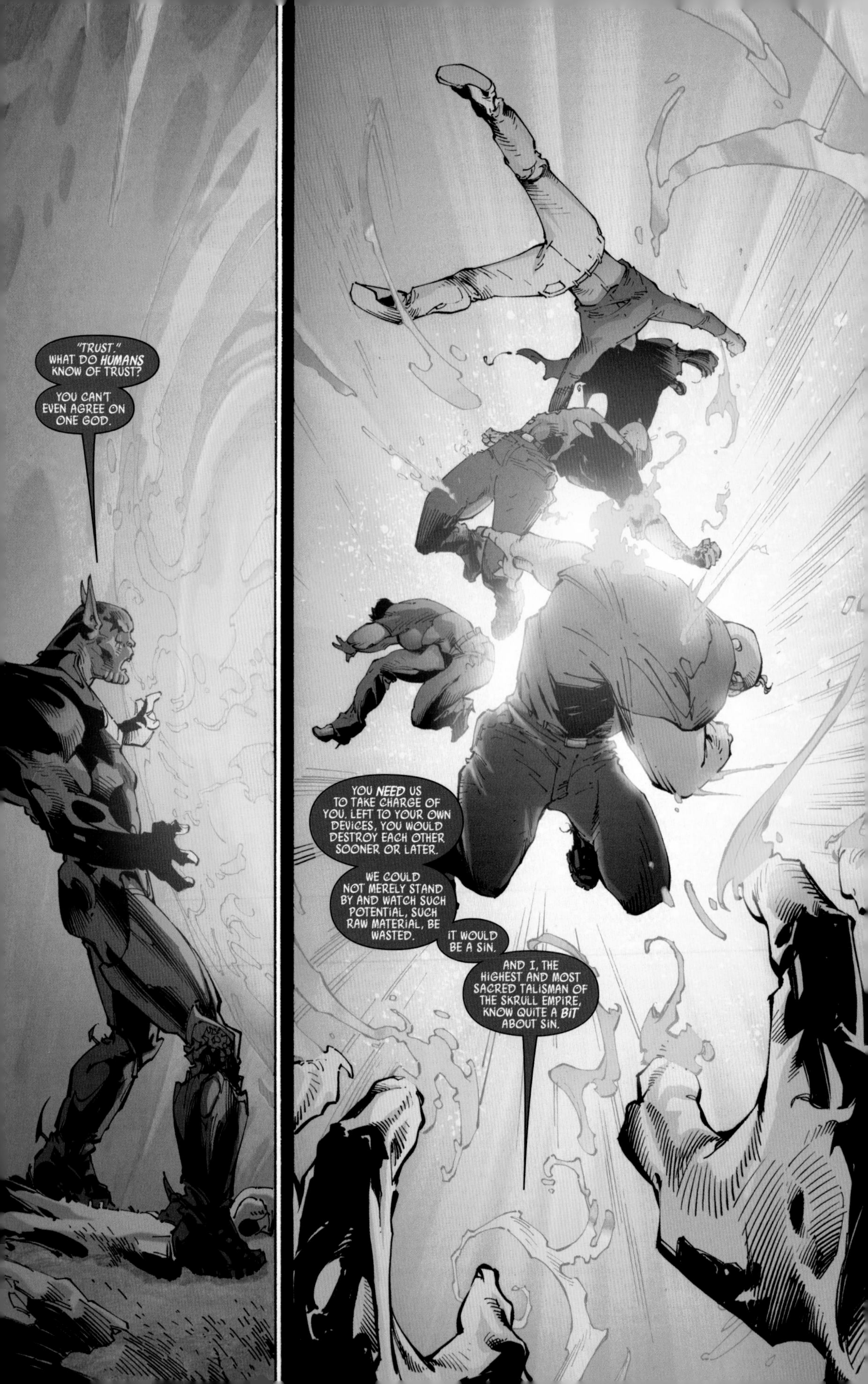
"TRUST." WHAT DO HUMANS KNOW OF TRUST?
YOU CAN'T EVEN AGREE ON ONE GOD.
YOU NEED US TO TAKE CHARGE OF YOU. LEFT TO YOUR OWN DEVICES, YOU WOULD DESTROY EACH OTHER SOONER OR LATER.
WE COULD NOT MERELY STAND BY AND WATCH SUCH POTENTIAL, SUCH RAW MATERIAL, BE WASTED.
IT WOULD BE A SIN.
AND I, THE HIGHEST AND MOST SACRED TALISMAN OF THE SKRULL EMPIRE, KNOW QUITE A BIT ABOUT SIN.

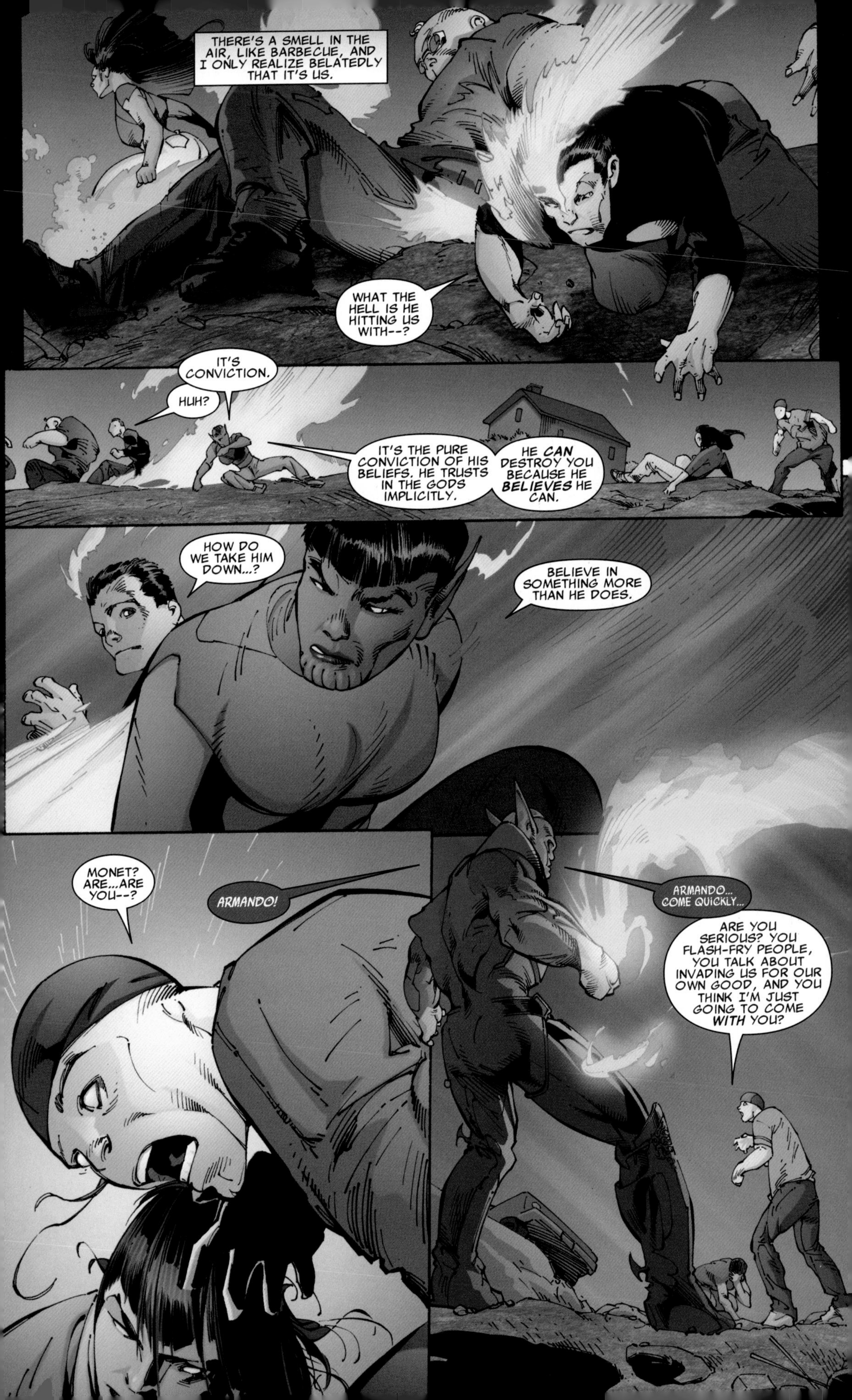
THERE'S A SMELL IN THE AIR, LIKE BARBECUE, AND I ONLY REALIZE BELATEDLY THAT IT'S US.
WHAT THE HELL IS HE HITTING US WITH--?
IT'S CONVICTION.
HUH?
IT'S THE PURE CONVICTION OF HIS BELIEFS. HE TRUSTS IN THE GODS IMPLICITLY.
HE CAN DESTROY YOU BECAUSE HE BELIEVES HE CAN.
HOW DO WE TAKE HIM DOWN...?
BELIEVE IN SOMETHING MORE THAN HE DOES.
MONET? ARE...ARE YOU--?
ARMANDO!
ARMANDO... COME QUICKLY...
ARE YOU SERIOUS? YOU FLASH-FRY PEOPLE, YOU TALK ABOUT INVADING US FOR OUR OWN GOOD, AND YOU THINK I'M JUST GOING TO COME WITH YOU?

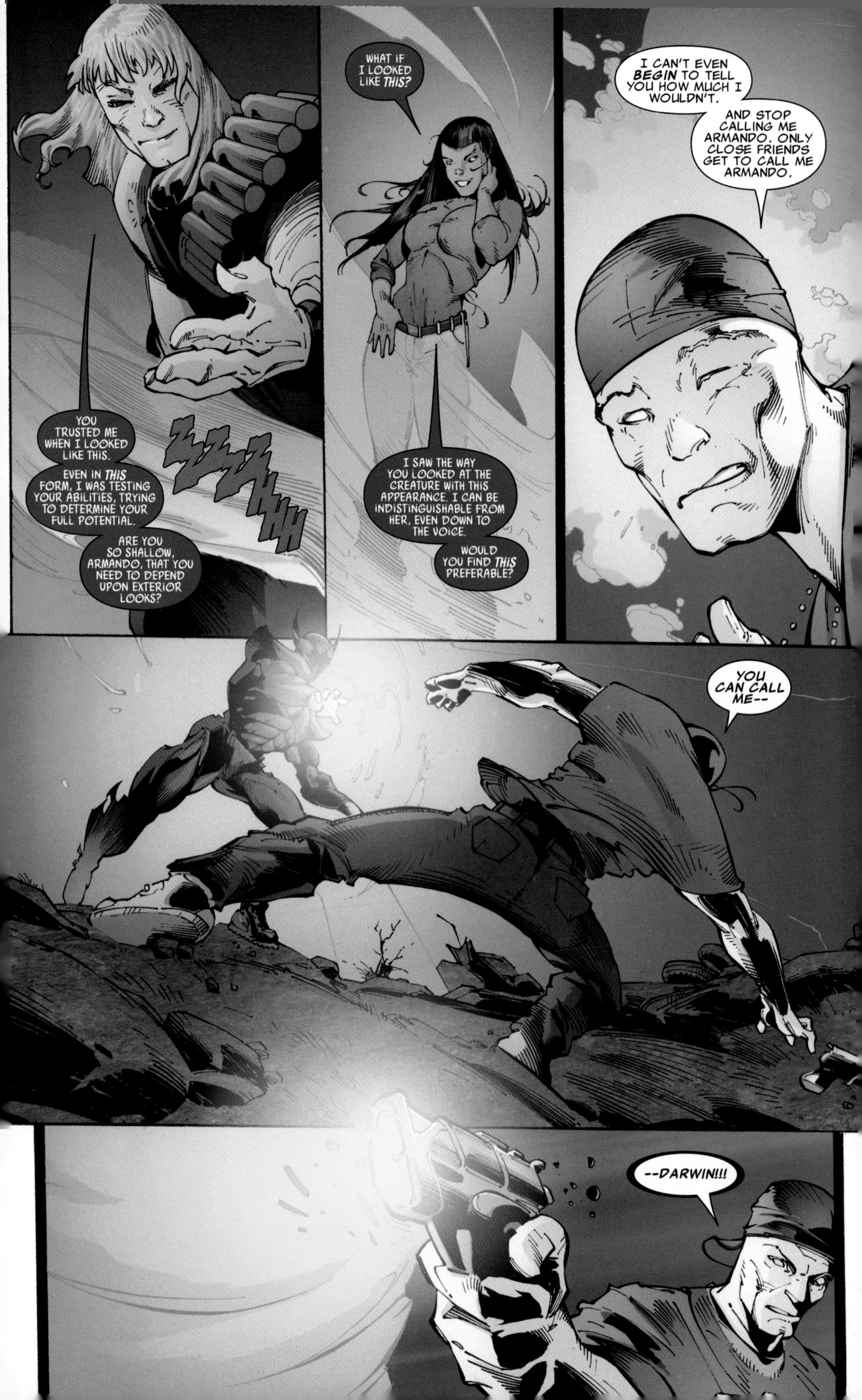

YOU TRUSTED ME WHEN I LOOKED LIKE THIS.
EVEN IN THIS FORM, I WAS TESTING YOUR ABILITIES, TRYING TO DETERMINE YOUR FULL POTENTIAL.
ARE YOU SO SHALLOW, ARMANDO, THAT YOU NEED TO DEPEND UPON EXTERIOR LOOKS?
ZZZZHHH
WHAT IF I LOOKED LIKE THIS?
I SAW THE WAY YOU LOOKED AT THE CREATURE WITH THIS APPEARANCE. I CAN BE INDISTINGUISHABLE FROM HER, EVEN DOWN TO THE VOICE.
WOULD YOU FIND THIS PREFERABLE?
I CAN'T EVEN BEGIN TO TELL YOU HOW MUCH I WOULDN'T.
AND STOP CALLING ME ARMANDO. ONLY CLOSE FRIENDS GET TO CALL ME ARMANDO.
YOU CAN CALL ME--
--DARWIN!!!

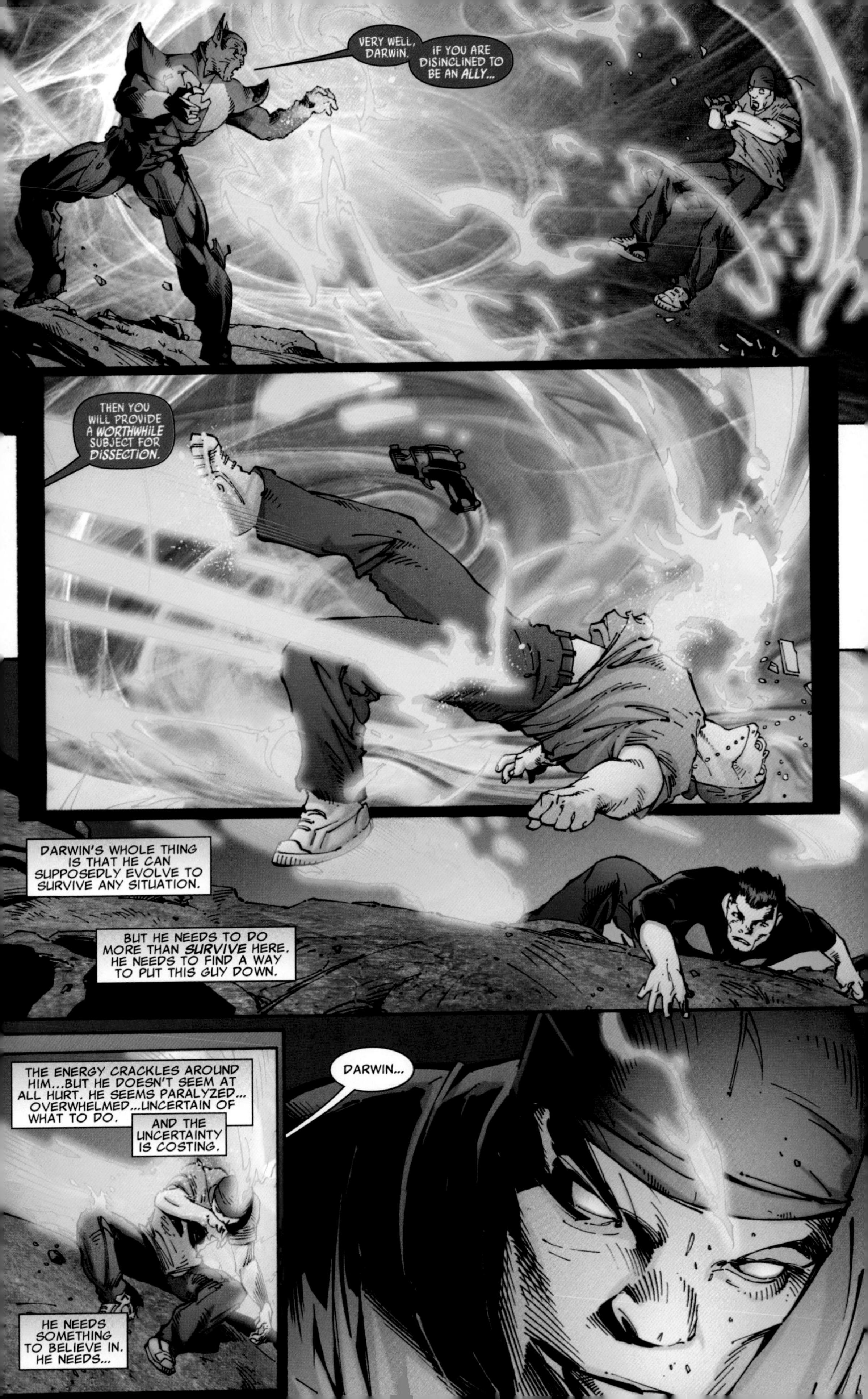
VERY WELL, DARWIN.
IF YOU ARE DISINCLINED TO BE AN ALLY...
THEN YOU WILL PROVIDE A WORTHWHILE SUBJECT FOR DISSECTION.
DARWIN'S WHOLE THING IS THAT HE CAN SUPPOSEDLY EVOLVE TO SURVIVE ANY SITUATION.
BUT HE NEEDS TO DO MORE THAN SURVIVE HERE. HE NEEDS TO FIND A WAY TO PUT THIS GUY DOWN.
THE ENERGY CRACKLES AROUND HIM...BUT HE DOESN'T SEEM AT ALL HURT. HE SEEMS PARALYZED... OVERWHELMED...UNCERTAIN OF WHAT TO DO.
AND THE UNCERTAINTY IS COSTING.
DARWIN...
HE NEEDS SOMETHING TO BELIEVE IN. HE NEEDS...

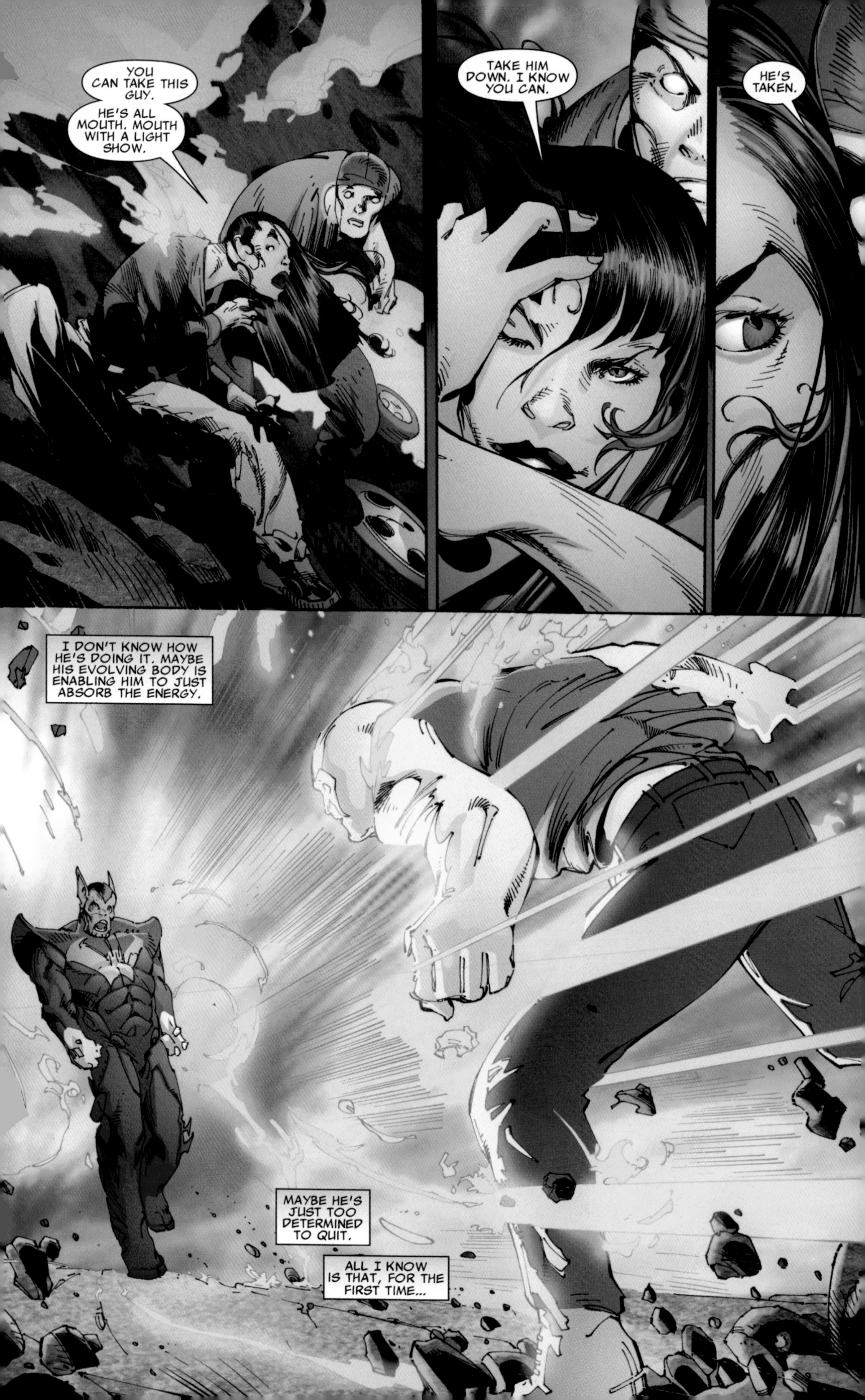
YOU CAN TAKE THIS GUY.
HE'S ALL MOUTH. MOUTH WITH A LIGHT SHOW.
TAKE HIM DOWN. I KNOW YOU CAN.
HE'S TAKEN.
I DON'T KNOW HOW HE'S DOING IT. MAYBE HIS EVOLVING BODY IS ENABLING HIM TO JUST ABSORB THE ENERGY.
MAYBE HE'S JUST TOO DETERMINED TO QUIT.
ALL I KNOW IS THAT, FOR THE FIRST TIME...

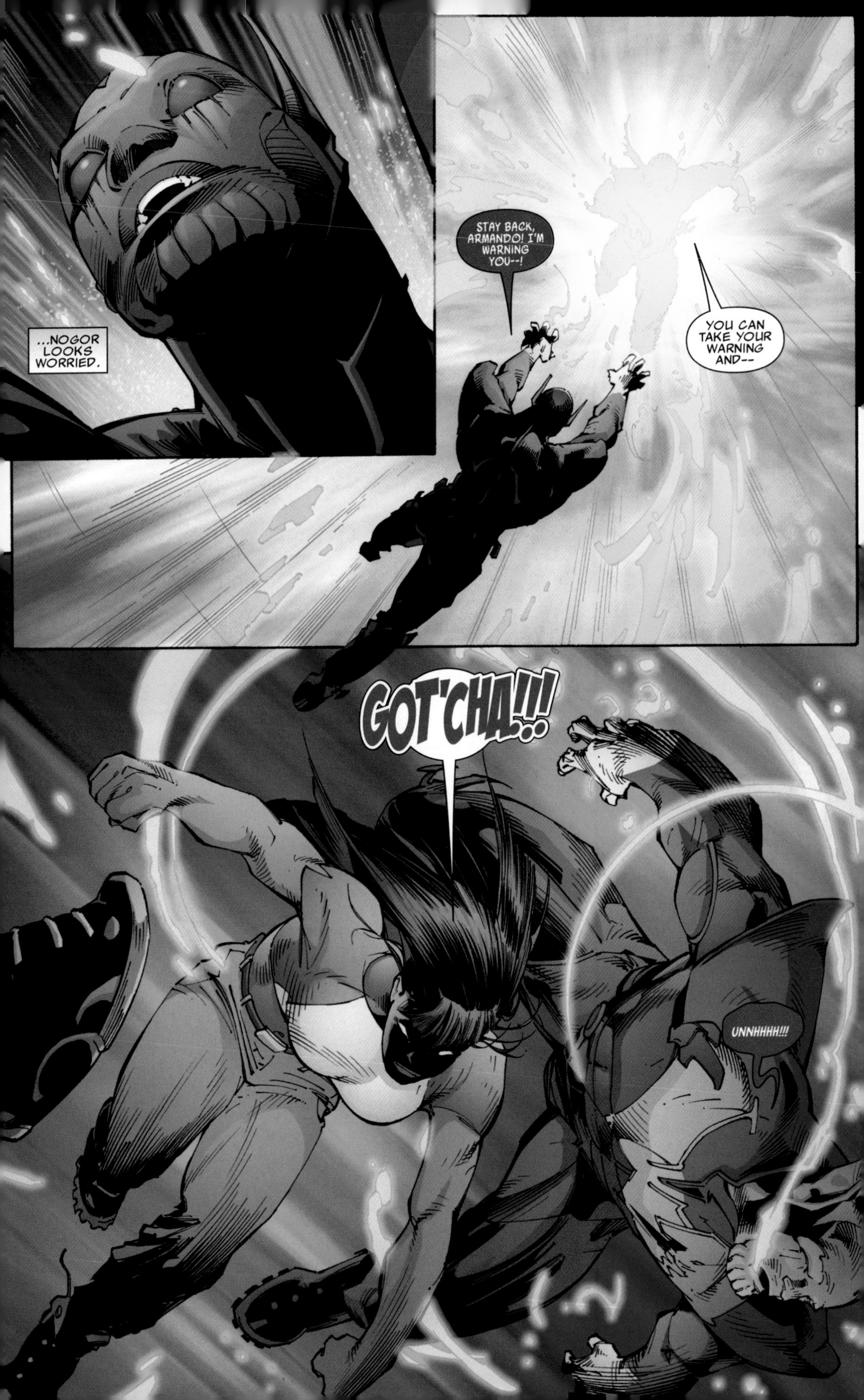
...NOGOR LOOKS WORRIED.
STAY BACK, ARMANDO! I'M WARNING YOU--!
YOU CAN TAKE YOUR WARNING AND--
GOT'CHA!!!
UNNHHHH!!!

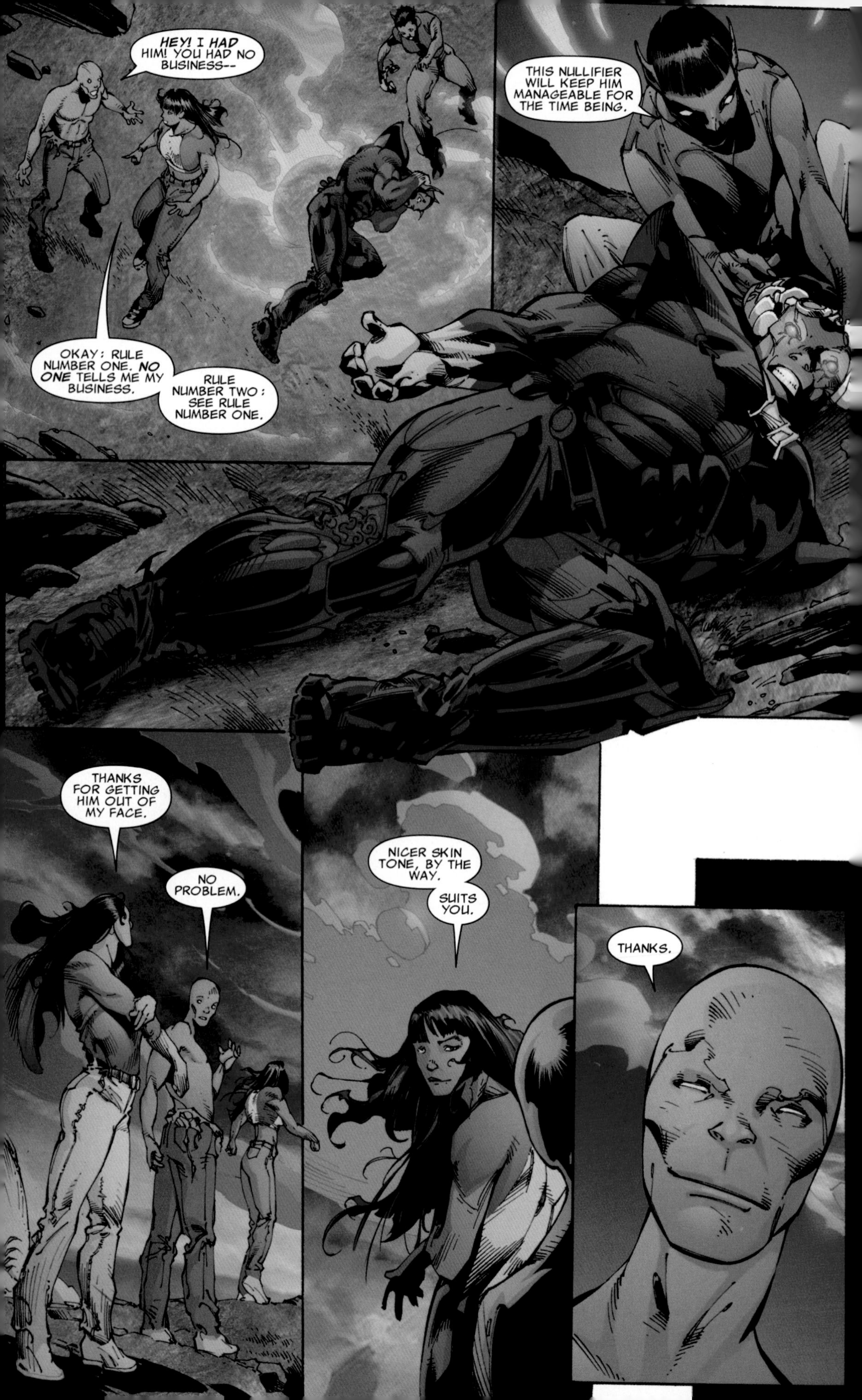
HEY! I HAD HIM! YOU HAD NO BUSINESS--
OKAY: RULE NUMBER ONE. NO ONE TELLS ME MY BUSINESS.
RULE NUMBER TWO: SEE RULE NUMBER ONE.
THIS NULLIFIER WILL KEEP HIM MANAGEABLE FOR THE TIME BEING.
THANKS FOR GETTING HIM OUT OF MY FACE.
NO PROBLEM.
NICER SKIN TONE, BY THE WAY.
SUITS YOU.
THANKS.

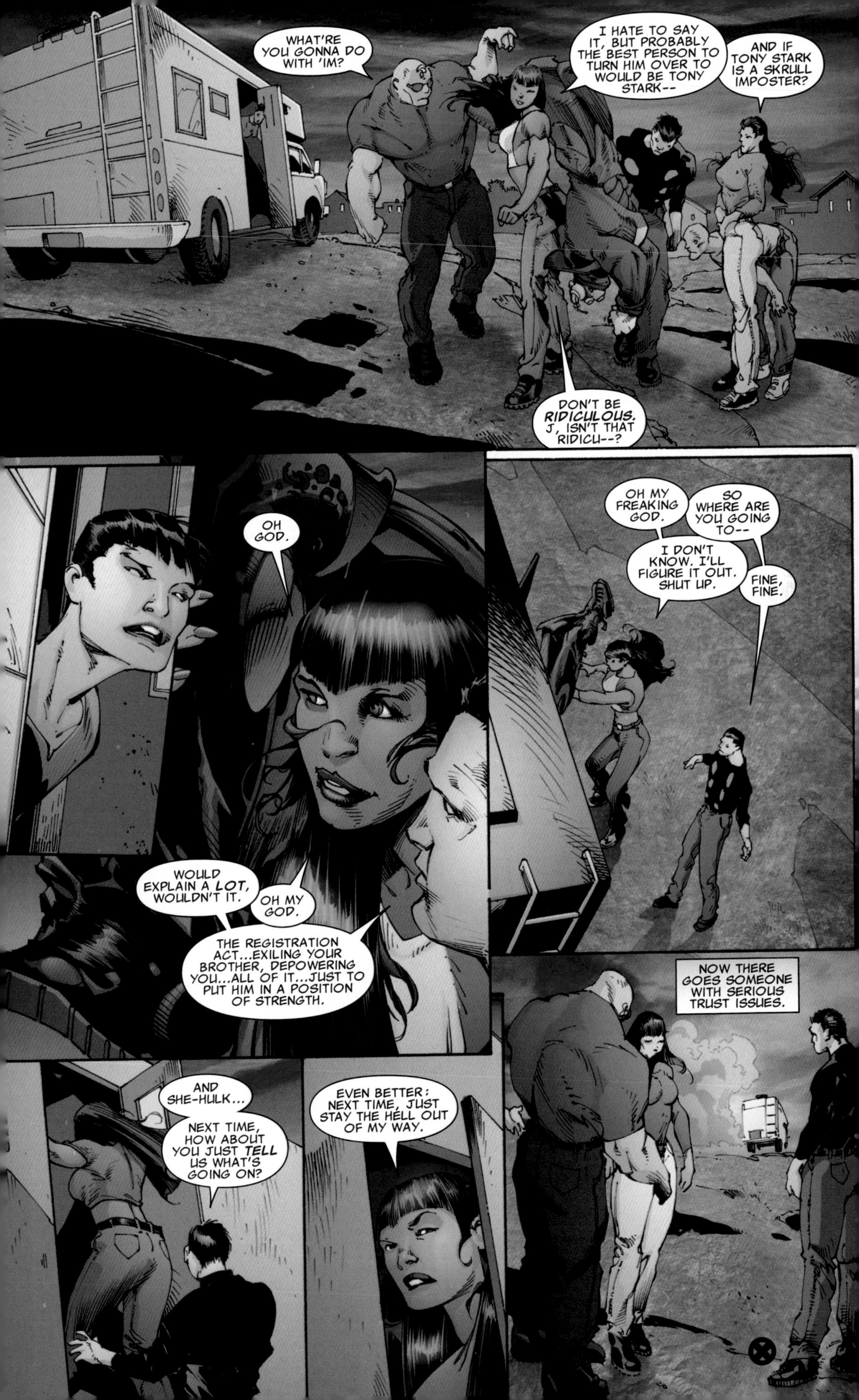
WHAT'RE YOU GONNA DO WITH 'IM?
I HATE TO SAY IT, BUT PROBABLY THE BEST PERSON TO TURN HIM OVER TO WOULD BE TONY STARK--
AND IF TONY STARK IS A SKRULL IMPOSTER?
DON'T BE RIDICULOUS. J, ISN'T THAT RIDICU--?
OH GOD.
WOULD EXPLAIN A LOT, WOULDN'T IT.
OH MY GOD.
THE REGISTRATION ACT...EXILING YOUR BROTHER, DEPOWERING YOU...ALL OF IT...JUST TO PUT HIM IN A POSITION OF STRENGTH.
OH MY FREAKING GOD.
SO WHERE ARE YOU GOING TO--
I DON'T KNOW. I'LL FIGURE IT OUT. SHUT UP.
FINE, FINE.
AND SHE-HULK...
NEXT TIME, HOW ABOUT YOU JUST TELL US WHAT'S GOING ON?
EVEN BETTER: NEXT TIME, JUST STAY THE HELL OUT OF MY WAY.
NOW THERE GOES SOMEONE WITH SERIOUS TRUST ISSUES.

32

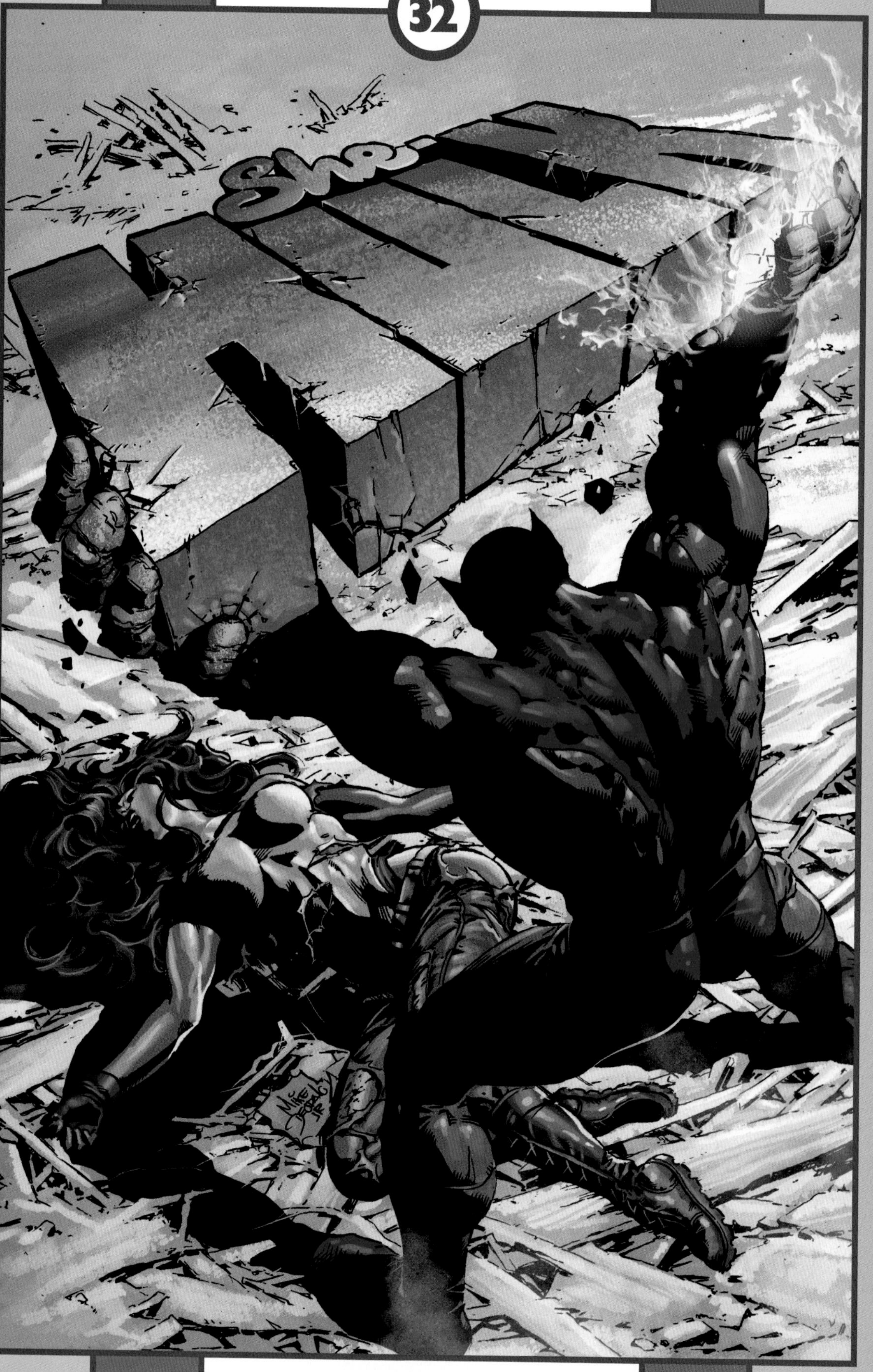

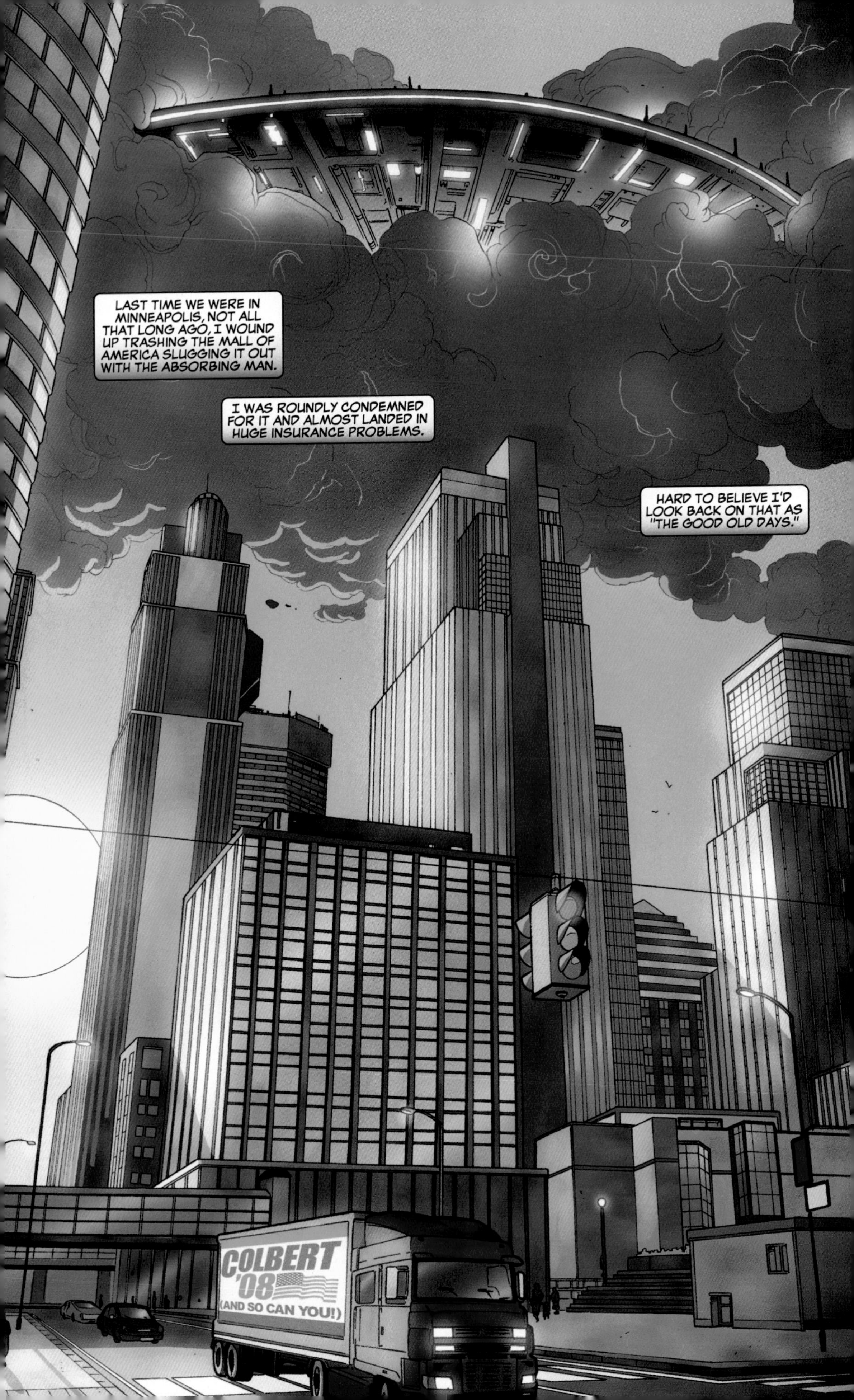
LAST TIME WE WERE IN MINNEAPOLIS, NOT ALL THAT LONG AGO, I WOUND UP TRASHING THE MALL OF AMERICA SLUGGING IT OUT WITH THE ABSORBING MAN.
I WAS ROUNDLY CONDEMNED FOR IT AND ALMOST LANDED IN HUGE INSURANCE PROBLEMS.
HARD TO BELIEVE I'D LOOK BACK ON THAT AS "THE GOOD OLD DAYS."
COLBERT '08
(AND SO CAN YOU!)

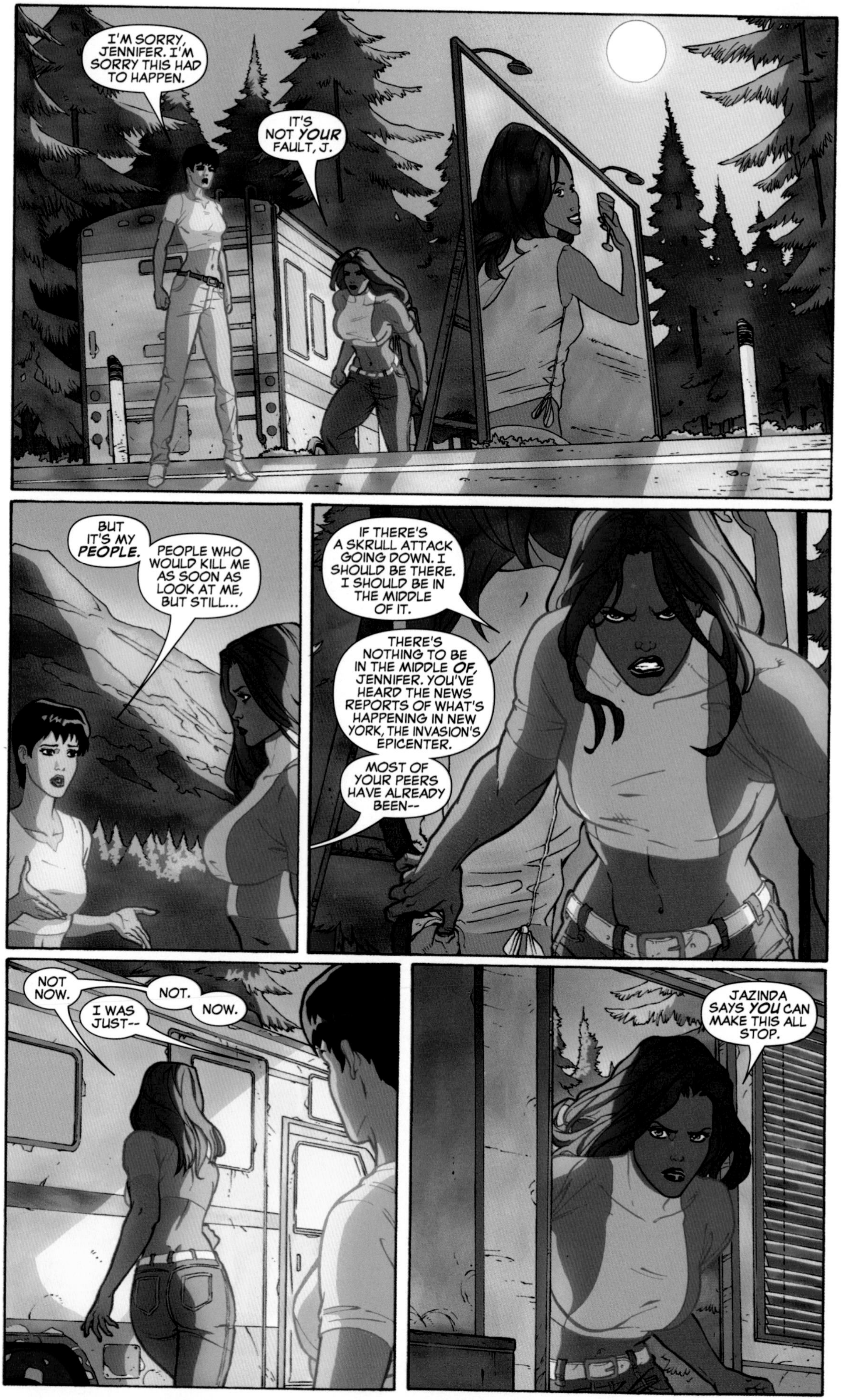

I'M SORRY, JENNIFER. I'M SORRY THIS HAD TO HAPPEN.
IT'S NOT YOUR FAULT, J.
BUT IT'S MY PEOPLE.
PEOPLE WHO WOULD KILL ME AS SOON AS LOOK AT ME, BUT STILL...
IF THERE'S A SKRULL ATTACK GOING DOWN. I SHOULD BE THERE. I SHOULD BE IN THE MIDDLE OF IT.
THERE'S NOTHING TO BE IN THE MIDDLE OF, JENNIFER. YOU'VE HEARD THE NEWS REPORTS OF WHAT'S HAPPENING IN NEW YORK, THE INVASION'S EPICENTER.
MOST OF YOUR PEERS HAVE ALREADY BEEN--
NOT NOW.
I WAS JUST--
NOT.
NOW.
JAZINDA SAYS YOU CAN MAKE THIS ALL STOP.

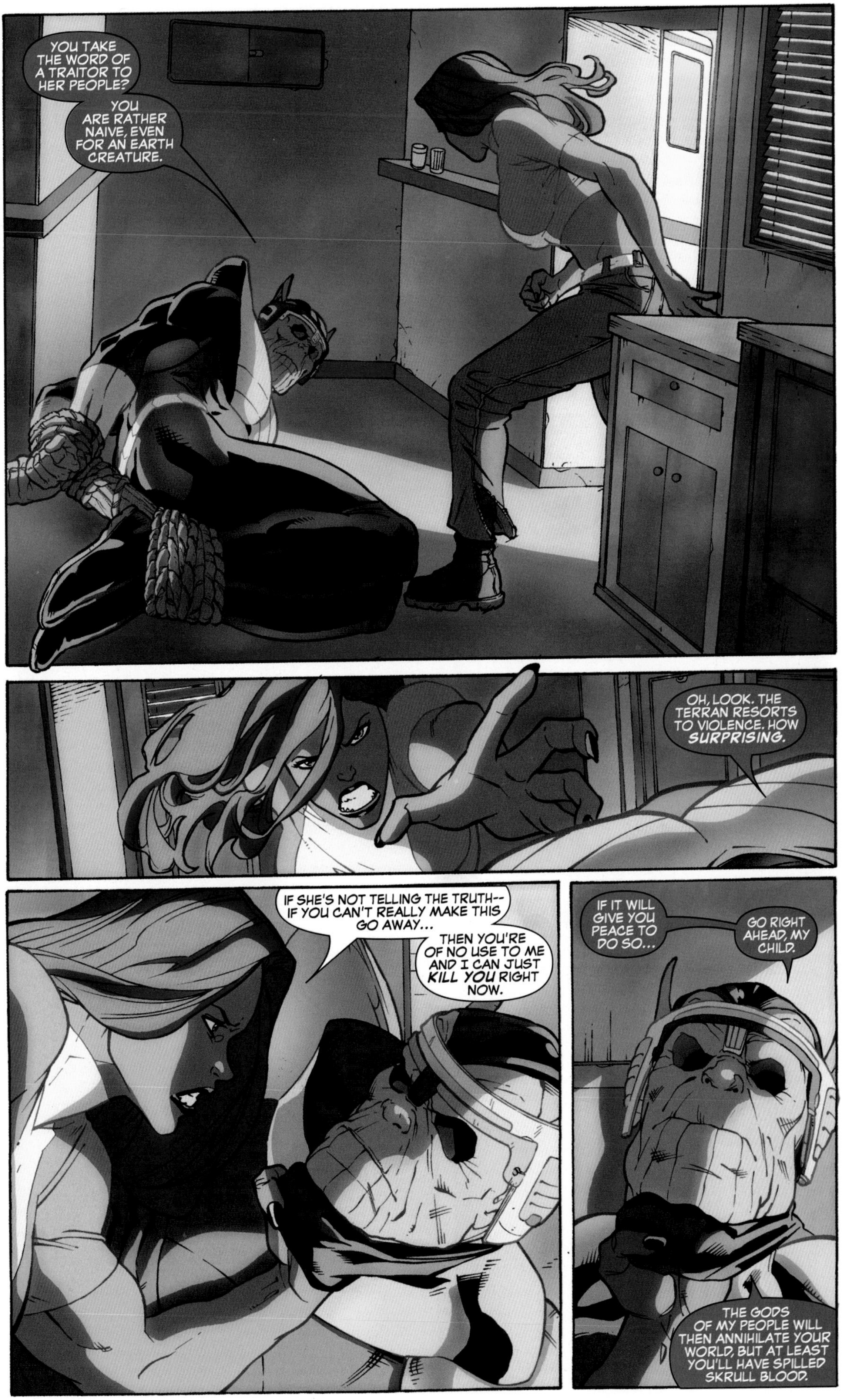
YOU TAKE THE WORD OF A TRAITOR TO HER PEOPLE?
YOU ARE RATHER NAIVE, EVEN FOR AN EARTH CREATURE.
OH, LOOK. THE TERRAN RESORTS TO VIOLENCE. HOW SURPRISING.
IF SHE'S NOT TELLING THE TRUTH-- IF YOU CAN'T REALLY MAKE THIS GO AWAY...
THEN YOU'RE OF NO USE TO ME AND I CAN JUST KILL YOU RIGHT NOW.
IF IT WILL GIVE YOU PEACE TO DO SO...
GO RIGHT AHEAD, MY CHILD.
THE GODS OF MY PEOPLE WILL THEN ANNIHILATE YOUR WORLD, BUT AT LEAST YOU'LL HAVE SPILLED SKRULL BLOOD.

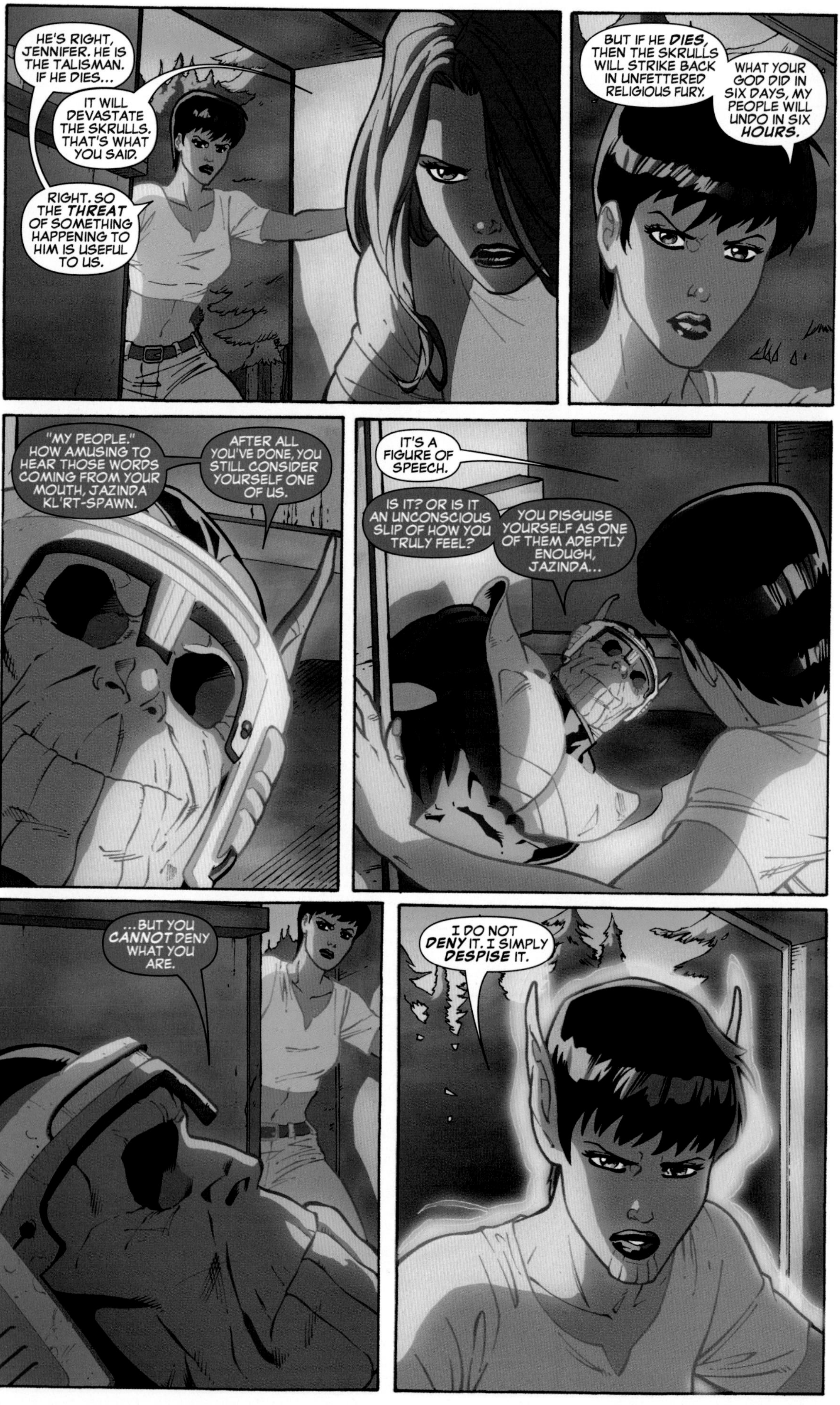
HE'S RIGHT, JENNIFER. HE IS THE TALISMAN. IF HE DIES...
IT WILL DEVASTATE THE SKRULLS. THAT'S WHAT YOU SAID.
RIGHT. SO THE THREAT OF SOMETHING HAPPENING TO HIM IS USEFUL TO US.
BUT IF HE DIES, THEN THE SKRULLS WILL STRIKE BACK IN UNFETTERED RELIGIOUS FURY.
WHAT YOUR GOD DID IN SIX DAYS, MY PEOPLE WILL UNDO IN SIX HOURS.
"MY PEOPLE." HOW AMUSING TO HEAR THOSE WORDS COMING FROM YOUR MOUTH, JAZINDA KL'RT-SPAWN.
AFTER ALL YOU'VE DONE, YOU STILL CONSIDER YOURSELF ONE OF US.
IT'S A FIGURE OF SPEECH.
IS IT? OR IS IT AN UNCONSCIOUS SLIP OF HOW YOU TRULY FEEL?
YOU DISGUISE YOURSELF AS ONE OF THEM ADEPTLY ENOUGH, JAZINDA...
...BUT YOU CANNOT DENY WHAT YOU ARE.
I DO NOT DENY IT. I SIMPLY DESPISE IT.

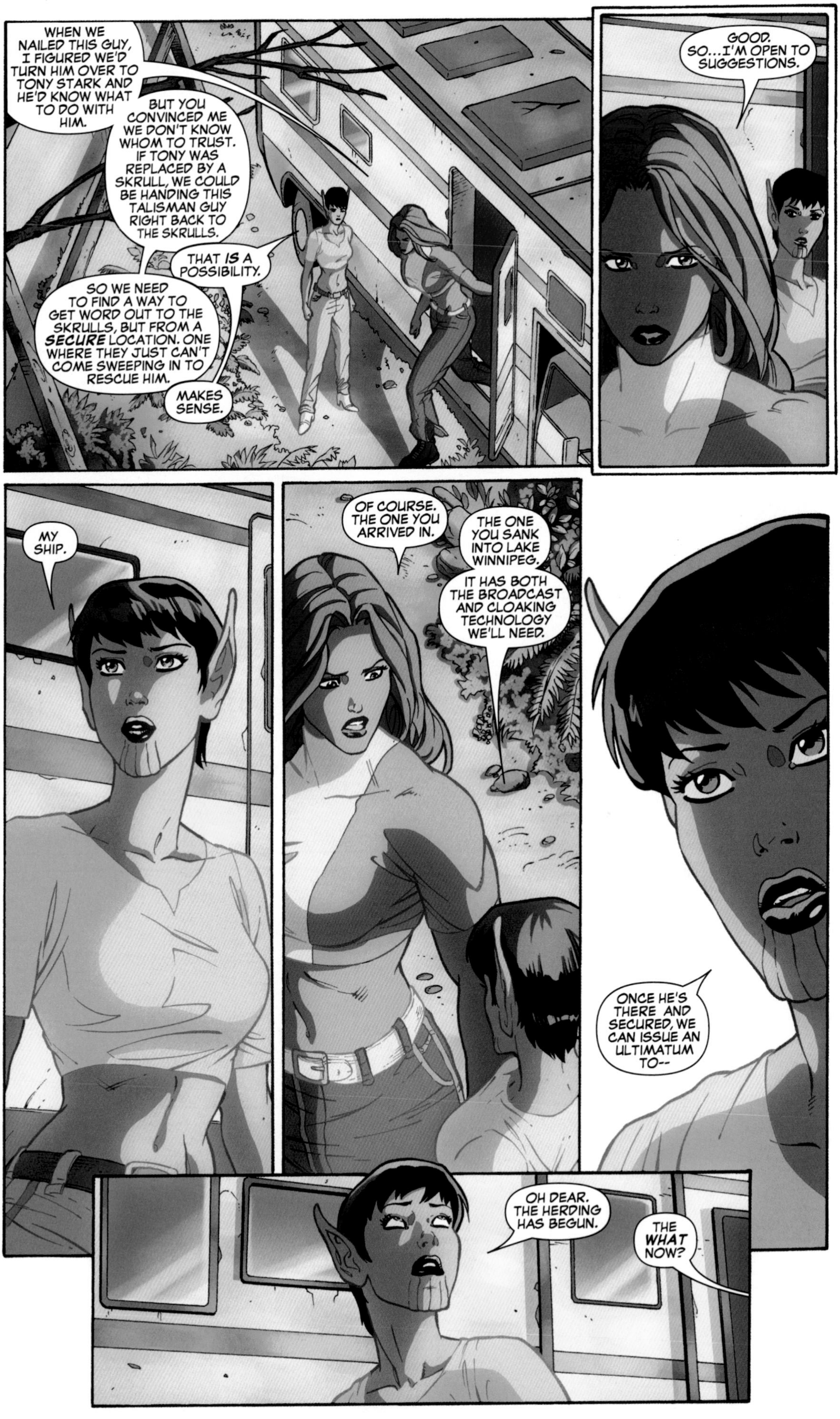
WHEN WE NAILED THIS GUY, I FIGURED WE'D TURN HIM OVER TO TONY STARK AND HE'D KNOW WHAT TO DO WITH HIM.
BUT YOU CONVINCED ME WE DON'T KNOW WHOM TO TRUST. IF TONY WAS REPLACED BY A SKRULL, WE COULD BE HANDING THIS TALISMAN GUY RIGHT BACK TO THE SKRULLS.
THAT IS A POSSIBILITY.
SO WE NEED TO FIND A WAY TO GET WORD OUT TO THE SKRULLS, BUT FROM A SECURE LOCATION. ONE WHERE THEY JUST CAN'T COME SWEEPING IN TO RESCUE HIM.
MAKES SENSE.
GOOD. SO...I'M OPEN TO SUGGESTIONS.
MY SHIP.
OF COURSE. THE ONE YOU ARRIVED IN.
THE ONE YOU SANK INTO LAKE WINNIPEG.
IT HAS BOTH THE BROADCAST AND CLOAKING TECHNOLOGY WE'LL NEED.
ONCE HE'S THERE AND SECURED, WE CAN ISSUE AN ULTIMATUM TO--
OH DEAR. THE HERDING HAS BEGUN.
THE WHAT NOW?

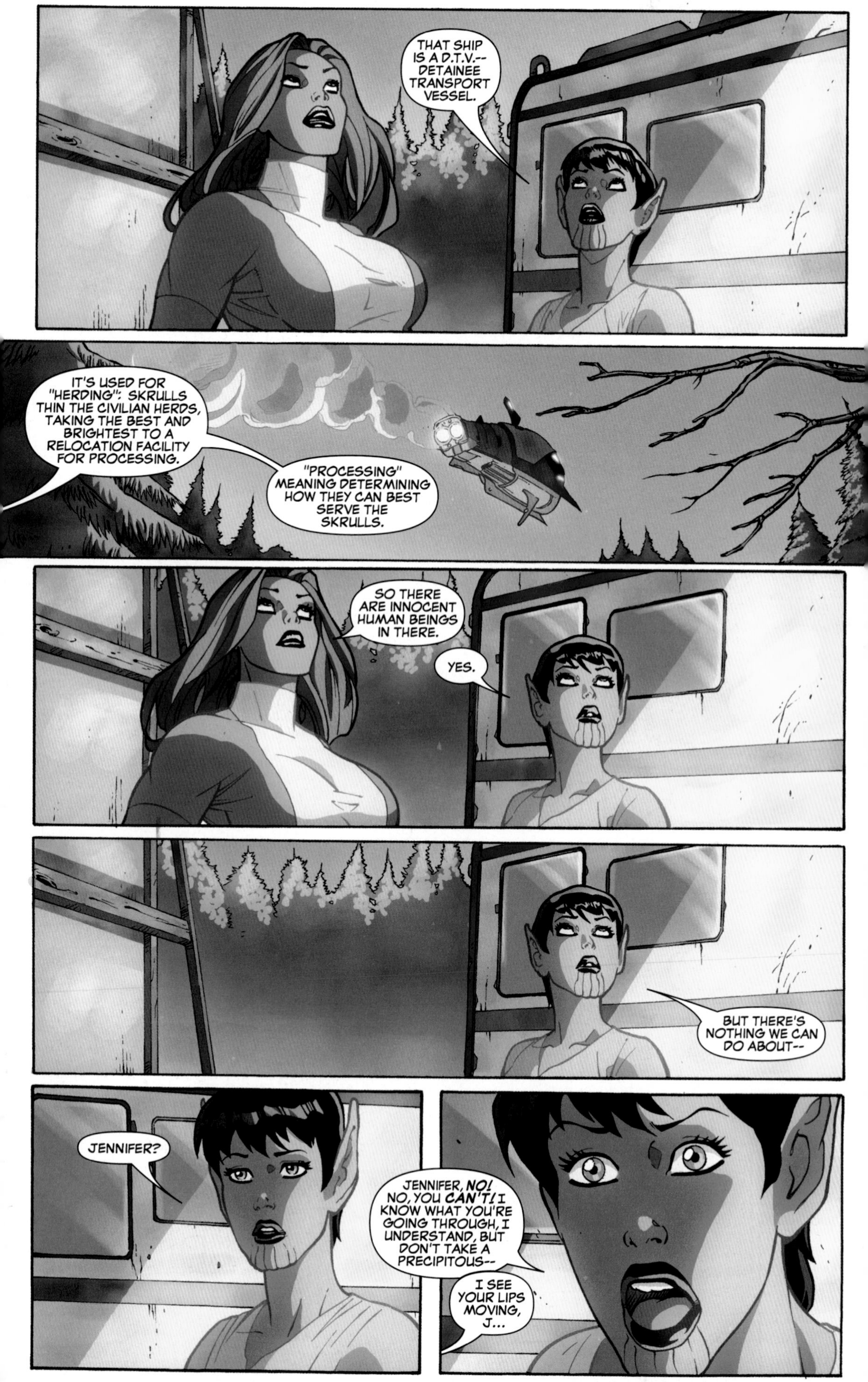

THAT SHIP IS A D.T.V.-- DETAINEE TRANSPORT VESSEL.
IT'S USED FOR "HERDING": SKRULLS THIN THE CIVILIAN HERDS, TAKING THE BEST AND BRIGHTEST TO A RELOCATION FACILITY FOR PROCESSING.
"PROCESSING" MEANING DETERMINING HOW THEY CAN BEST SERVE THE SKRULLS.
SO THERE ARE INNOCENT HUMAN BEINGS IN THERE.
YES.
BUT THERE'S NOTHING WE CAN DO ABOUT--
JENNIFER?
JENNIFER, NO! NO, YOU CAN'T! I KNOW WHAT YOU'RE GOING THROUGH, I UNDERSTAND, BUT DON'T TAKE A PRECIPITOUS--
I SEE YOUR LIPS MOVING, J...

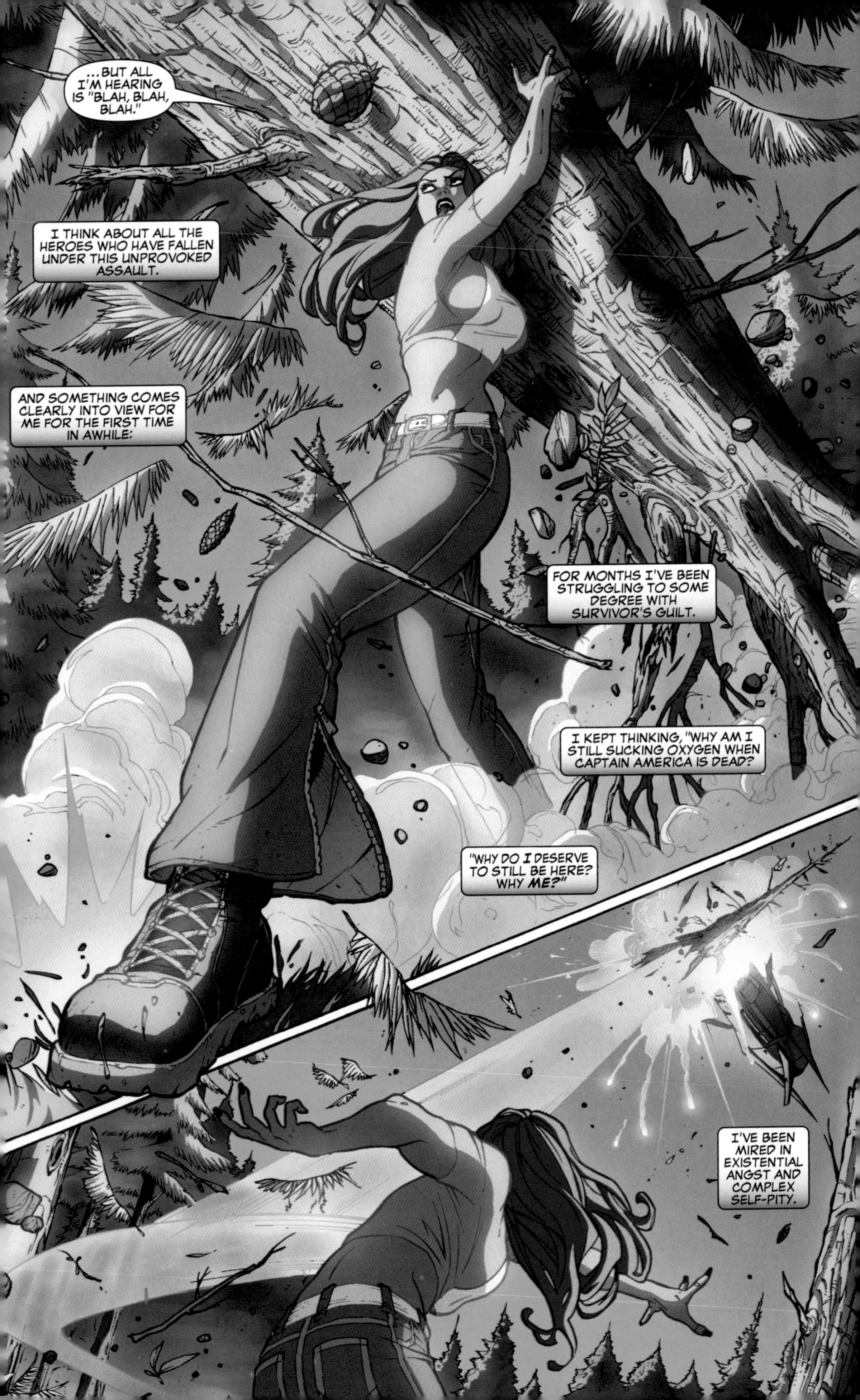
...BUT ALL I'M HEARING IS "BLAH, BLAH, BLAH."
I THINK ABOUT ALL THE HEROES WHO HAVE FALLEN UNDER THIS UNPROVOKED ASSAULT.
AND SOMETHING COMES CLEARLY INTO VIEW FOR ME FOR THE FIRST TIME IN AWHILE:
FOR MONTHS I'VE BEEN STRUGGLING TO SOME DEGREE WITH SURVIVOR'S GUILT.
I KEPT THINKING, "WHY AM I STILL SUCKING OXYGEN WHEN CAPTAIN AMERICA IS DEAD?
"WHY DO I DESERVE TO STILL BE HERE? WHY ME?"
I'VE BEEN MIRED IN EXISTENTIAL ANGST AND COMPLEX SELF-PITY.

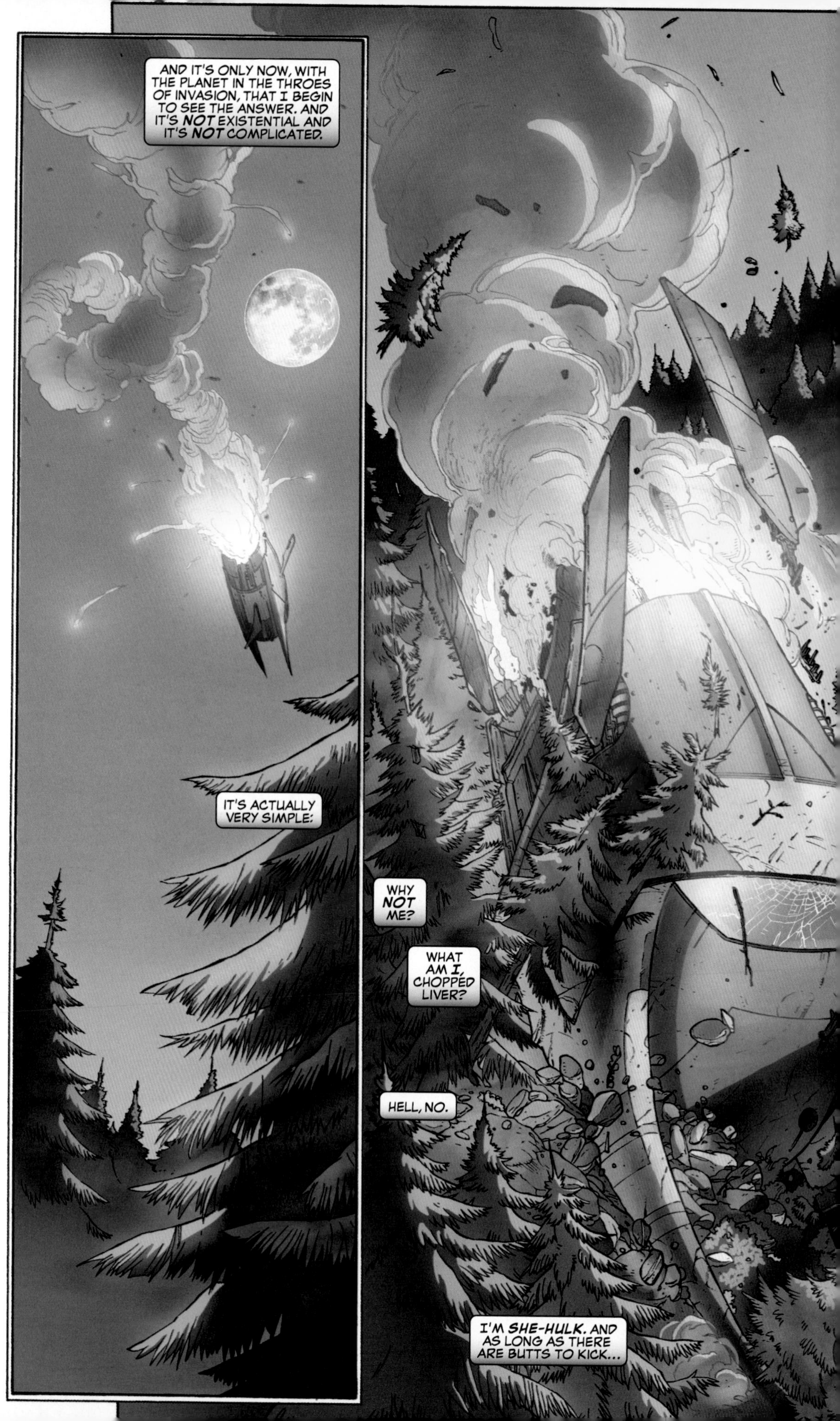
AND IT'S ONLY NOW, WITH THE PLANET IN THE THROES OF INVASION, THAT I BEGIN TO SEE THE ANSWER. AND IT'S NOT EXISTENTIAL AND IT'S NOT COMPLICATED.
IT'S ACTUALLY VERY SIMPLE:
WHY NOT ME?
WHAT AM I, CHOPPED LIVER?
HELL, NO.
I'M SHE-HULK. AND AS LONG AS THERE ARE BUTTS TO KICK...

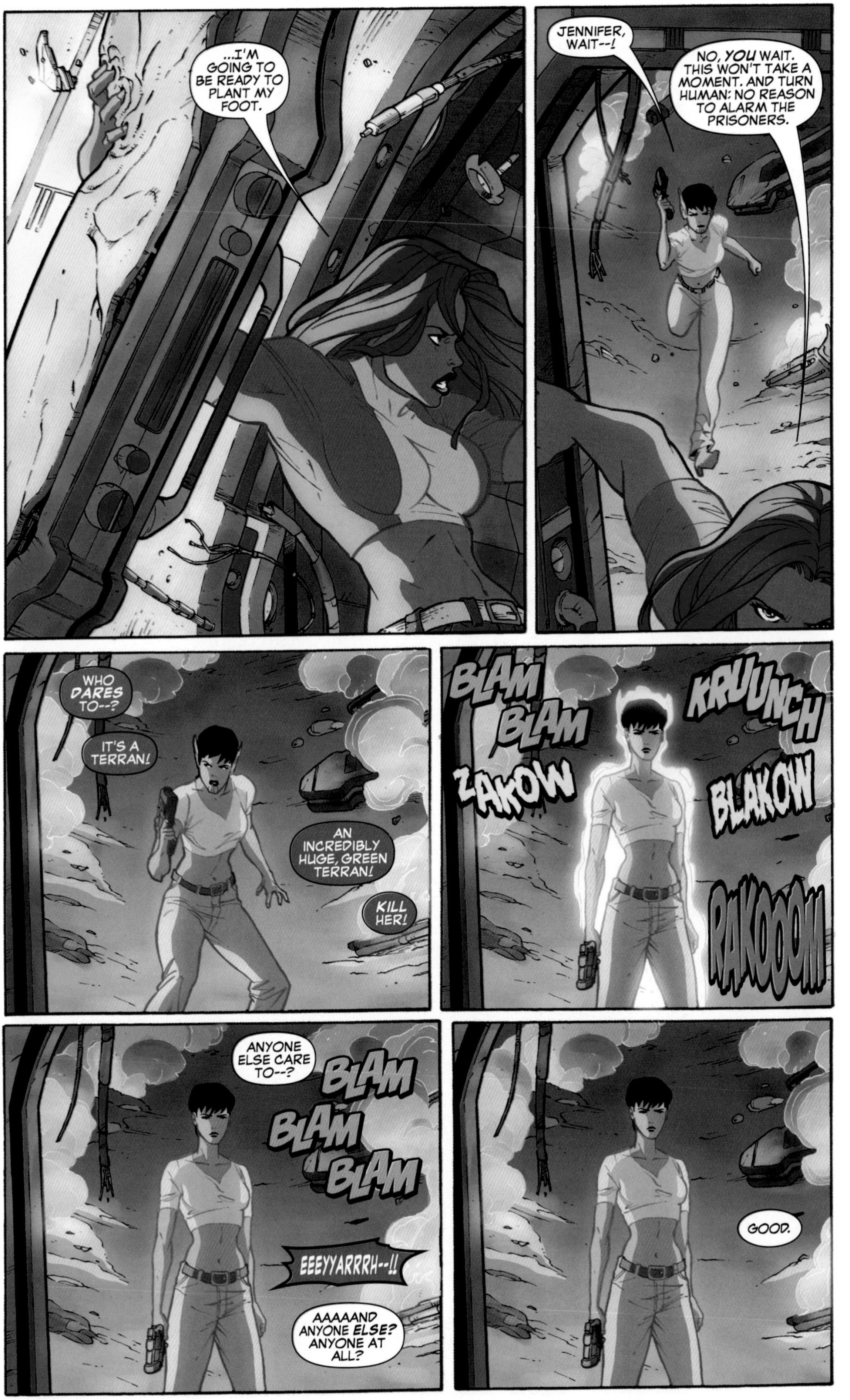

...I'M GOING TO BE READY TO PLANT MY FOOT.
JENNIFER, WAIT--!
NO, YOU WAIT. THIS WON'T TAKE A MOMENT. AND TURN HUMAN: NO REASON TO ALARM THE PRISONERS.
WHO DARES TO--?
IT'S A TERRAN!
AN INCREDIBLY HUGE, GREEN TERRAN!
KILL HER!
BLAM
BLAM
ZAKOW
KRUUNCH
BLAKOW
RAKOOOM
ANYONE ELSE CARE TO--?
BLAM
BLAM
BLAM
EEEYYARRRH--!!
AAAAAND ANYONE ELSE? ANYONE AT ALL?
GOOD.

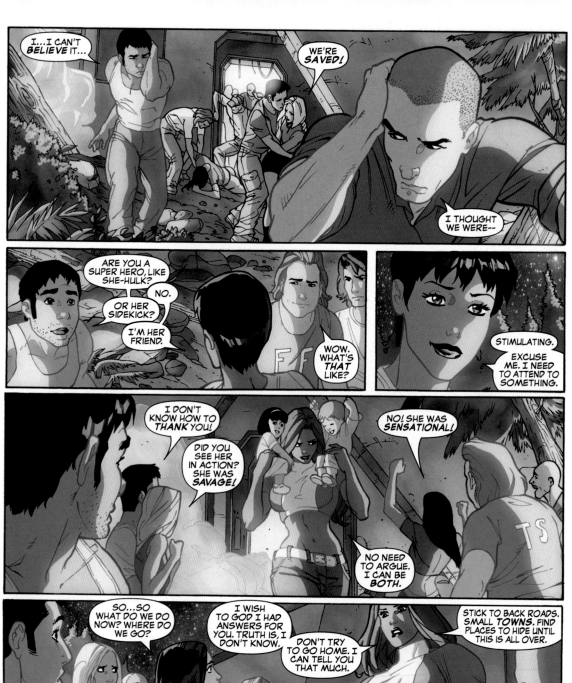

I...I CAN'T *BELIEVE* IT...

WE'RE *SAVED!*

I THOUGHT WE WERE--

ARE YOU A SUPER HERO, LIKE SHE-HULK?

NO.

OR HER SIDEKICK?

I'M HER FRIEND.

WOW. WHAT'S *THAT* LIKE?

STIMULATING. EXCUSE ME. I NEED TO ATTEND TO SOMETHING.

I DON'T KNOW HOW TO *THANK* YOU!

DID YOU SEE HER IN ACTION? SHE WAS *SAVAGE!*

NO! SHE WAS *SENSATIONAL!*

NO NEED TO ARGUE. I CAN BE *BOTH.*

SO...SO WHAT DO WE DO NOW? WHERE DO WE GO?

I WISH TO GOD I HAD ANSWERS FOR YOU. TRUTH IS, I DON'T KNOW.

DON'T TRY TO GO HOME. I CAN TELL YOU THAT MUCH.

STICK TO BACK ROADS. SMALL *TOWNS.* FIND PLACES TO HIDE UNTIL THIS IS ALL OVER.

WHAT IF IT'S ALL OVER ALREADY? WHAT IF *THIS* IS HOW IT ENDS? WITH THOSE... THOSE *THINGS* IN CHARGE?

IT WON'T. TRUST ME. WE'LL BEAT THEM.

BECAUSE HEROES *ALWAYS* BEAT THE BAD GUYS, RIGHT?

RIGHT.

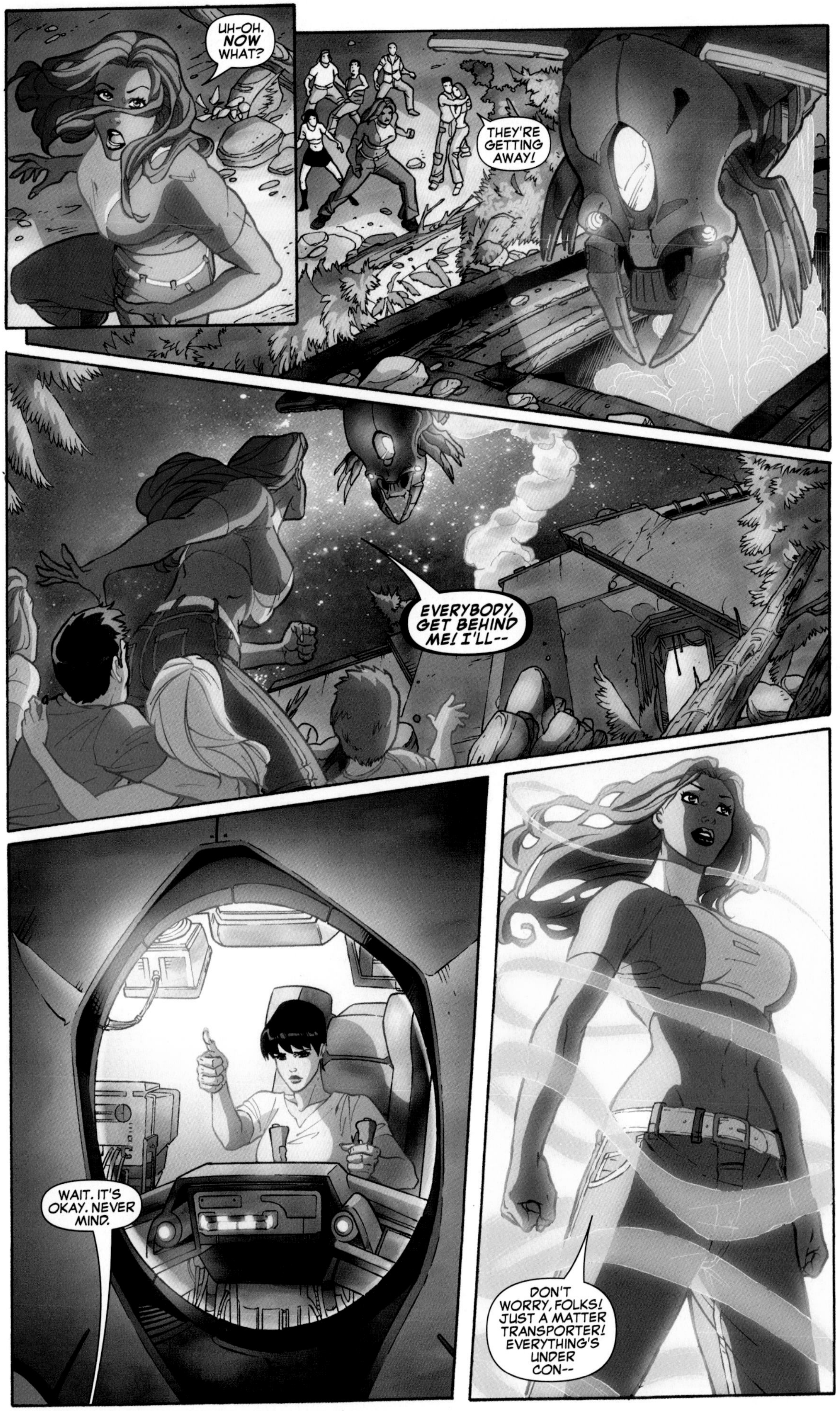
UH-OH. **NOW** WHAT?
THEY'RE GETTING AWAY!
EVERYBODY, GET BEHIND ME! I'LL--
WAIT. IT'S OKAY. NEVER MIND.
DON'T WORRY, FOLKS! JUST A MATTER TRANSPORTER! EVERYTHING'S UNDER CON--

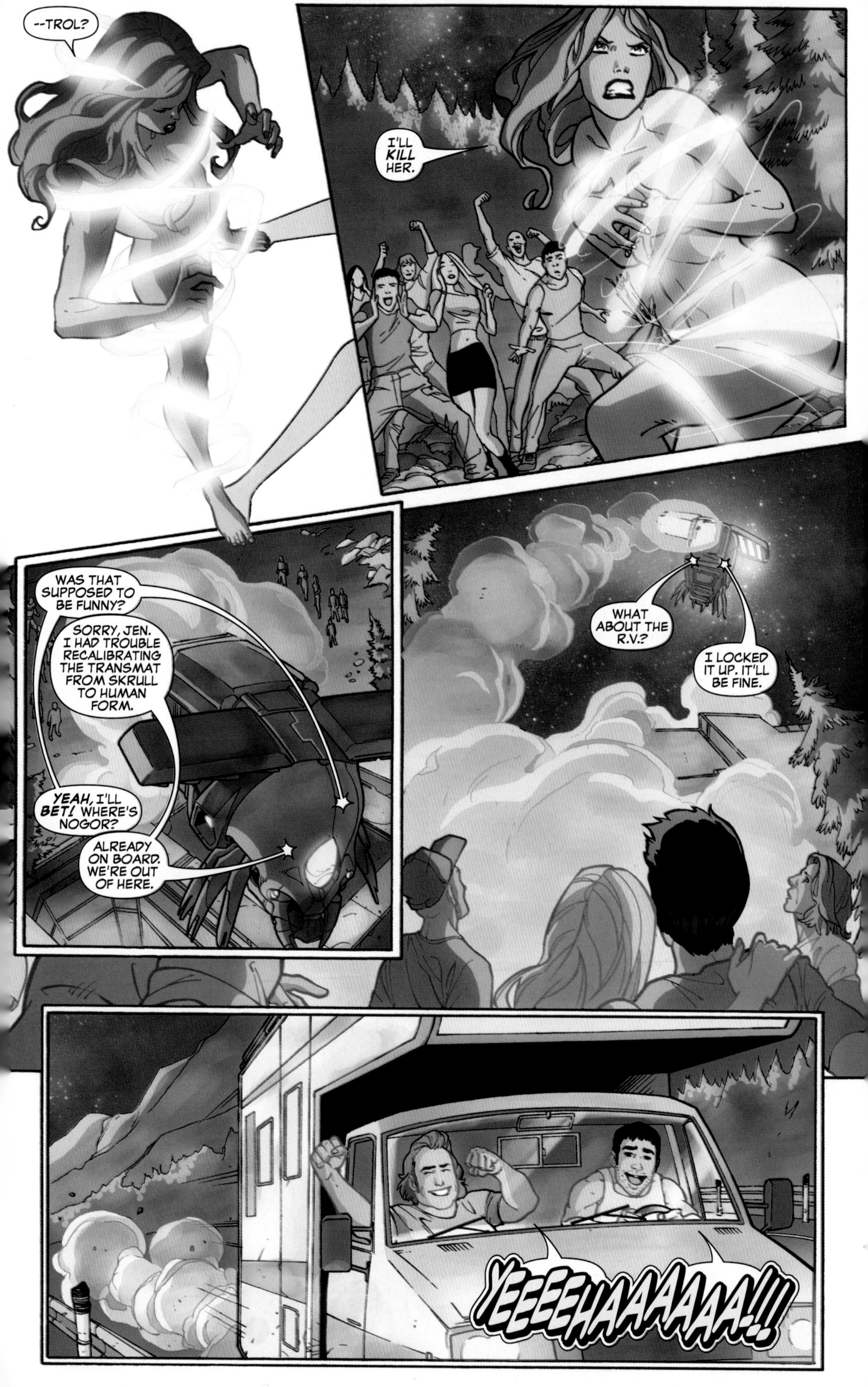
--TROL?
I'LL KILL HER.
WAS THAT SUPPOSED TO BE FUNNY?
SORRY, JEN. I HAD TROUBLE RECALIBRATING THE TRANSMAT FROM SKRULL TO HUMAN FORM.
YEAH, I'LL BET! WHERE'S NOGOR?
ALREADY ON BOARD. WE'RE OUT OF HERE.
WHAT ABOUT THE R.V.?
I LOCKED IT UP. IT'LL BE FINE.
YEEEEHAAAAAAA!!!

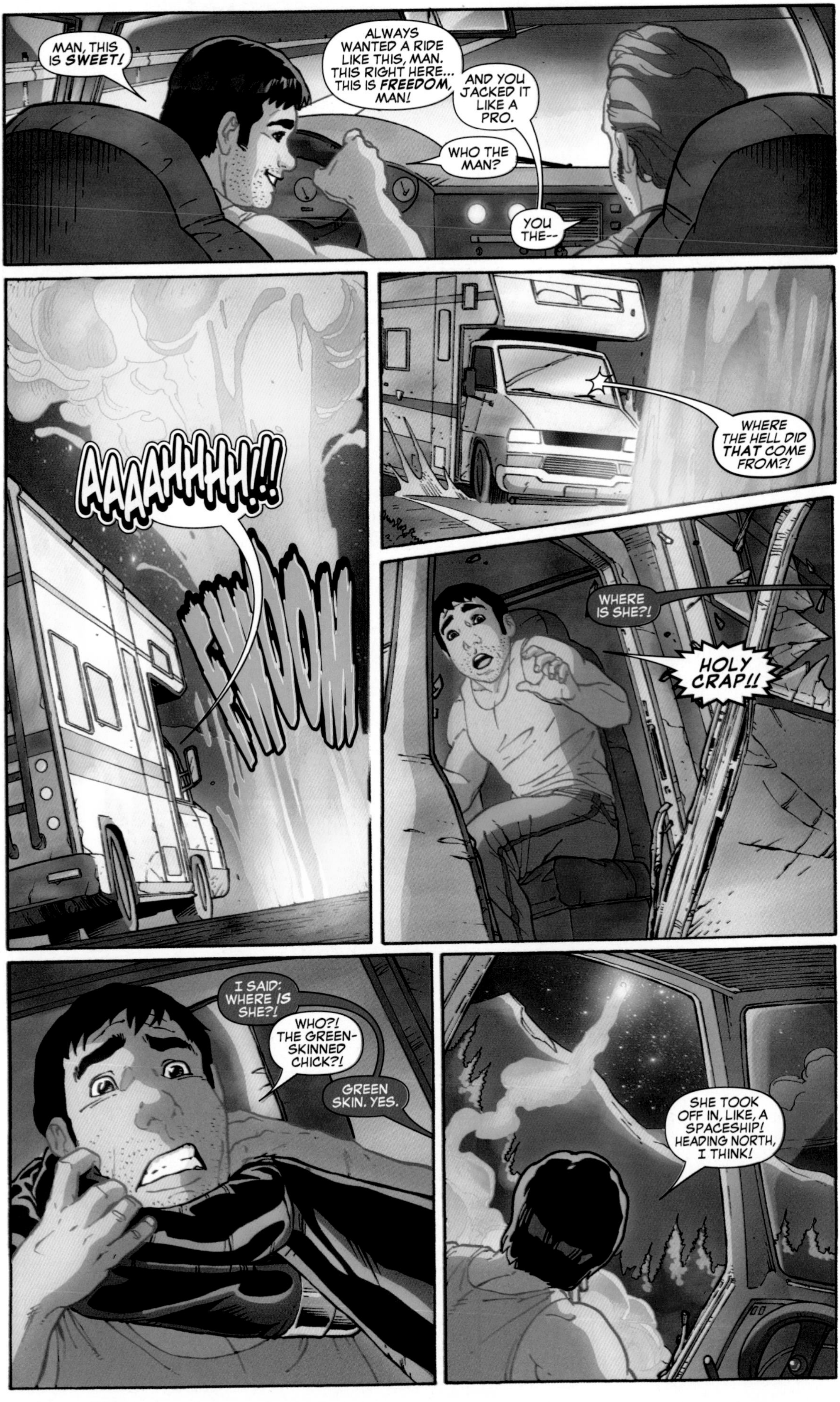
MAN, THIS IS SWEET!
ALWAYS WANTED A RIDE LIKE THIS, MAN. THIS RIGHT HERE... THIS IS FREEDOM, MAN!
AND YOU JACKED IT LIKE A PRO.
WHO THE MAN?
YOU THE--
AAAAHHHH!!!
FWOOM
WHERE THE HELL DID THAT COME FROM?!
WHERE IS SHE?!
HOLY CRAP!!
I SAID: WHERE IS SHE?!
WHO?! THE GREEN-SKINNED CHICK?!
GREEN SKIN. YES.
SHE TOOK OFF IN, LIKE, A SPACESHIP! HEADING NORTH, I THINK!

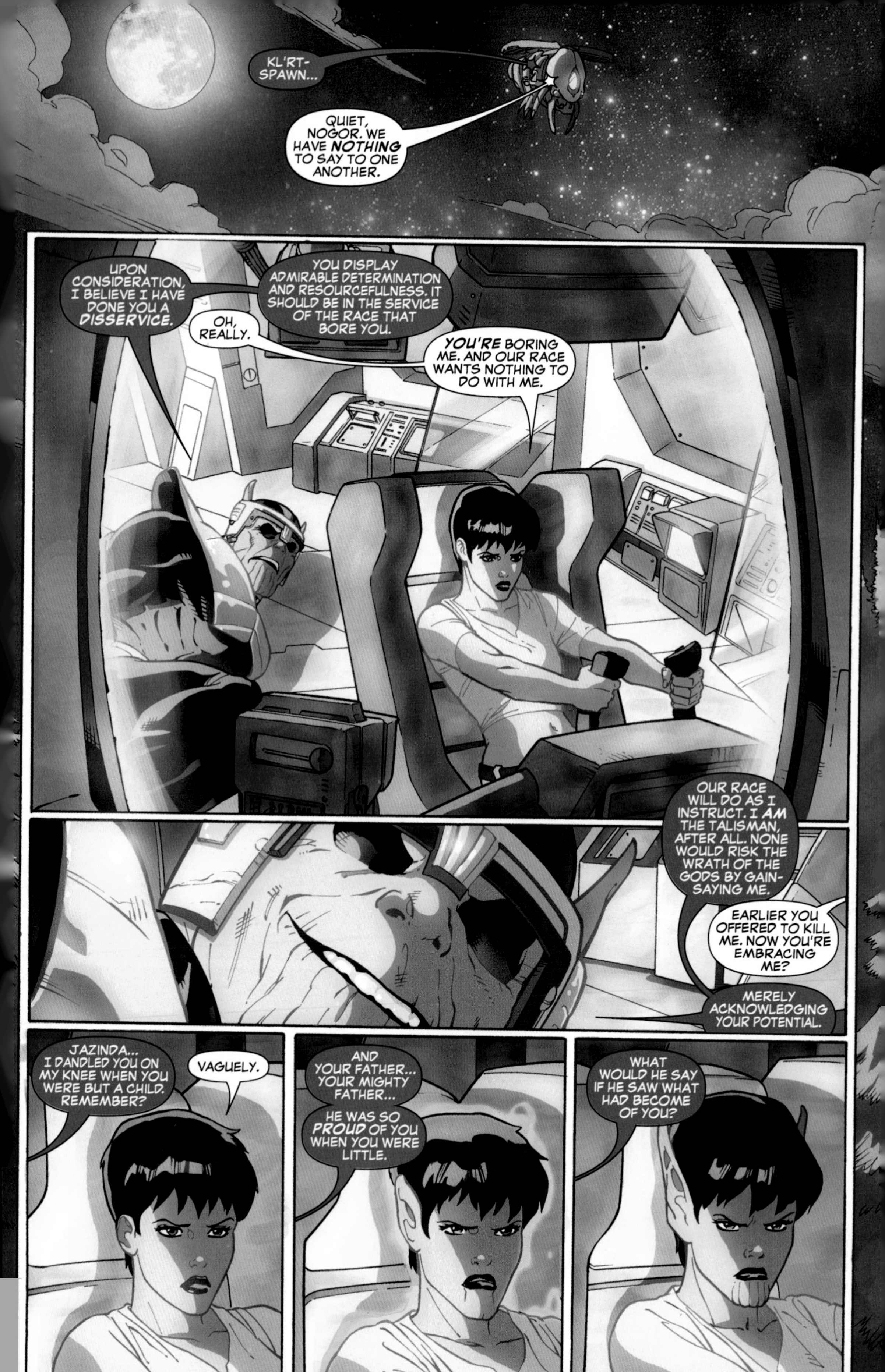
KL'RT-SPAWN...
QUIET, NOGOR. WE HAVE NOTHING TO SAY TO ONE ANOTHER.
UPON CONSIDERATION, I BELIEVE I HAVE DONE YOU A DISSERVICE.
YOU DISPLAY ADMIRABLE DETERMINATION AND RESOURCEFULNESS. IT SHOULD BE IN THE SERVICE OF THE RACE THAT BORE YOU.
OH, REALLY.
YOU'RE BORING ME. AND OUR RACE WANTS NOTHING TO DO WITH ME.
OUR RACE WILL DO AS I INSTRUCT. I AM THE TALISMAN, AFTER ALL. NONE WOULD RISK THE WRATH OF THE GODS BY GAIN-SAYING ME.
EARLIER YOU OFFERED TO KILL ME. NOW YOU'RE EMBRACING ME?
MERELY ACKNOWLEDGING YOUR POTENTIAL.
JAZINDA... I DANDLED YOU ON MY KNEE WHEN YOU WERE BUT A CHILD. REMEMBER?
VAGUELY.
AND YOUR FATHER... YOUR MIGHTY FATHER...
HE WAS SO PROUD OF YOU WHEN YOU WERE LITTLE.
WHAT WOULD HE SAY IF HE SAW WHAT HAD BECOME OF YOU?

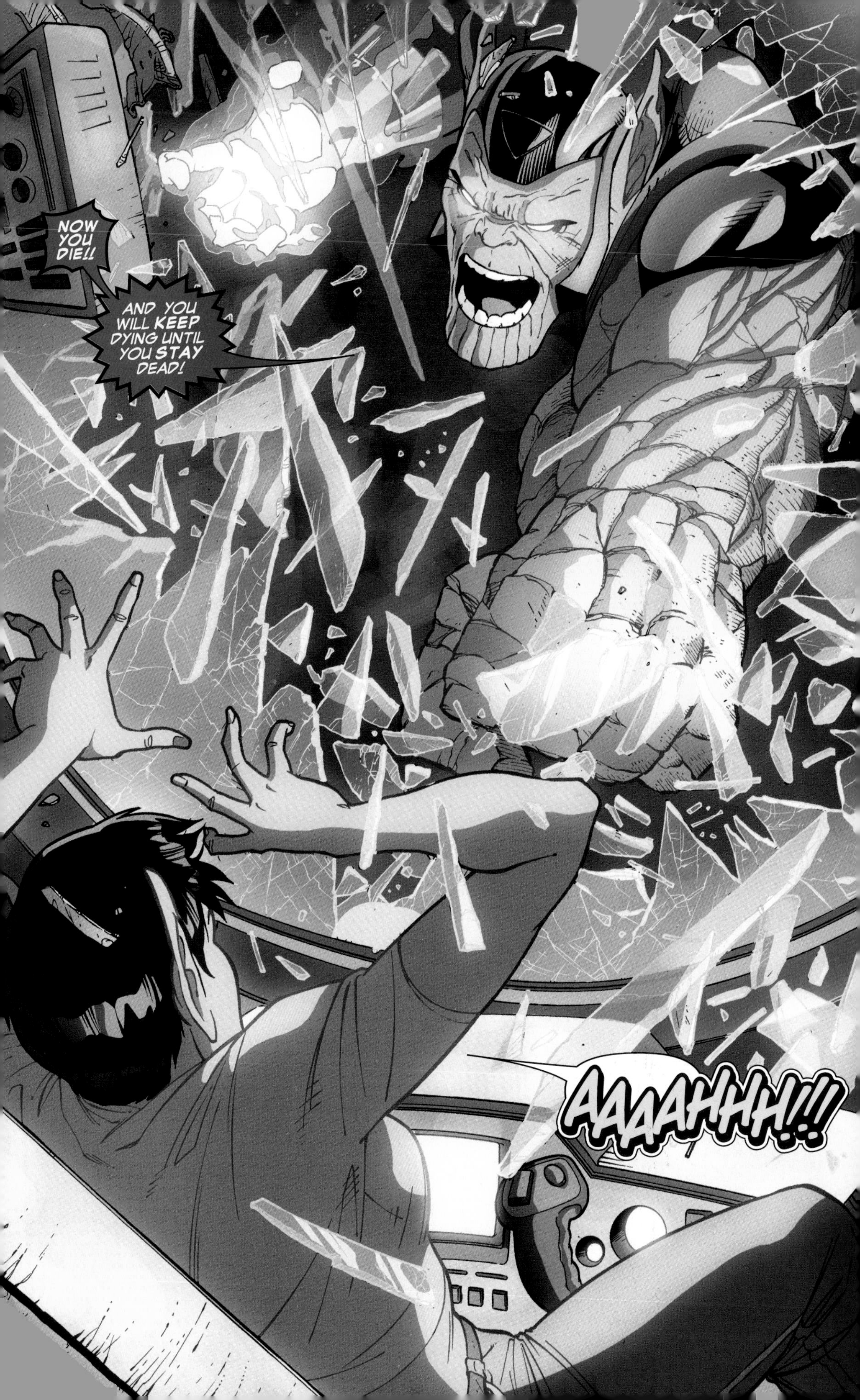
NOW YOU DIE!!
AND YOU WILL KEEP DYING UNTIL YOU STAY DEAD!
AAAAHHH!!!

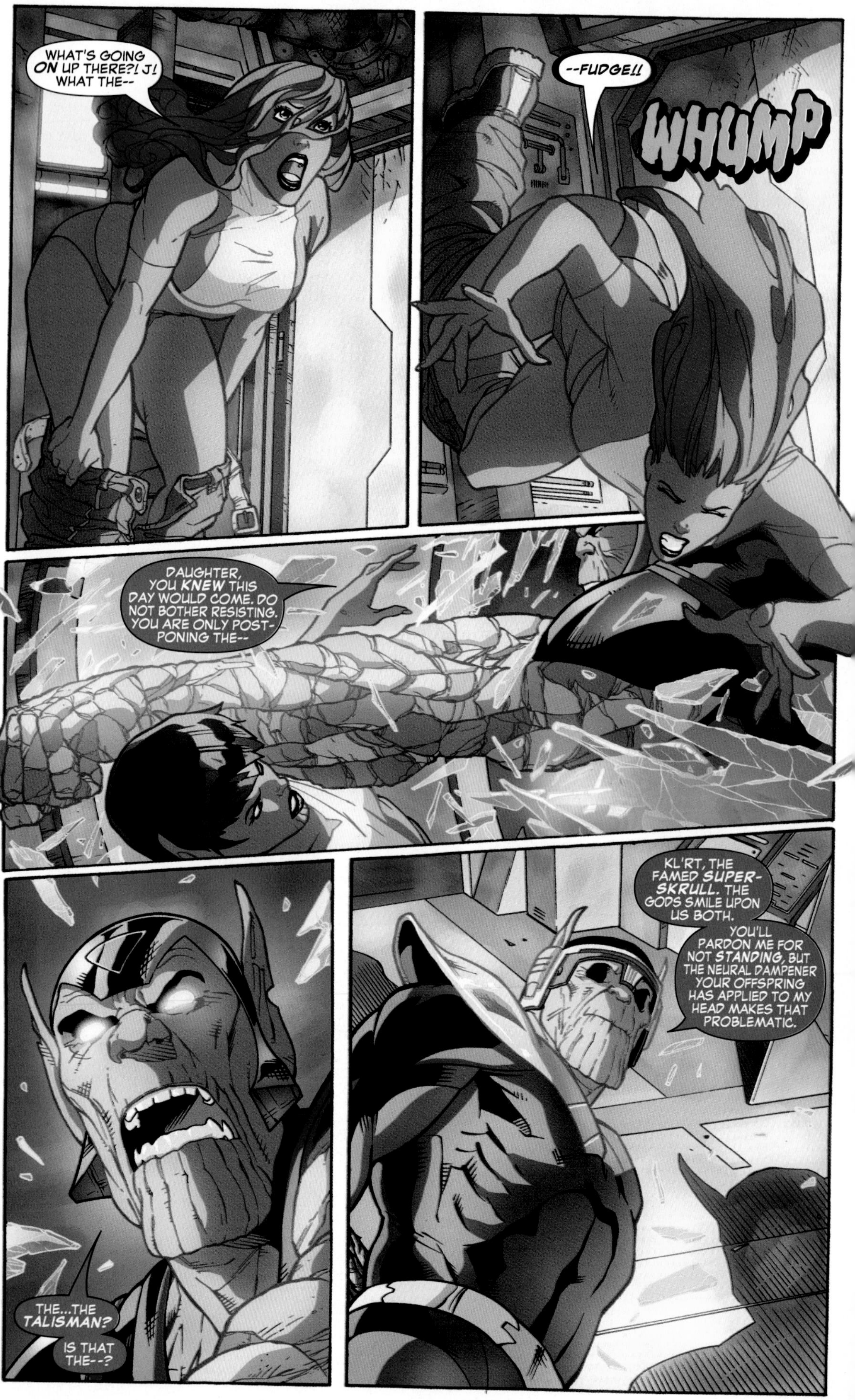
WHAT'S GOING ON UP THERE?! J! WHAT THE--
--FUDGE!!
WHUMP
DAUGHTER, YOU KNEW THIS DAY WOULD COME. DO NOT BOTHER RESISTING. YOU ARE ONLY POSTPONING THE--
THE...THE TALISMAN?
IS THAT THE--?
KL'RT, THE FAMED SUPER-SKRULL. THE GODS SMILE UPON US BOTH.
YOU'LL PARDON ME FOR NOT STANDING, BUT THE NEURAL DAMPENER YOUR OFFSPRING HAS APPLIED TO MY HEAD MAKES THAT PROBLEMATIC.

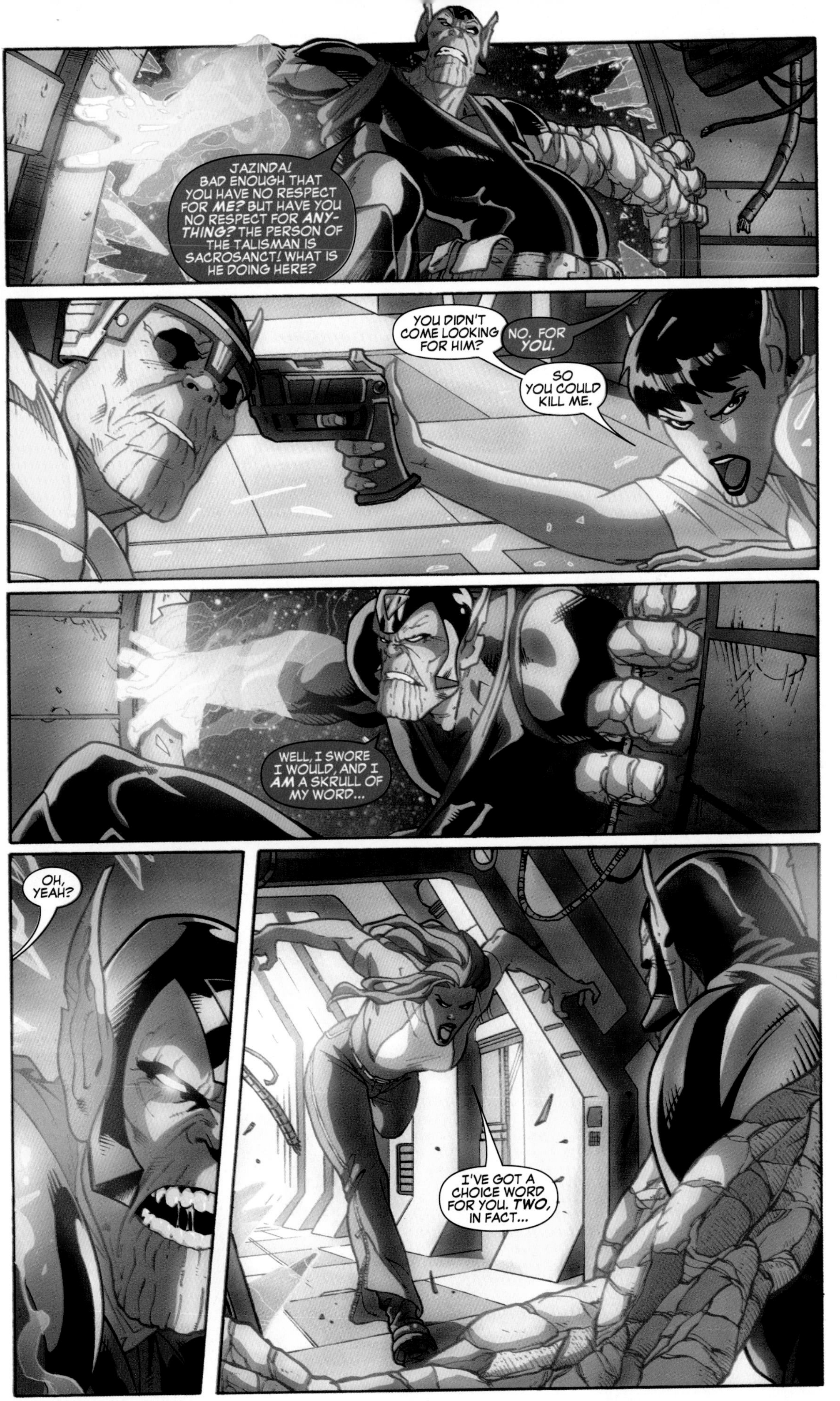
JAZINDA! BAD ENOUGH THAT YOU HAVE NO RESPECT FOR ME? BUT HAVE YOU NO RESPECT FOR ANY-THING? THE PERSON OF THE TALISMAN IS SACROSANCT! WHAT IS HE DOING HERE?
YOU DIDN'T COME LOOKING FOR HIM?
NO. FOR YOU.
SO YOU COULD KILL ME.
WELL, I SWORE I WOULD, AND I AM A SKRULL OF MY WORD...
OH, YEAH?
I'VE GOT A CHOICE WORD FOR YOU. TWO, IN FACT...

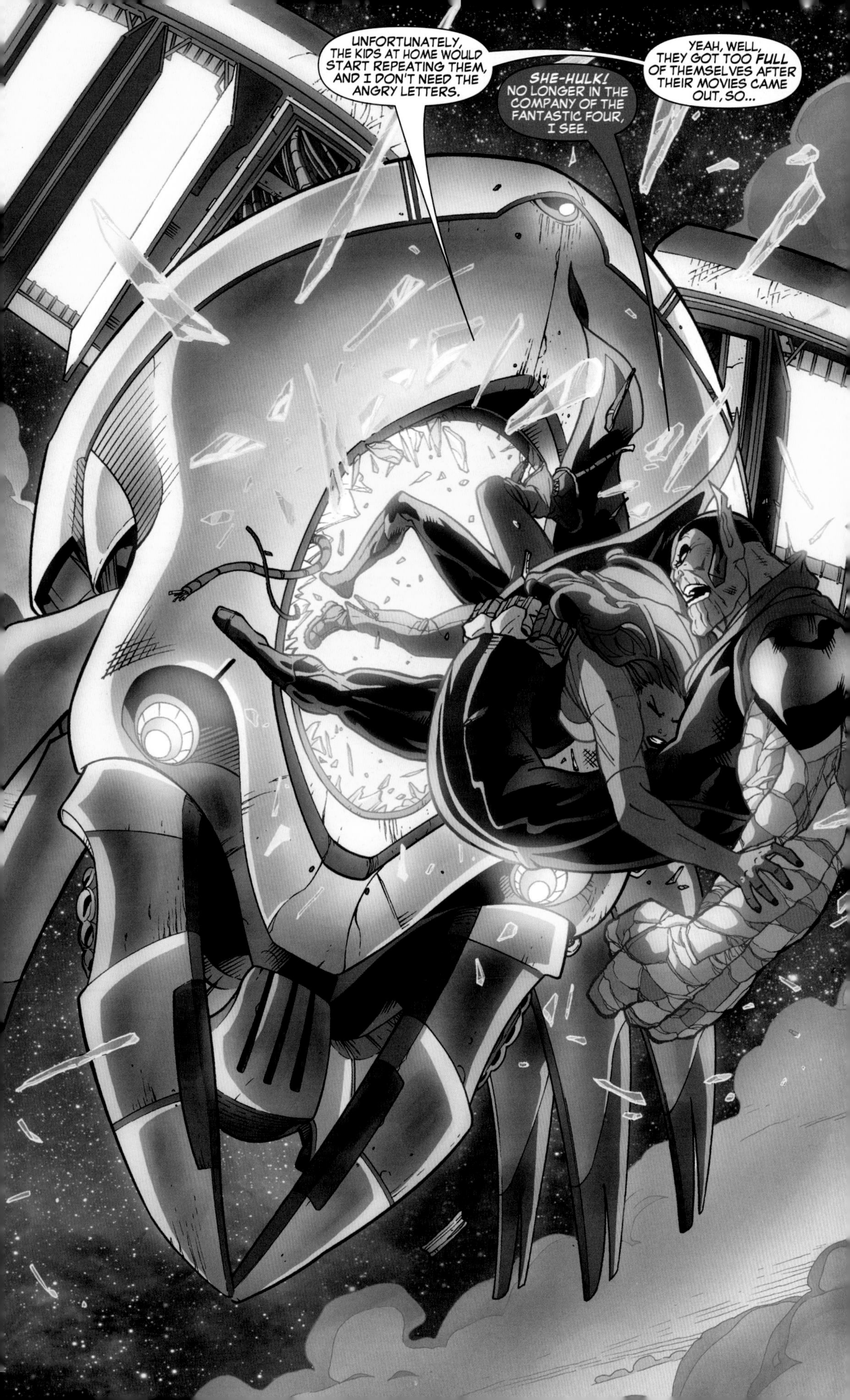

UNFORTUNATELY, THE KIDS AT HOME WOULD START REPEATING THEM, AND I DON'T NEED THE ANGRY LETTERS.
SHE-HULK! NO LONGER IN THE COMPANY OF THE FANTASTIC FOUR, I SEE.
YEAH, WELL, THEY GOT TOO FULL OF THEMSELVES AFTER THEIR MOVIES CAME OUT, SO...

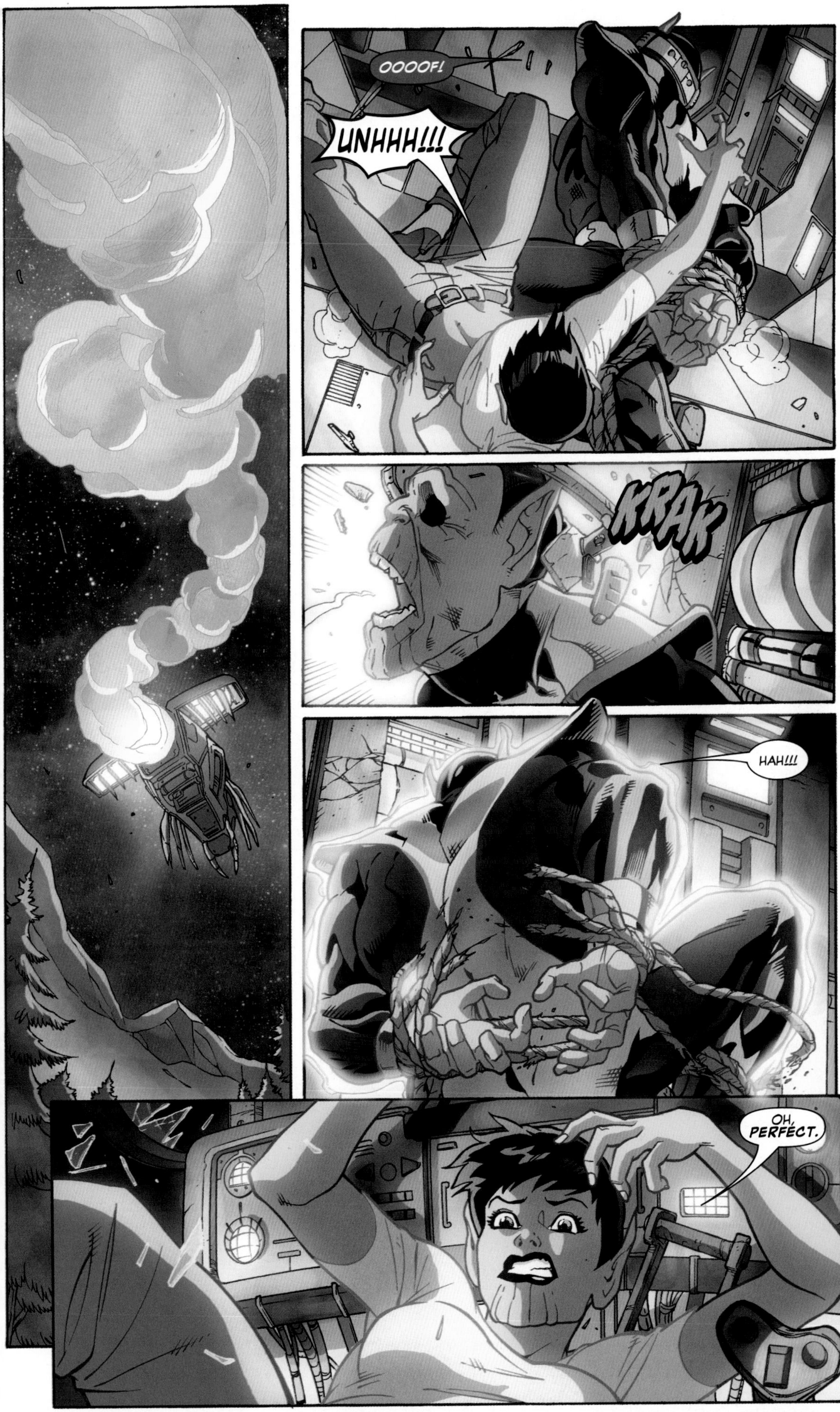
OOOOF!
UNHHH!!!
KRAK
HAH!!!
OH, PERFECT.

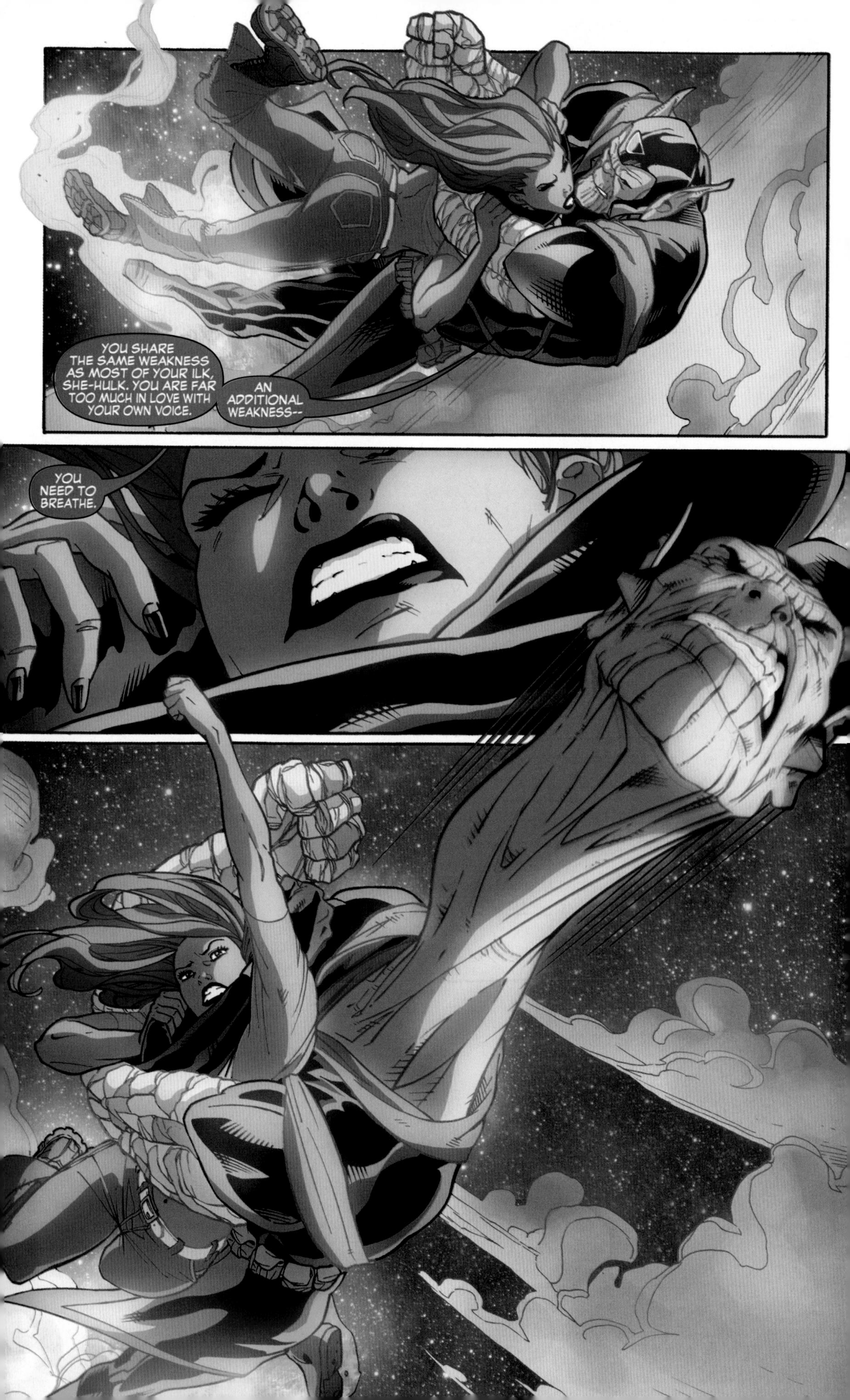
YOU SHARE THE SAME WEAKNESS AS MOST OF YOUR ILK, SHE-HULK. YOU ARE FAR TOO MUCH IN LOVE WITH YOUR OWN VOICE.
AN ADDITIONAL WEAKNESS--
YOU NEED TO BREATHE.

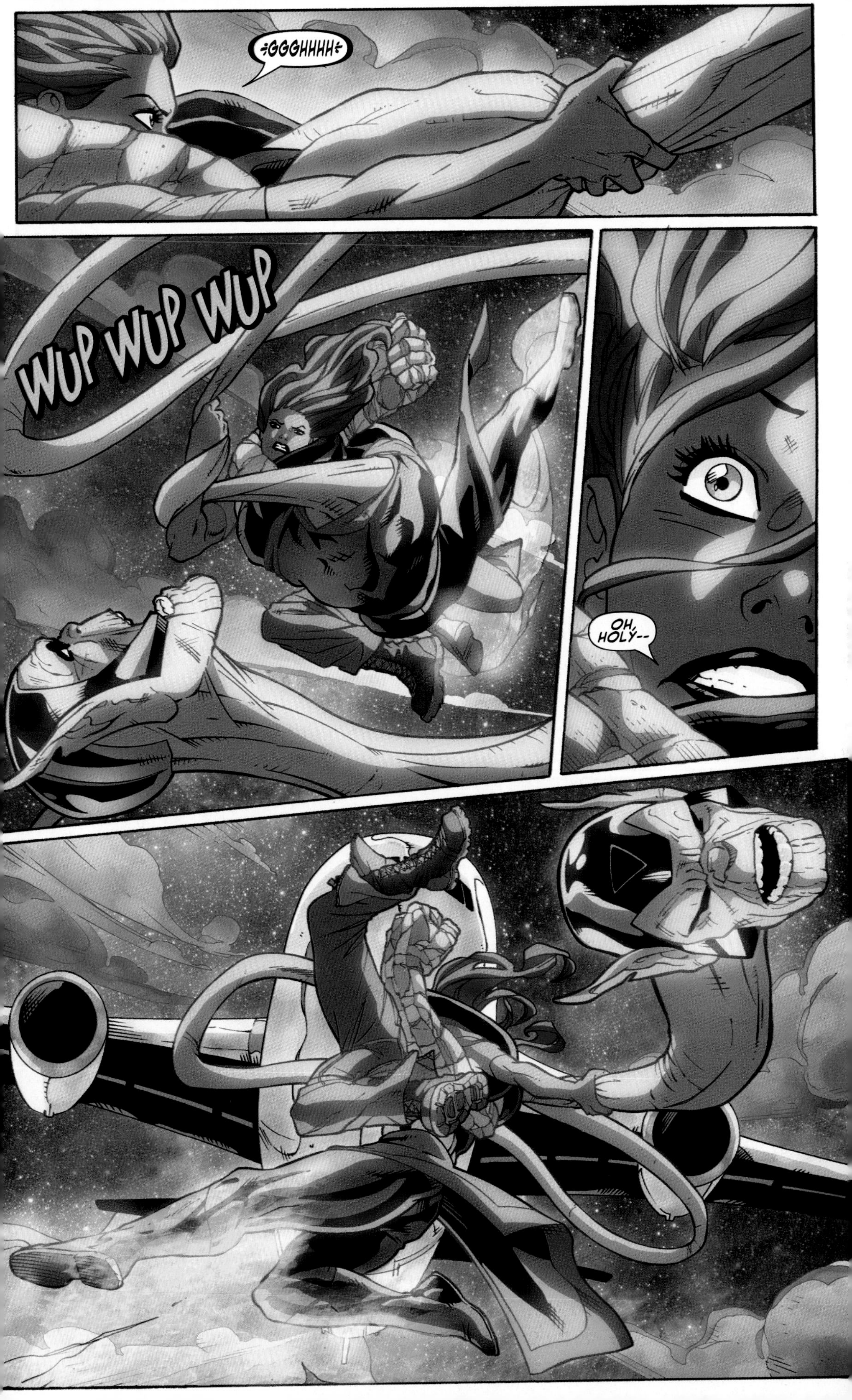

GGGHHHH
WUP WUP WUP
OH, HOLY--

YOU FOOL! YOU ANNIHILATED THE CONTROLS! I CAN'T COURSE-CORRECT US!

THAT SHOULD NOT CONCERN YOU, SHOULD IT?

YOU IMAGINE THAT, SHOULD YOU DIE IN THE CRASH, YOU WILL SIMPLY RETURN TO LIFE.

BUT NOT IF THE POWER OF THE GODS IS WITHDRAWING YOUR ILL-GOTTEN RESURRECTION POWER FROM YOU AND TURNING IT OVER TO ONE WHO RIGHTLY DESERVES IT.

NAMELY MYSEL--

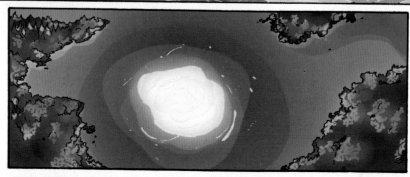

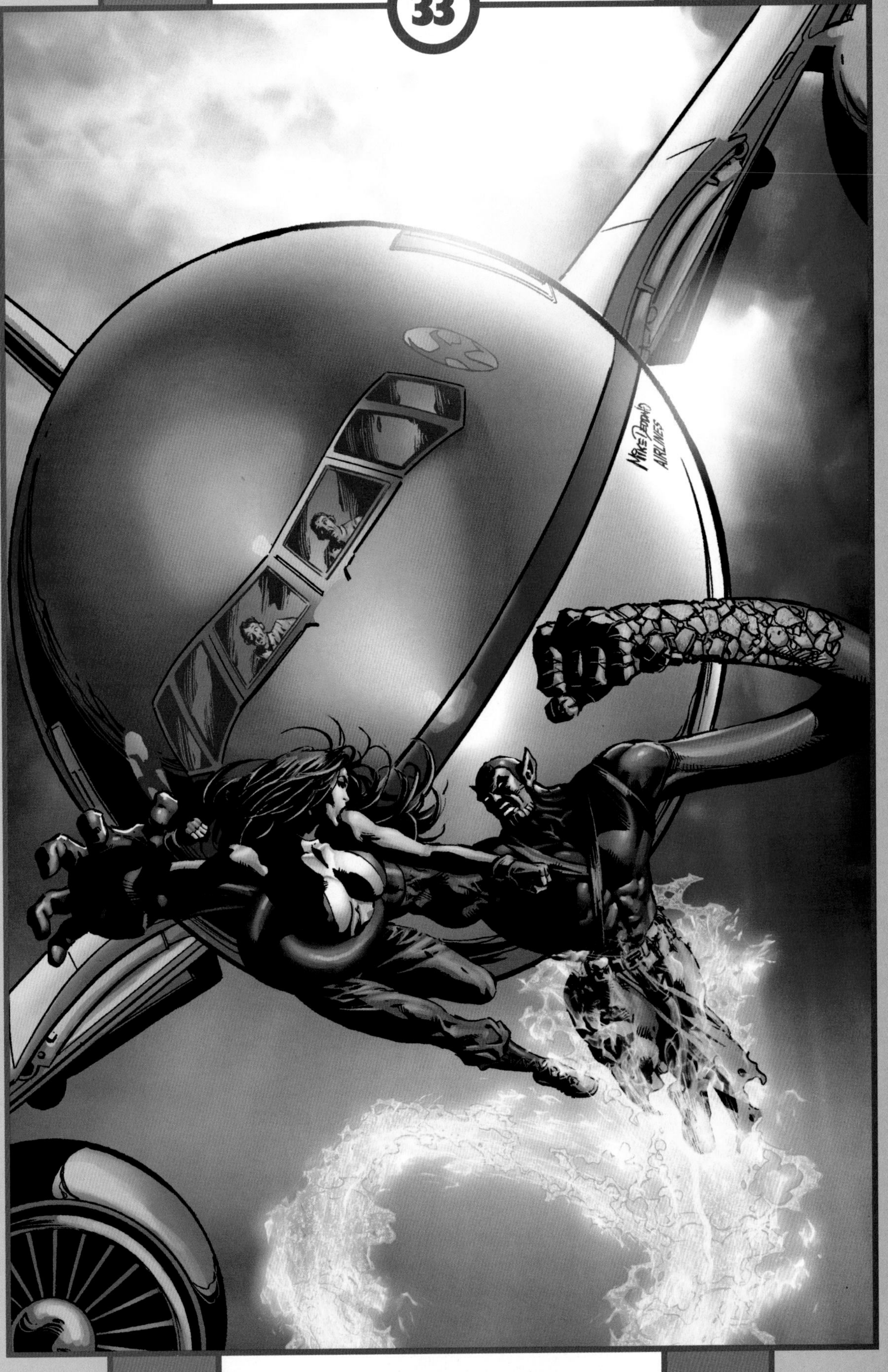
MIKE DEODATO
AIRLINES

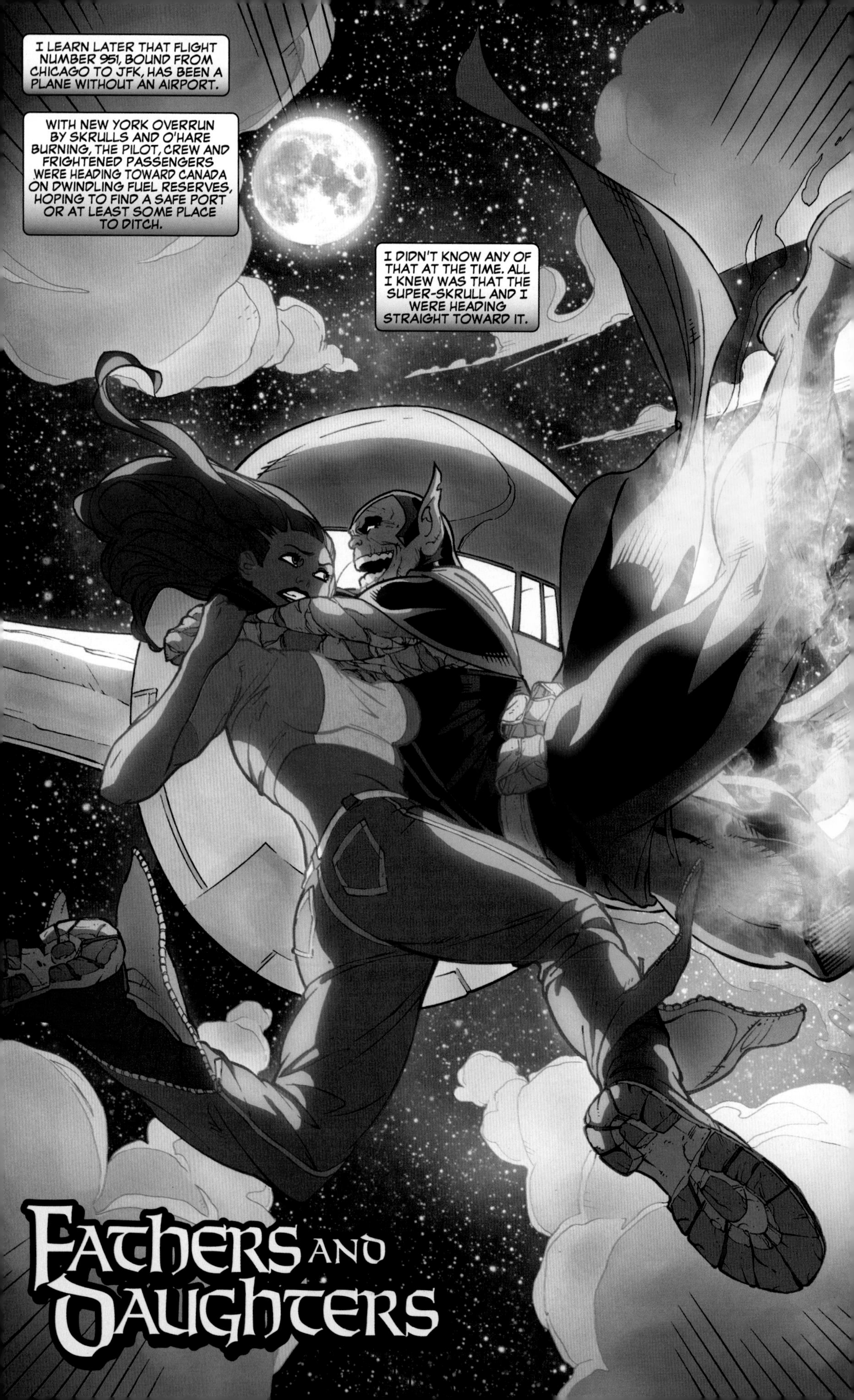
I LEARN LATER THAT FLIGHT NUMBER 951, BOUND FROM CHICAGO TO JFK, HAS BEEN A PLANE WITHOUT AN AIRPORT.
WITH NEW YORK OVERRUN BY SKRULLS AND O'HARE BURNING, THE PILOT, CREW AND FRIGHTENED PASSENGERS WERE HEADING TOWARD CANADA ON DWINDLING FUEL RESERVES, HOPING TO FIND A SAFE PORT OR AT LEAST SOME PLACE TO DITCH.
I DIDN'T KNOW ANY OF THAT AT THE TIME. ALL I KNEW WAS THAT THE SUPER-SKRULL AND I WERE HEADING STRAIGHT TOWARD IT.
FATHERS AND DAUGHTERS

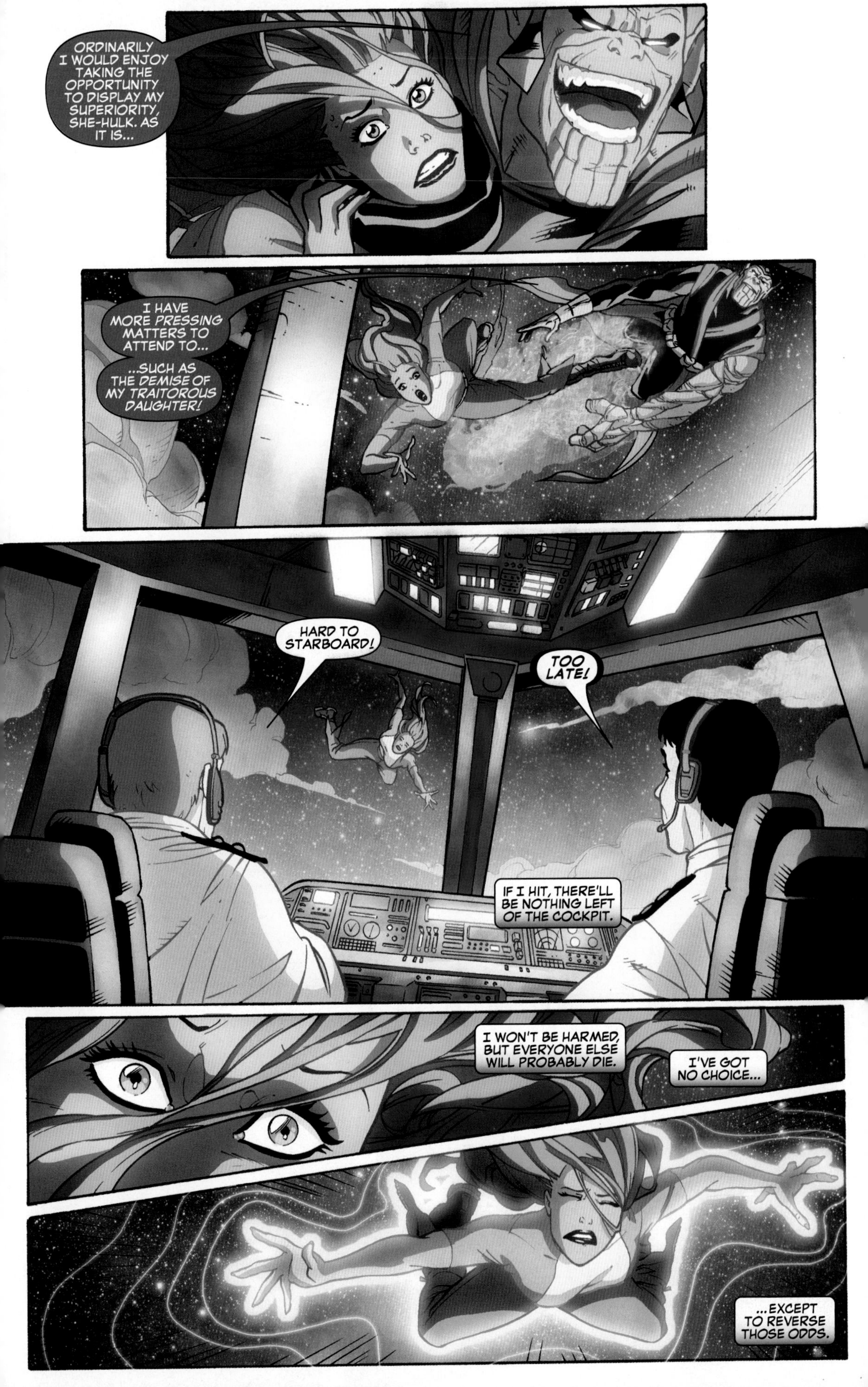
ORDINARILY I WOULD ENJOY TAKING THE OPPORTUNITY TO DISPLAY MY SUPERIORITY, SHE-HULK. AS IT IS...
I HAVE MORE PRESSING MATTERS TO ATTEND TO...
...SUCH AS THE DEMISE OF MY TRAITOROUS DAUGHTER!
HARD TO STARBOARD!
TOO LATE!
IF I HIT, THERE'LL BE NOTHING LEFT OF THE COCKPIT.
I WON'T BE HARMED, BUT EVERYONE ELSE WILL PROBABLY DIE.
I'VE GOT NO CHOICE...
...EXCEPT TO REVERSE THOSE ODDS.

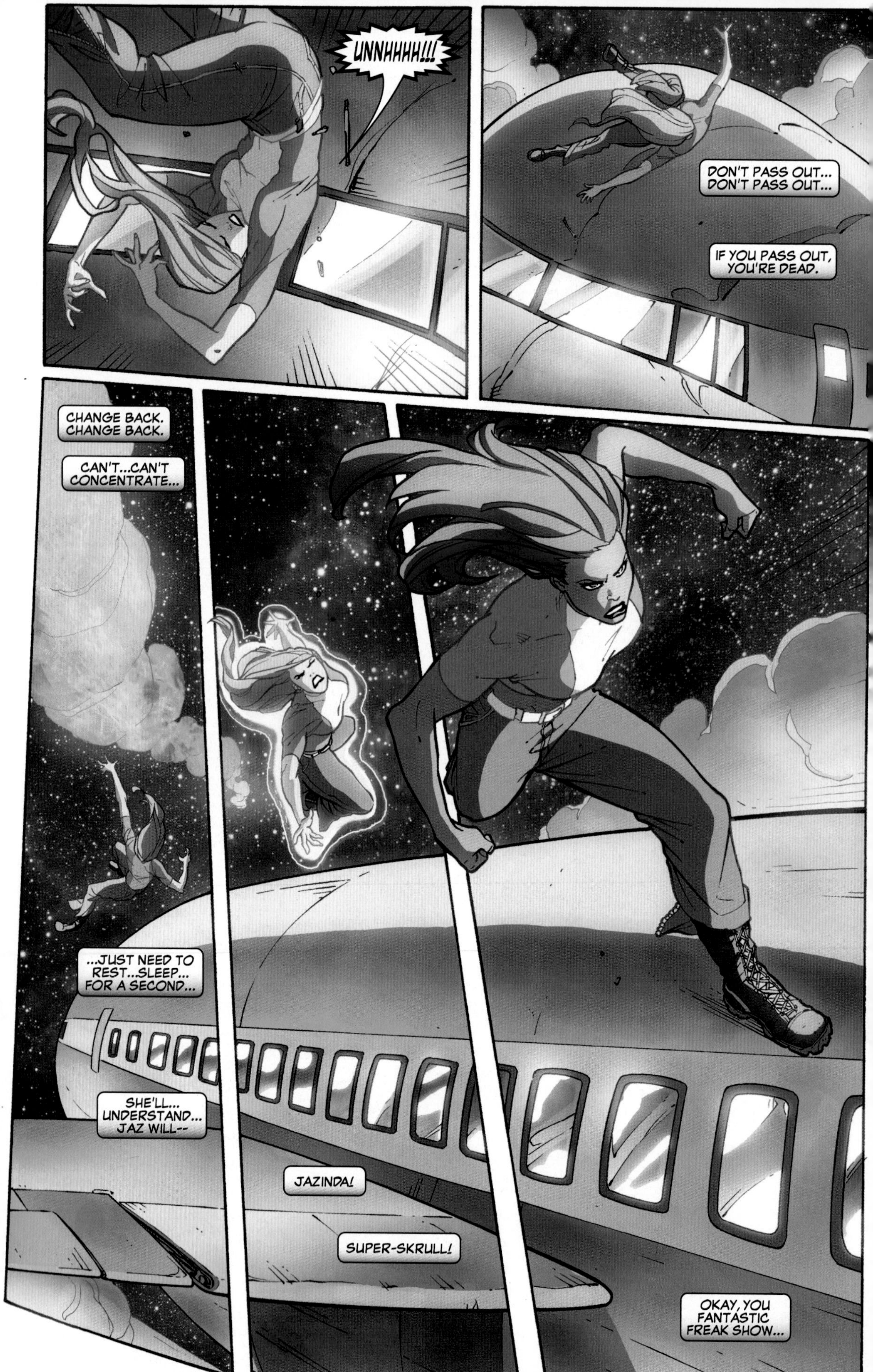
UNNHHHH!!!
DON'T PASS OUT... DON'T PASS OUT...
IF YOU PASS OUT, YOU'RE DEAD.
CHANGE BACK. CHANGE BACK.
CAN'T...CAN'T CONCENTRATE...
...JUST NEED TO REST...SLEEP... FOR A SECOND...
SHE'LL... UNDERSTAND... JAZ WILL--
JAZINDA!
SUPER-SKRULL!
OKAY, YOU FANTASTIC FREAK SHOW...

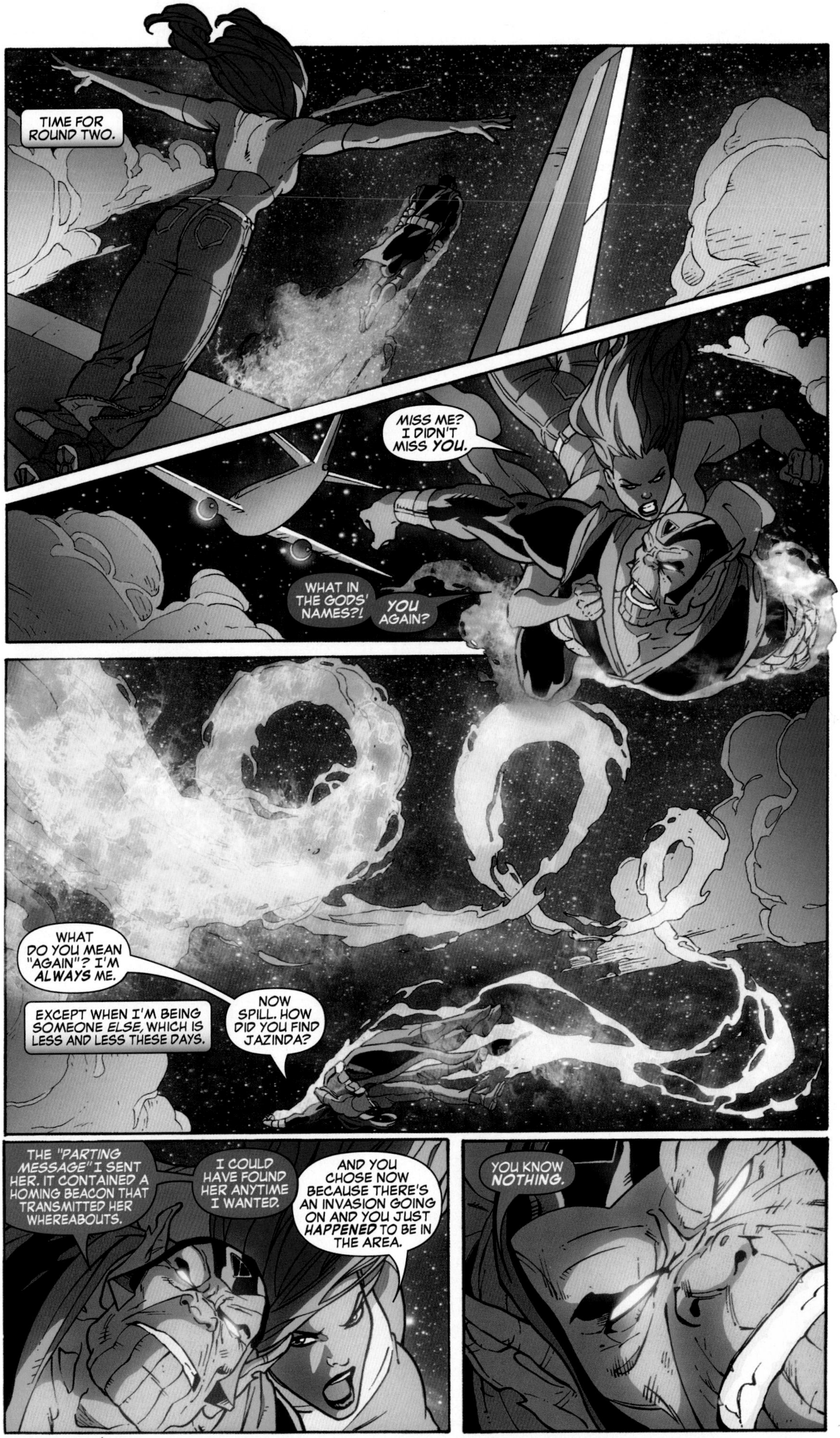
TIME FOR ROUND TWO.
MISS ME? I DIDN'T MISS YOU.
WHAT IN THE GODS' NAMES?!
YOU AGAIN?
WHAT DO YOU MEAN "AGAIN"? I'M ALWAYS ME.
EXCEPT WHEN I'M BEING SOMEONE ELSE, WHICH IS LESS AND LESS THESE DAYS.
NOW SPILL. HOW DID YOU FIND JAZINDA?
THE "PARTING MESSAGE" I SENT HER. IT CONTAINED A HOMING BEACON THAT TRANSMITTED HER WHEREABOUTS.
I COULD HAVE FOUND HER ANYTIME I WANTED.
AND YOU CHOSE NOW BECAUSE THERE'S AN INVASION GOING ON AND YOU JUST HAPPENED TO BE IN THE AREA.
YOU KNOW NOTHING.

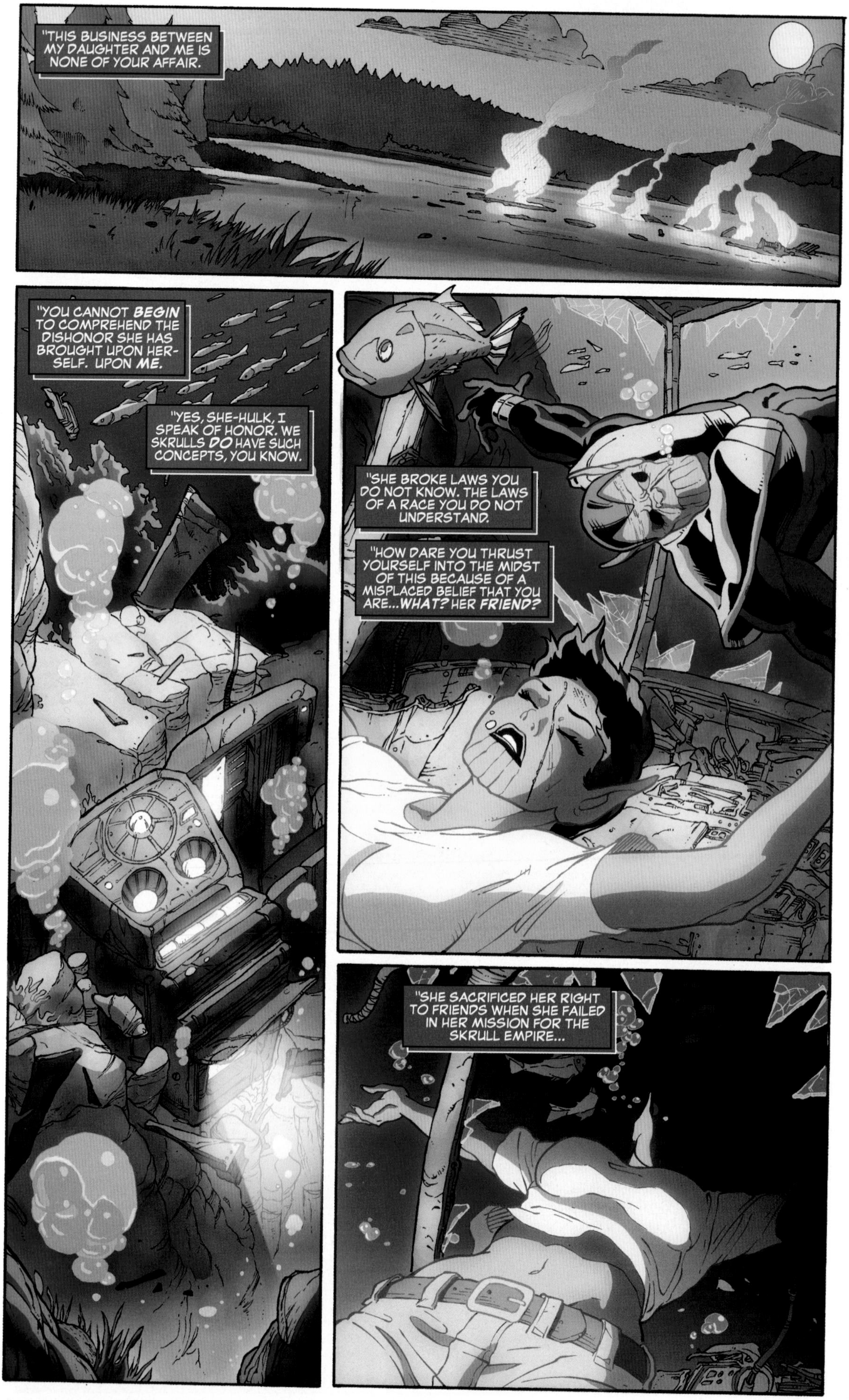
"THIS BUSINESS BETWEEN MY DAUGHTER AND ME IS NONE OF YOUR AFFAIR.
"YOU CANNOT BEGIN TO COMPREHEND THE DISHONOR SHE HAS BROUGHT UPON HER-SELF. UPON ME.
"YES, SHE-HULK, I SPEAK OF HONOR. WE SKRULLS DO HAVE SUCH CONCEPTS, YOU KNOW.
"SHE BROKE LAWS YOU DO NOT KNOW. THE LAWS OF A RACE YOU DO NOT UNDERSTAND.
"HOW DARE YOU THRUST YOURSELF INTO THE MIDST OF THIS BECAUSE OF A MISPLACED BELIEF THAT YOU ARE...WHAT? HER FRIEND?
"SHE SACRIFICED HER RIGHT TO FRIENDS WHEN SHE FAILED IN HER MISSION FOR THE SKRULL EMPIRE...

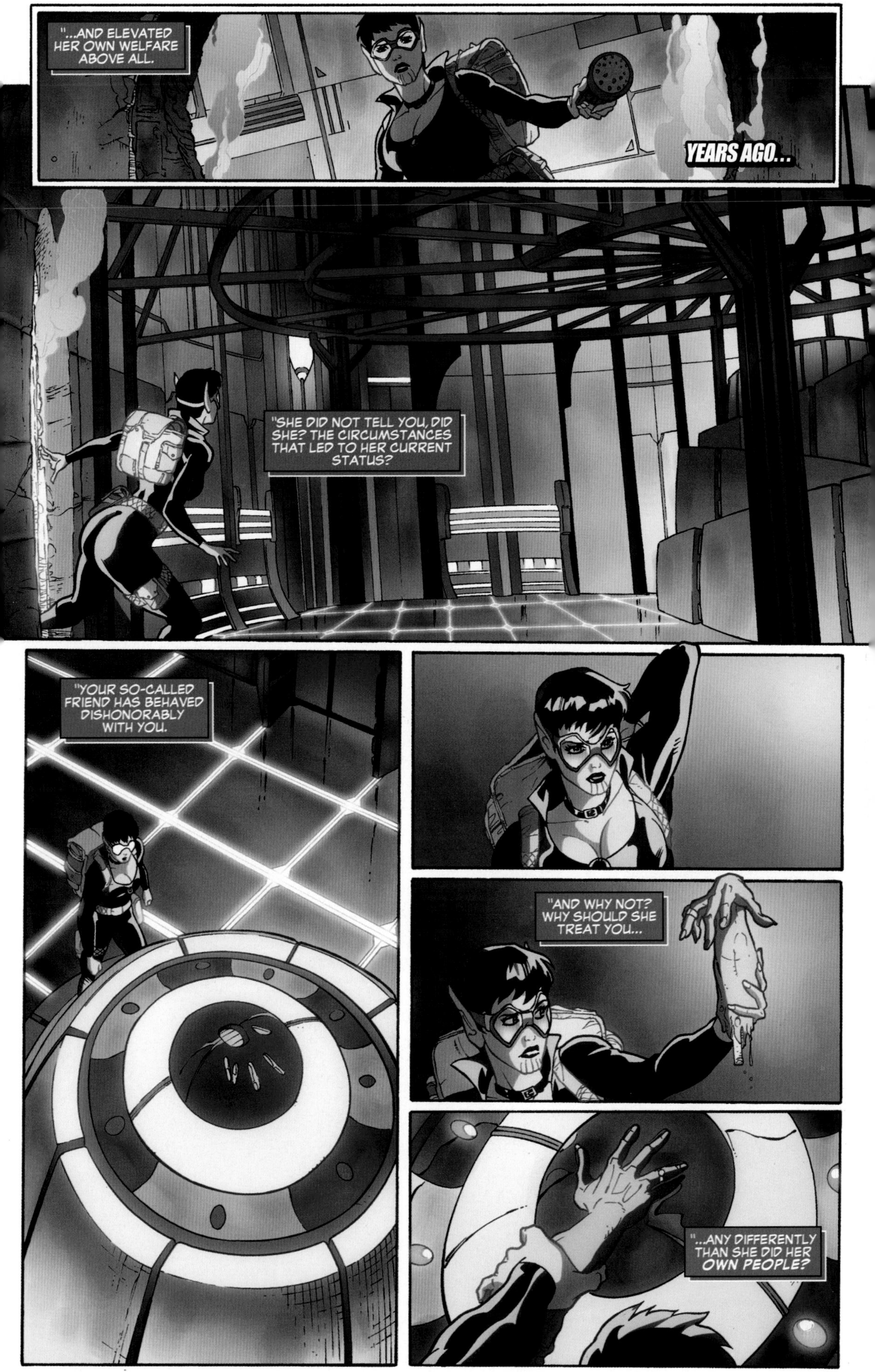
"...AND ELEVATED HER OWN WELFARE ABOVE ALL.
YEARS AGO...
"SHE DID NOT TELL YOU, DID SHE? THE CIRCUMSTANCES THAT LED TO HER CURRENT STATUS?
"YOUR SO-CALLED FRIEND HAS BEHAVED DISHONORABLY WITH YOU.
"AND WHY NOT? WHY SHOULD SHE TREAT YOU...
"...ANY DIFFERENTLY THAN SHE DID HER *OWN PEOPLE*?

"SHE WAS ENTRUSTED WITH A GREAT MISSION. A MISSION INVOLVING THE RETRIEVAL OF A SACRED ARTIFACT RIGHTFULLY BELONGING TO THE SKRULLS.

"SHE BOTCHED IT."

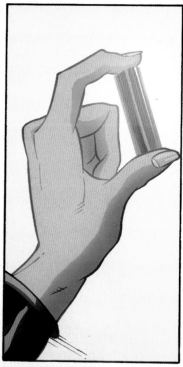

THERE SHE IS!

SHE CUT THE HAND OFF HIGH MINISTER TUNIS-VAR TO PENETRATE SECURITY!

NO MERCY! PRY THE GEM FROM HER COLD, DEAD FINGERS!

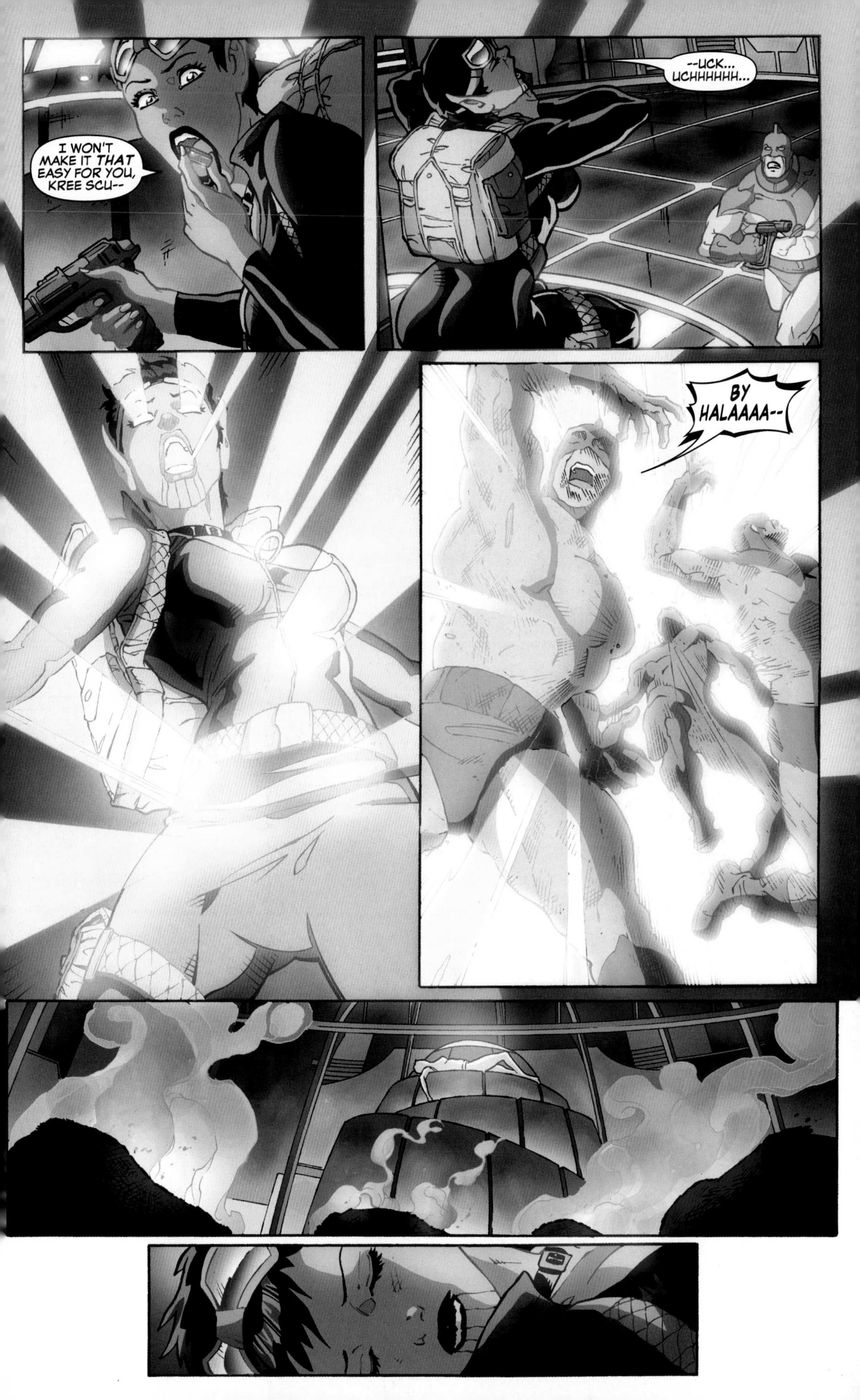
I WON'T MAKE IT THAT EASY FOR YOU, KREE SCU--
--UCK... UCHHHHHH...
BY HALAAAA--

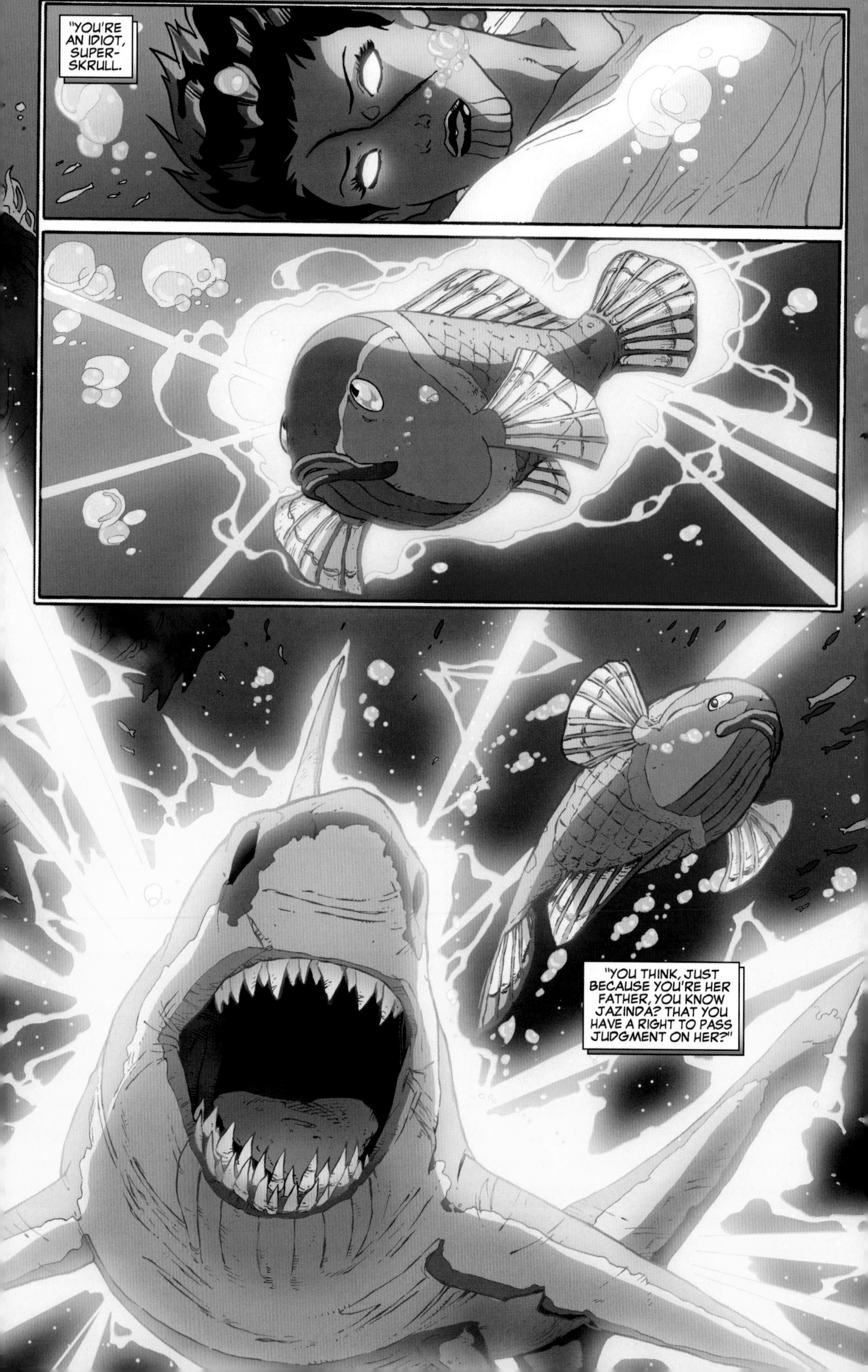
"YOU'RE AN IDIOT, SUPER-SKRULL.
"YOU THINK, JUST BECAUSE YOU'RE HER FATHER, YOU KNOW JAZINDA? THAT YOU HAVE A RIGHT TO PASS JUDGMENT ON HER?"

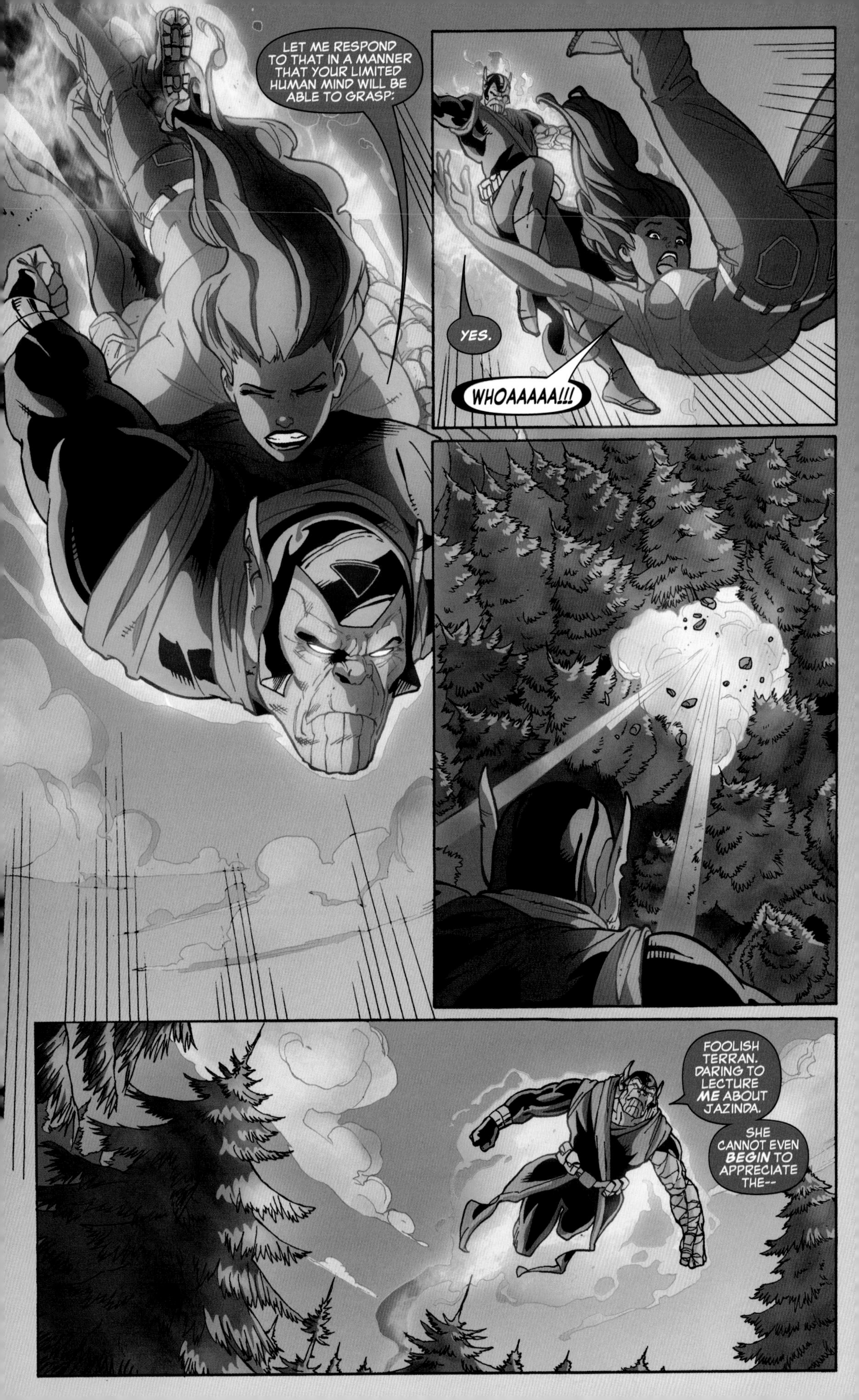
LET ME RESPOND TO THAT IN A MANNER THAT YOUR LIMITED HUMAN MIND WILL BE ABLE TO GRASP:
YES.
WHOAAAAA!!!
FOOLISH TERRAN. DARING TO LECTURE ME ABOUT JAZINDA.
SHE CANNOT EVEN BEGIN TO APPRECIATE THE--

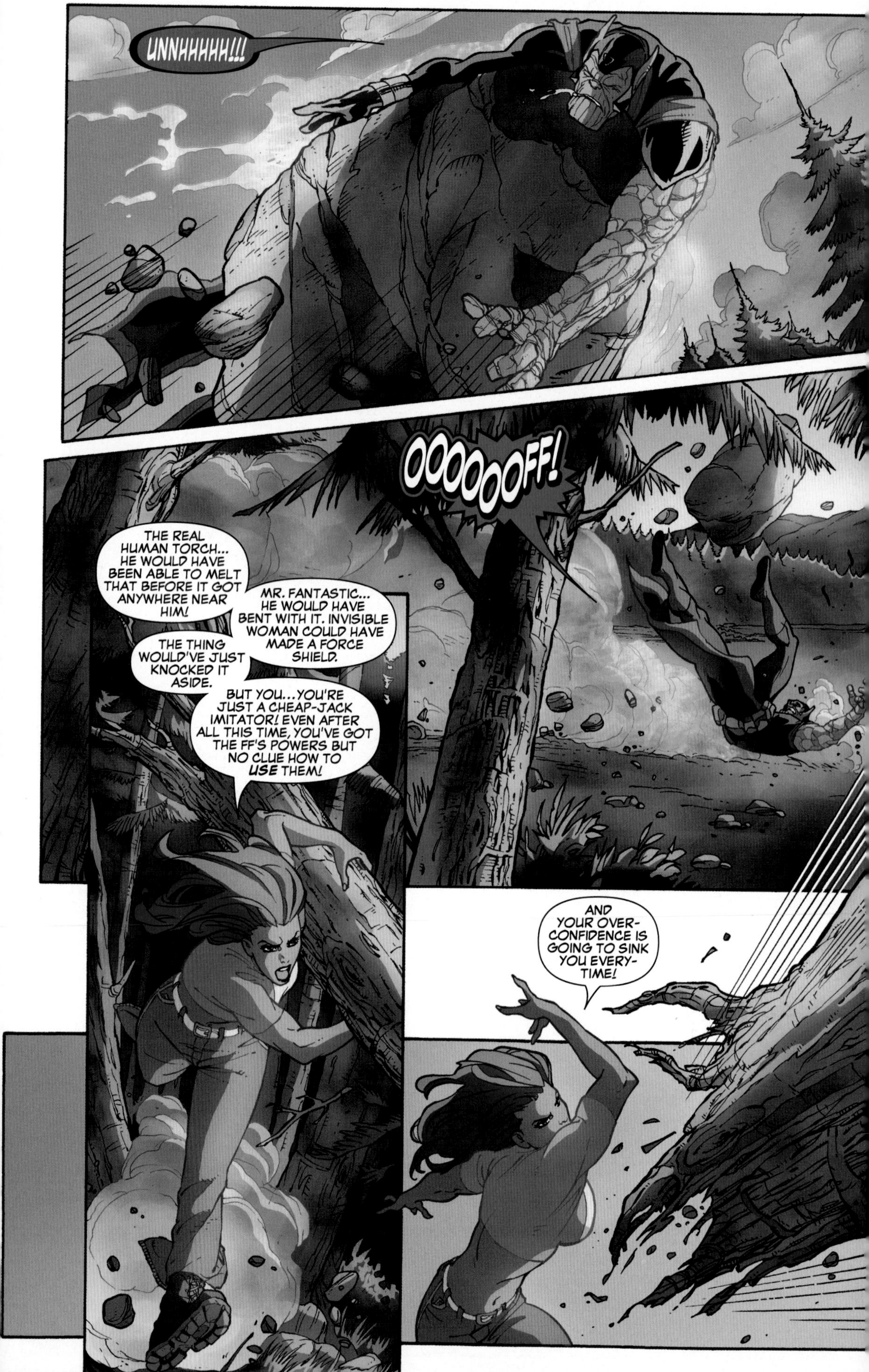
UNNHHHHH!!!
OOOOOOFF!
THE REAL HUMAN TORCH... HE WOULD HAVE BEEN ABLE TO MELT THAT BEFORE IT GOT ANYWHERE NEAR HIM!
MR. FANTASTIC... HE WOULD HAVE BENT WITH IT. INVISIBLE WOMAN COULD HAVE MADE A FORCE SHIELD.
THE THING WOULD'VE JUST KNOCKED IT ASIDE.
BUT YOU...YOU'RE JUST A CHEAP-JACK IMITATOR! EVEN AFTER ALL THIS TIME, YOU'VE GOT THE FF'S POWERS BUT NO CLUE HOW TO USE THEM!
AND YOUR OVER-CONFIDENCE IS GOING TO SINK YOU EVERY-TIME!

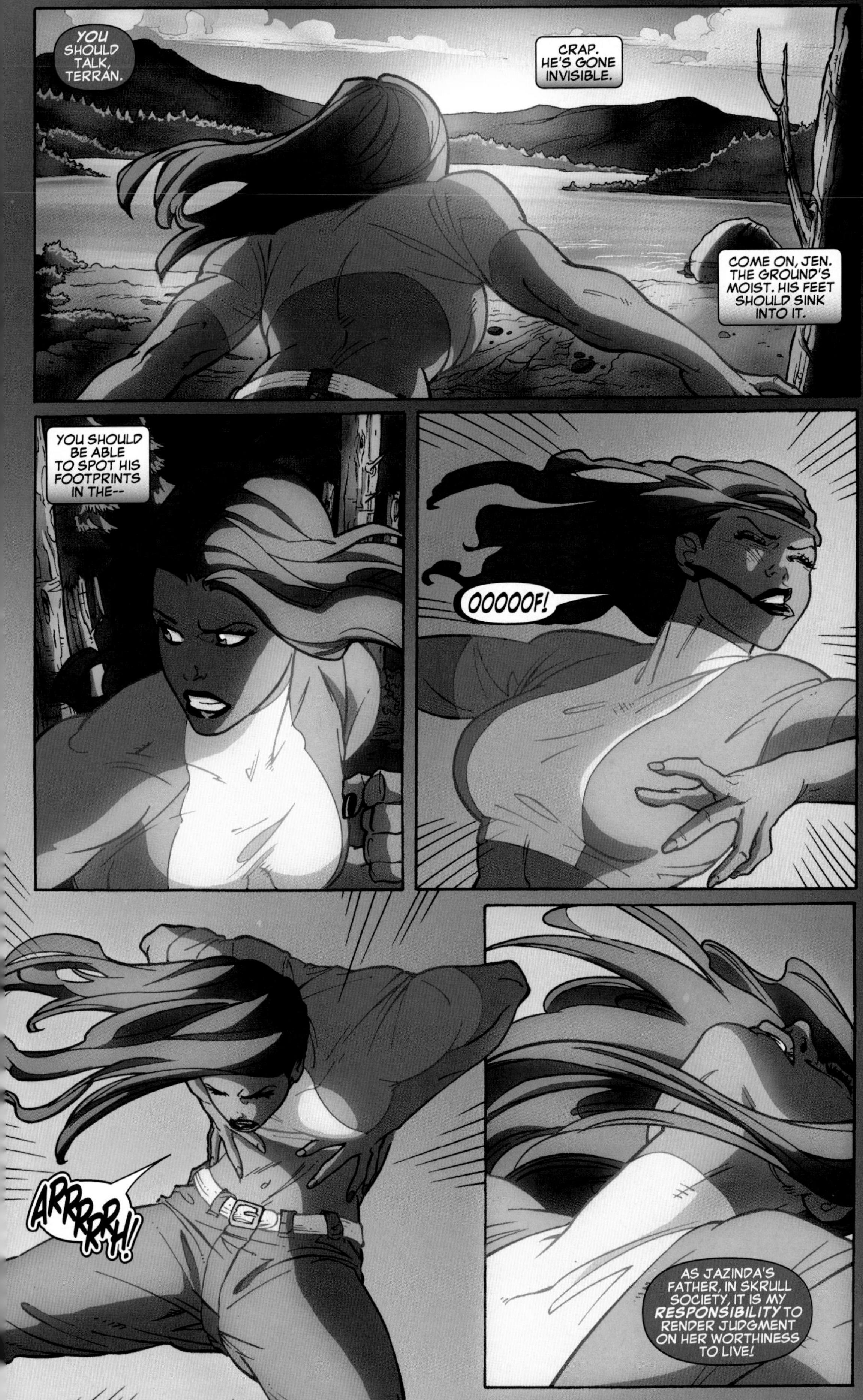
YOU SHOULD TALK, TERRAN.
CRAP. HE'S GONE INVISIBLE.
COME ON, JEN. THE GROUND'S MOIST. HIS FEET SHOULD SINK INTO IT.
YOU SHOULD BE ABLE TO SPOT HIS FOOTPRINTS IN THE--
OOOOOF!
ARRRRRH!
AS JAZINDA'S FATHER, IN SKRULL SOCIETY, IT IS MY RESPONSIBILITY TO RENDER JUDGMENT ON HER WORTHINESS TO LIVE!

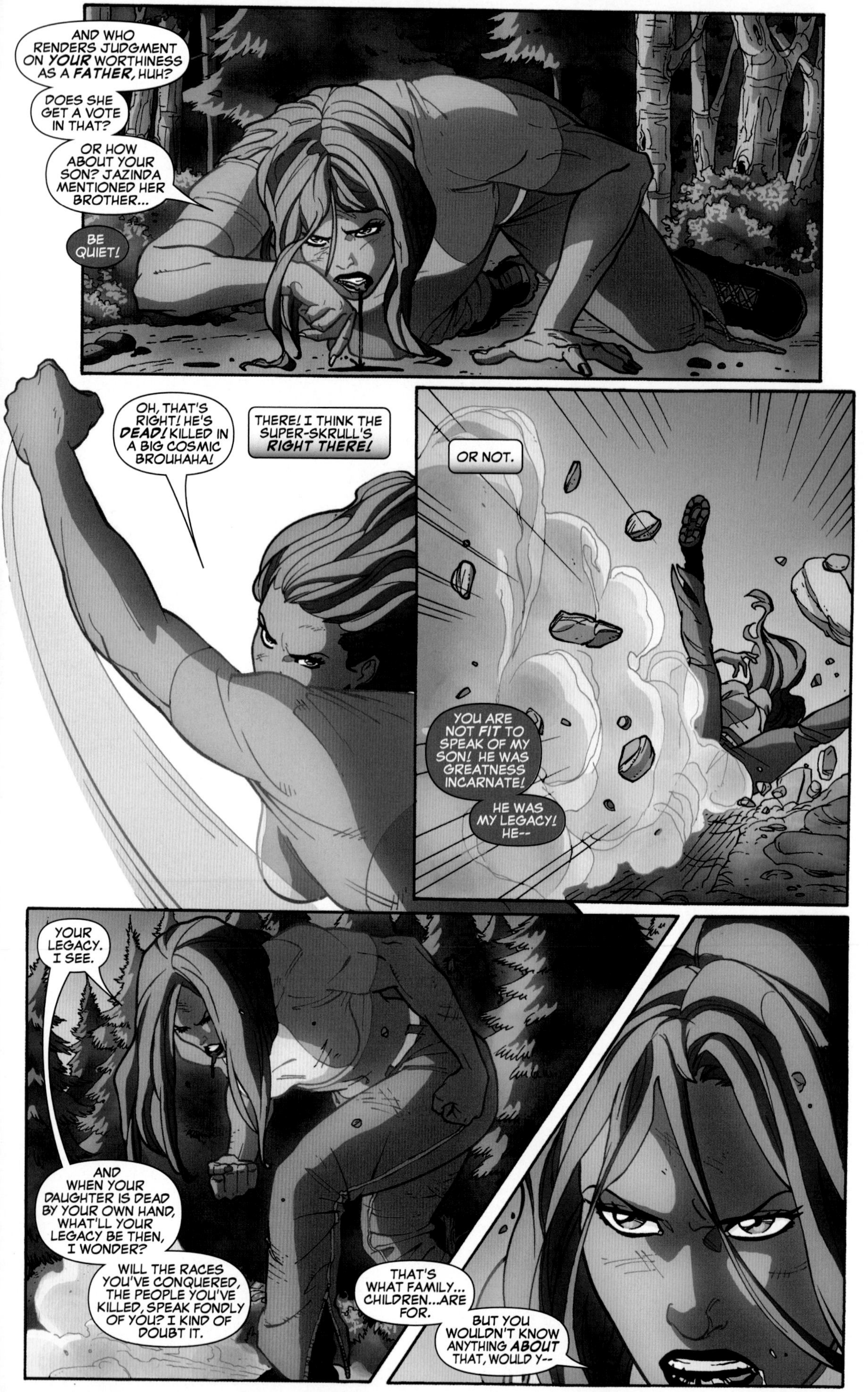
AND WHO RENDERS JUDGMENT ON YOUR WORTHINESS AS A FATHER, HUH?
DOES SHE GET A VOTE IN THAT?
OR HOW ABOUT YOUR SON? JAZINDA MENTIONED HER BROTHER...
BE QUIET!
OH, THAT'S RIGHT! HE'S DEAD! KILLED IN A BIG COSMIC BROUHAHA!
THERE! I THINK THE SUPER-SKRULL'S RIGHT THERE!
OR NOT.
YOU ARE NOT FIT TO SPEAK OF MY SON! HE WAS GREATNESS INCARNATE!
HE WAS MY LEGACY! HE--
YOUR LEGACY. I SEE.
AND WHEN YOUR DAUGHTER IS DEAD BY YOUR OWN HAND, WHAT'LL YOUR LEGACY BE THEN, I WONDER?
WILL THE RACES YOU'VE CONQUERED, THE PEOPLE YOU'VE KILLED, SPEAK FONDLY OF YOU? I KIND OF DOUBT IT.
THAT'S WHAT FAMILY... CHILDREN...ARE FOR.
BUT YOU WOULDN'T KNOW ANYTHING ABOUT THAT, WOULD Y--

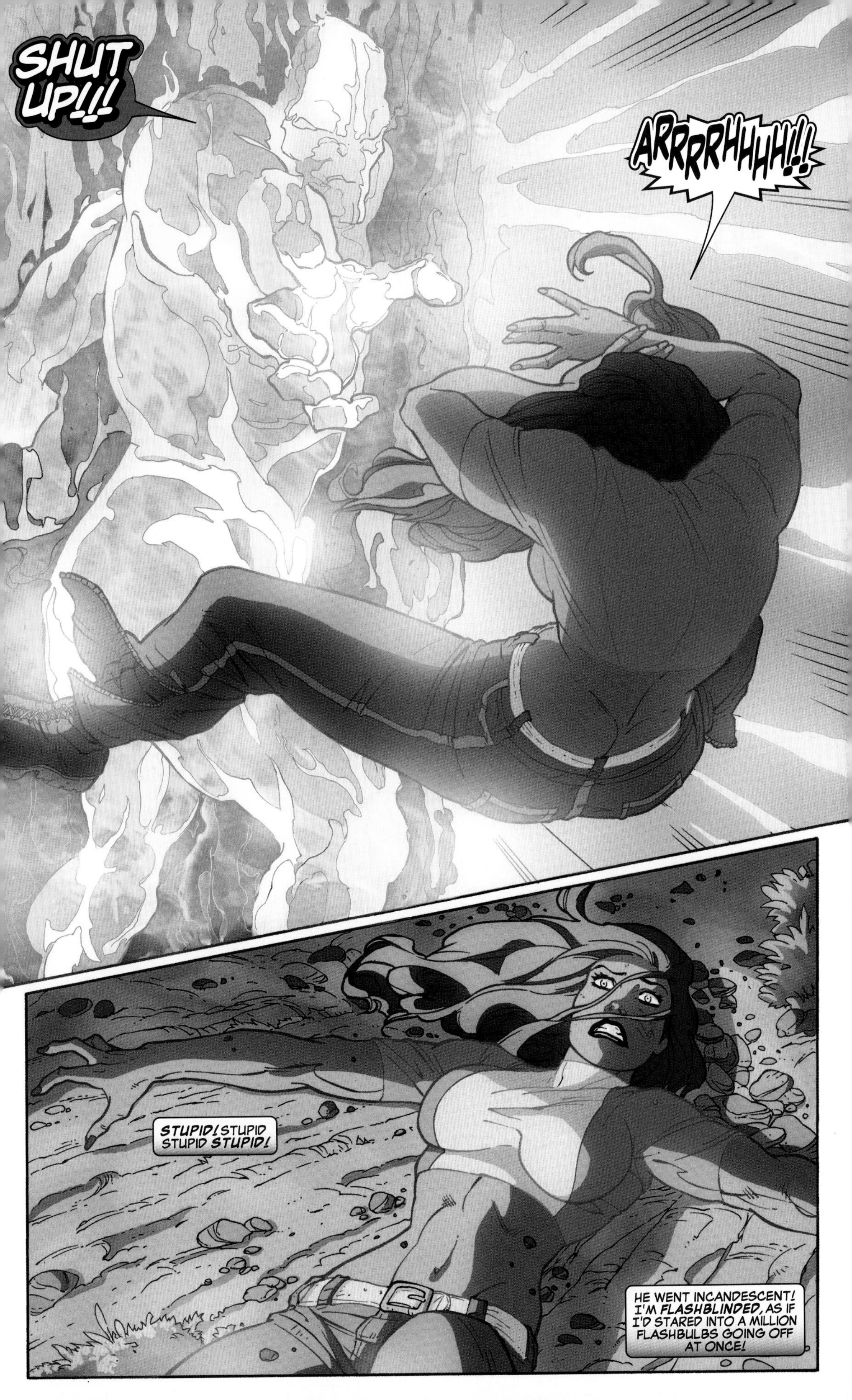
SHUT UP!!!
ARRRRHHHH!!!
STUPID! STUPID STUPID STUPID!
HE WENT INCANDESCENT! I'M FLASHBLINDED, AS IF I'D STARED INTO A MILLION FLASHBULBS GOING OFF AT ONCE!

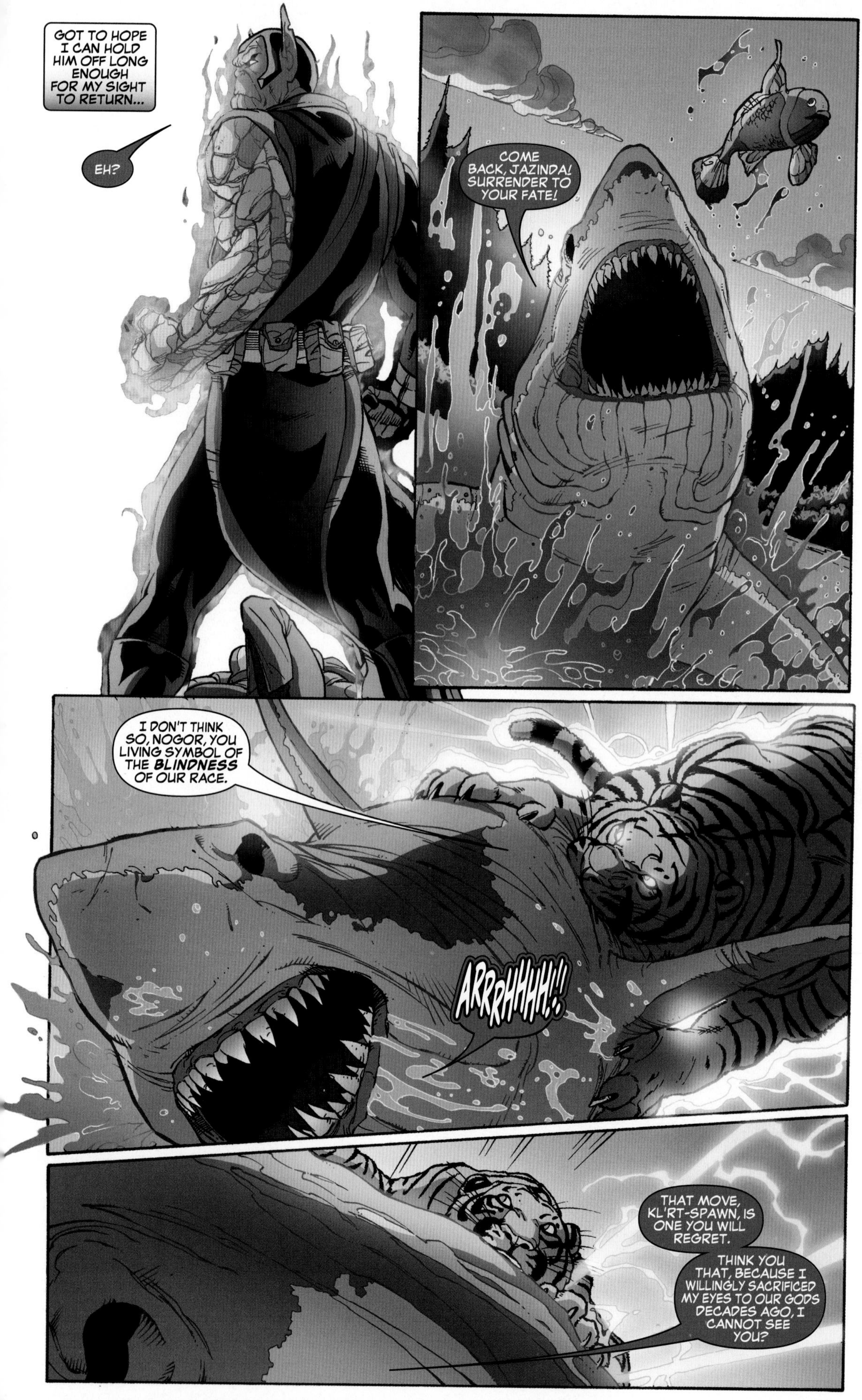
GOT TO HOPE I CAN HOLD HIM OFF LONG ENOUGH FOR MY SIGHT TO RETURN...
EH?
COME BACK, JAZINDA! SURRENDER TO YOUR FATE!
I DON'T THINK SO, NOGOR, YOU LIVING SYMBOL OF THE BLINDNESS OF OUR RACE.
ARRRHHHH!!!
THAT MOVE, KL'RT-SPAWN, IS ONE YOU WILL REGRET.
THINK YOU THAT, BECAUSE I WILLINGLY SACRIFICED MY EYES TO OUR GODS DECADES AGO, I CANNOT SEE YOU?

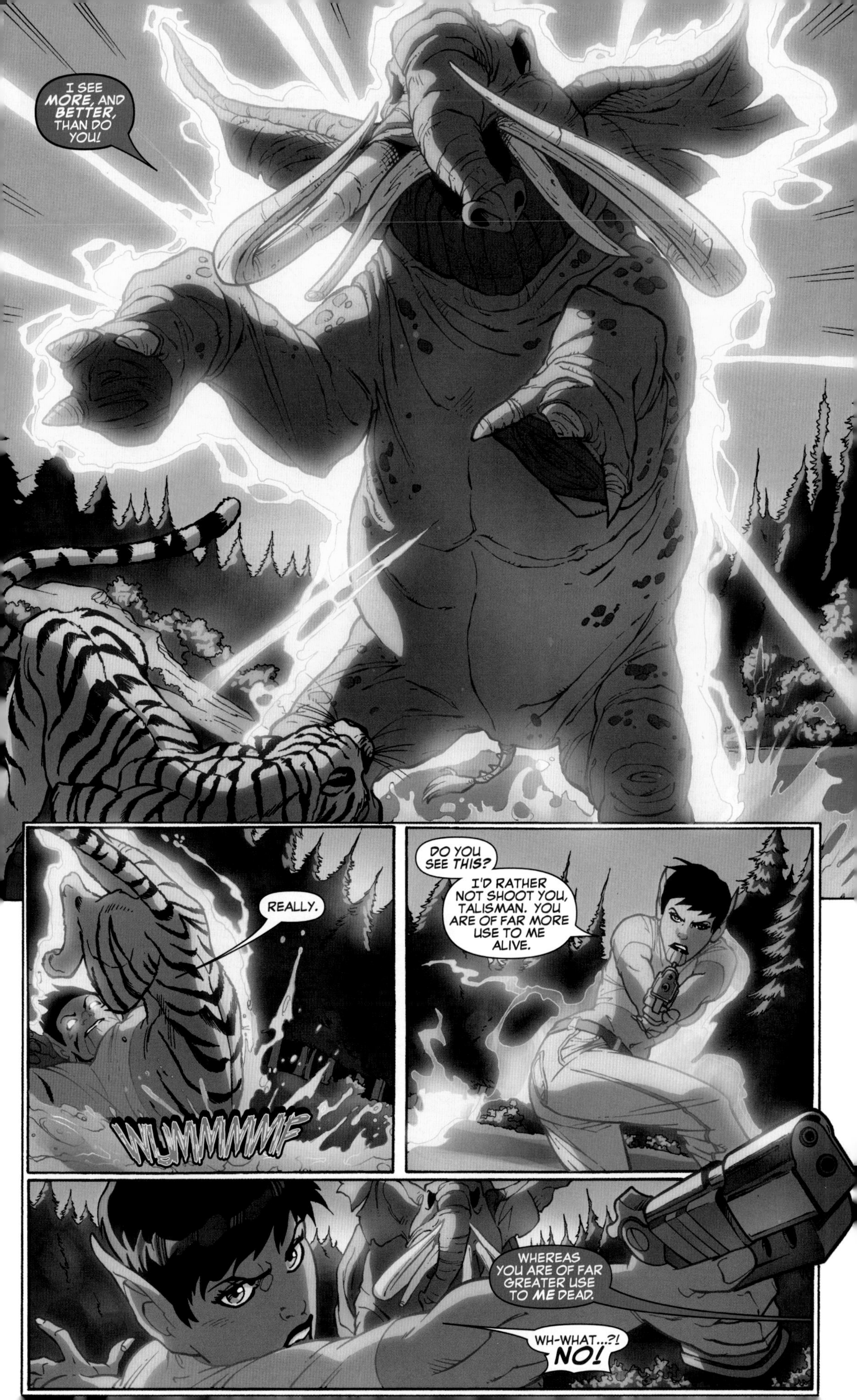
I SEE MORE, AND BETTER, THAN DO YOU!
REALLY.
WUMMMMF
DO YOU SEE THIS?
I'D RATHER NOT SHOOT YOU, TALISMAN. YOU ARE OF FAR MORE USE TO ME ALIVE.
WHEREAS YOU ARE OF FAR GREATER USE TO ME DEAD.
WH-WHAT...?! NO!

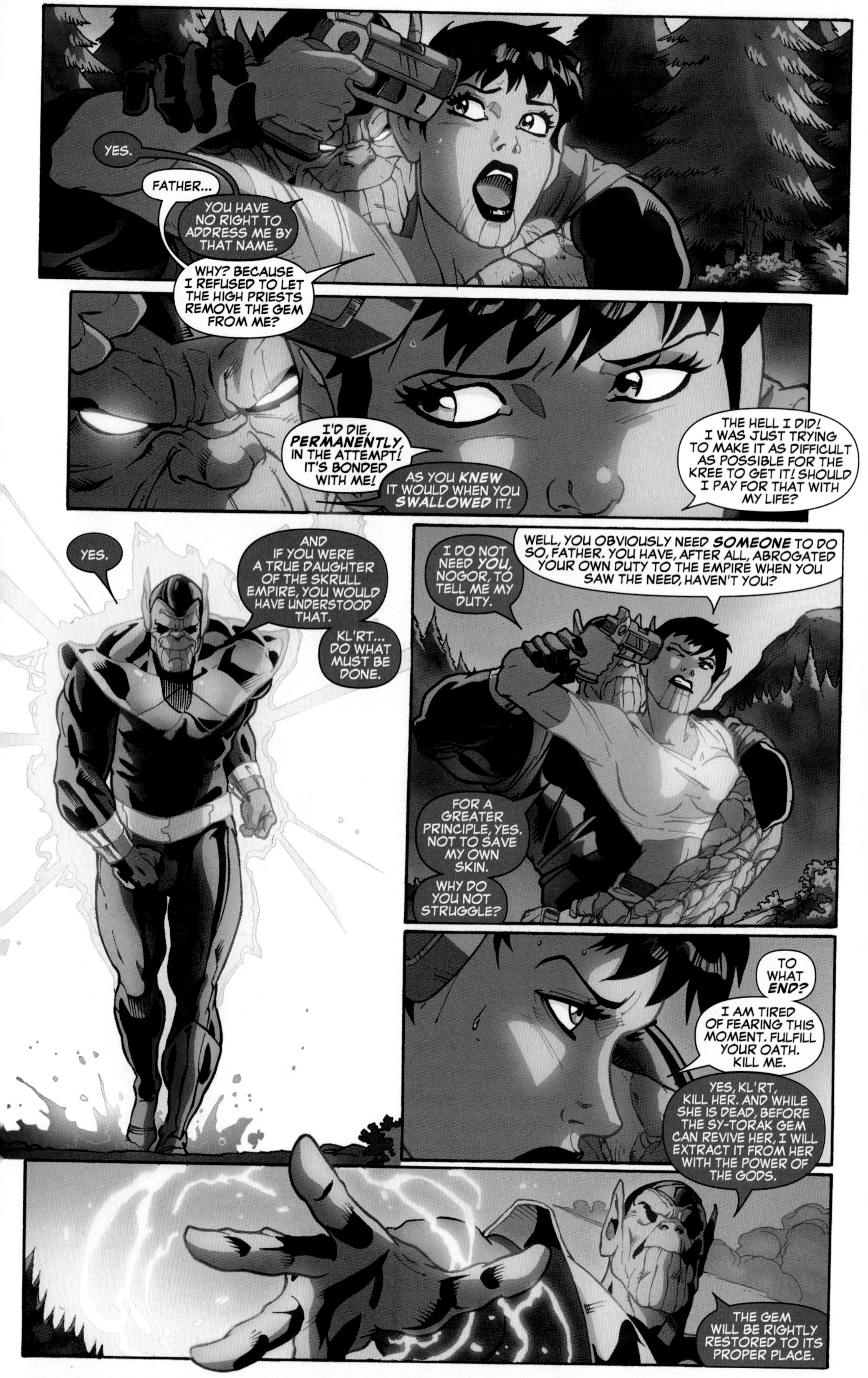
YES.
FATHER...
YOU HAVE NO RIGHT TO ADDRESS ME BY THAT NAME.
WHY? BECAUSE I REFUSED TO LET THE HIGH PRIESTS REMOVE THE GEM FROM ME?
I'D DIE, PERMANENTLY, IN THE ATTEMPT! IT'S BONDED WITH ME!
AS YOU KNEW IT WOULD WHEN YOU SWALLOWED IT!
THE HELL I DID! I WAS JUST TRYING TO MAKE IT AS DIFFICULT AS POSSIBLE FOR THE KREE TO GET IT! SHOULD I PAY FOR THAT WITH MY LIFE?
YES.
AND IF YOU WERE A TRUE DAUGHTER OF THE SKRULL EMPIRE, YOU WOULD HAVE UNDERSTOOD THAT.
KL'RT... DO WHAT MUST BE DONE.
I DO NOT NEED YOU, NOGOR, TO TELL ME MY DUTY.
WELL, YOU OBVIOUSLY NEED SOMEONE TO DO SO, FATHER. YOU HAVE, AFTER ALL, ABROGATED YOUR OWN DUTY TO THE EMPIRE WHEN YOU SAW THE NEED, HAVEN'T YOU?
FOR A GREATER PRINCIPLE, YES. NOT TO SAVE MY OWN SKIN.
WHY DO YOU NOT STRUGGLE?
TO WHAT END?
I AM TIRED OF FEARING THIS MOMENT. FULFILL YOUR OATH. KILL ME.
YES, KL'RT, KILL HER. AND WHILE SHE IS DEAD, BEFORE THE SY-TORAK GEM CAN REVIVE HER, I WILL EXTRACT IT FROM HER WITH THE POWER OF THE GODS.
THE GEM WILL BE RIGHTLY RESTORED TO ITS PROPER PLACE.

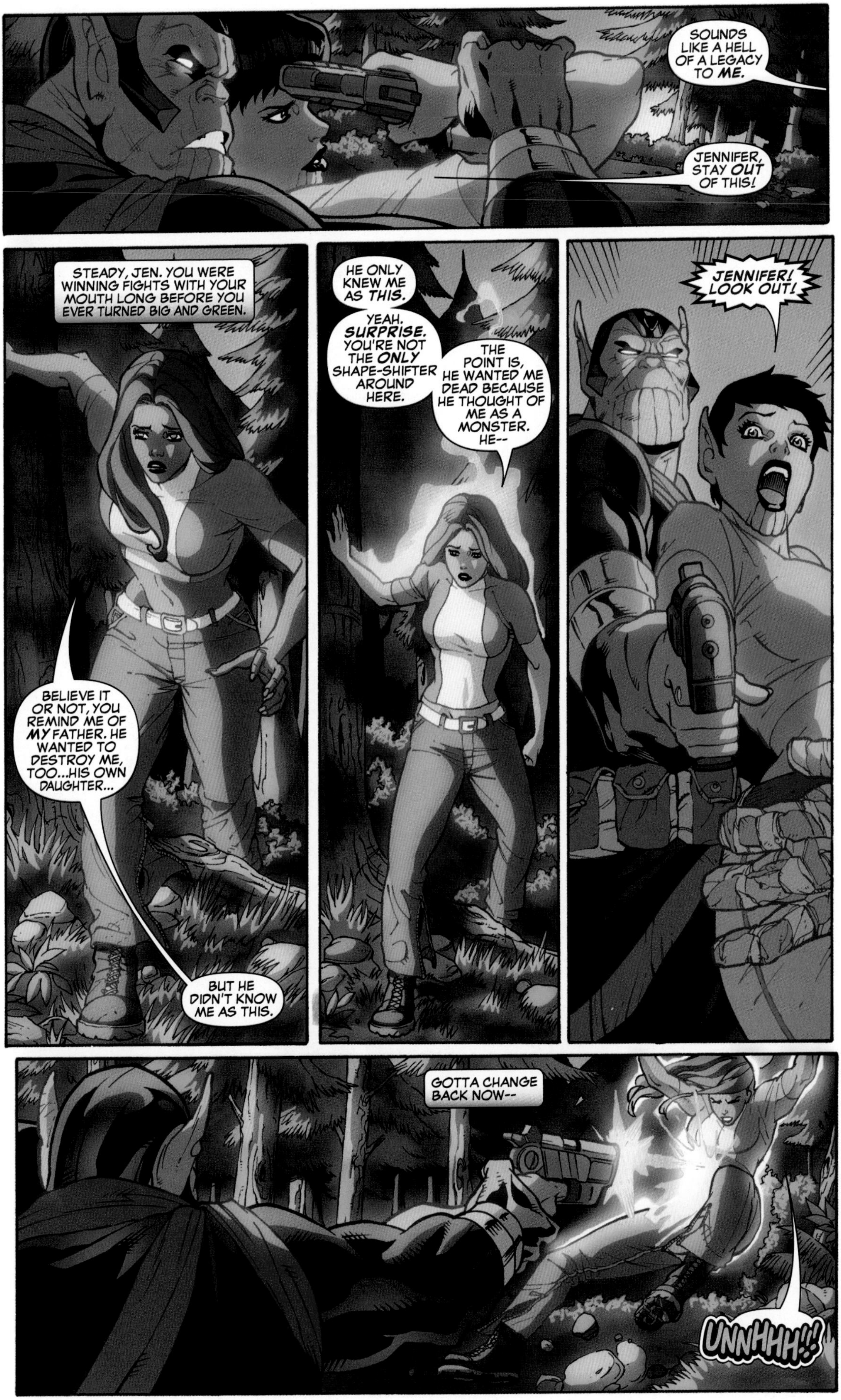
SOUNDS LIKE A HELL OF A LEGACY TO ME.
JENNIFER, STAY OUT OF THIS!
STEADY, JEN. YOU WERE WINNING FIGHTS WITH YOUR MOUTH LONG BEFORE YOU EVER TURNED BIG AND GREEN.
BELIEVE IT OR NOT, YOU REMIND ME OF MY FATHER. HE WANTED TO DESTROY ME, TOO...HIS OWN DAUGHTER...
BUT HE DIDN'T KNOW ME AS THIS.
HE ONLY KNEW ME AS THIS.
YEAH. SURPRISE. YOU'RE NOT THE ONLY SHAPE-SHIFTER AROUND HERE.
THE POINT IS, HE WANTED ME DEAD BECAUSE HE THOUGHT OF ME AS A MONSTER. HE--
JENNIFER! LOOK OUT!
GOTTA CHANGE BACK NOW--
UNNHHH!!

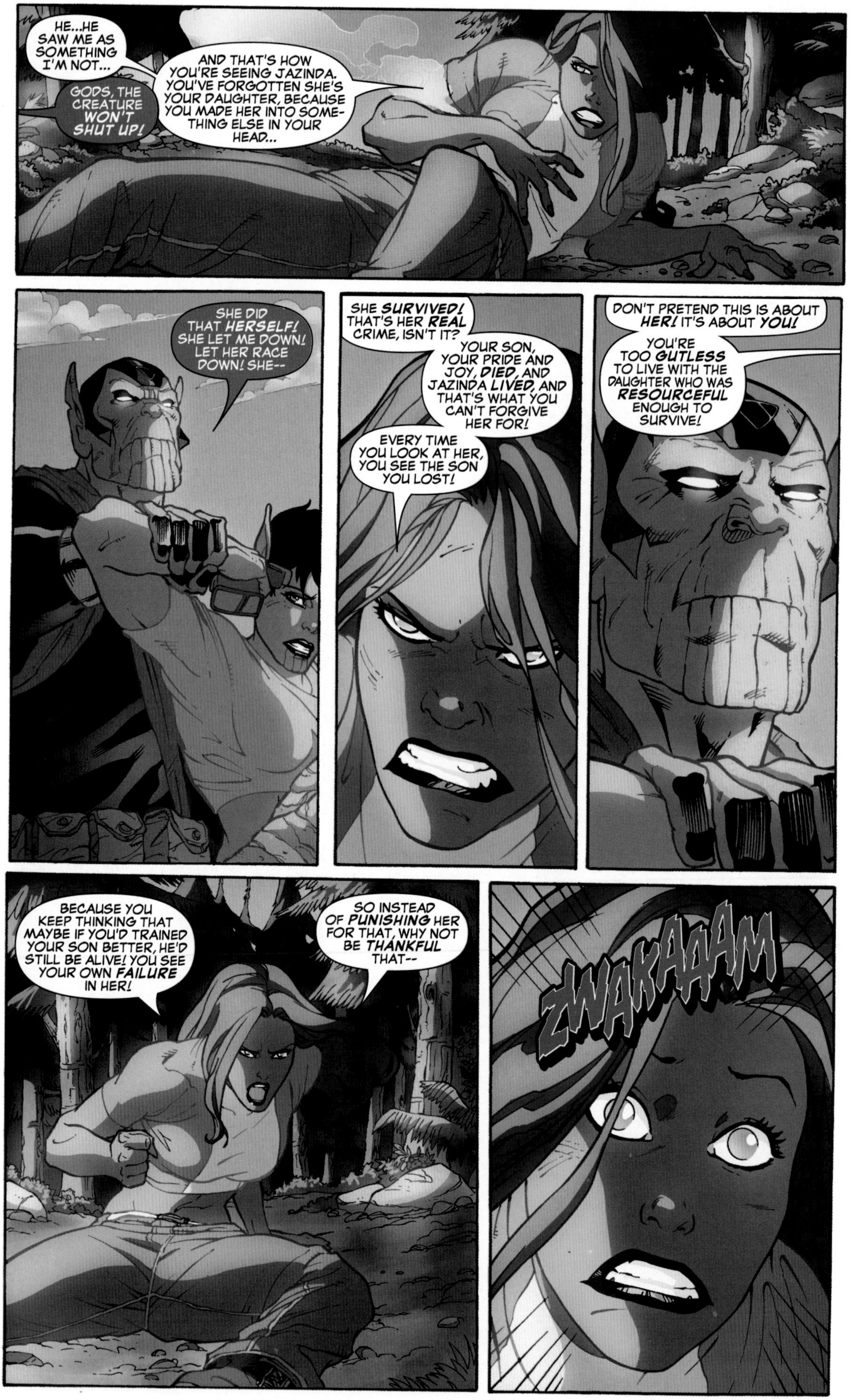

HE...HE SAW ME AS SOMETHING I'M NOT...
GODS, THE CREATURE WON'T SHUT UP!
AND THAT'S HOW YOU'RE SEEING JAZINDA. YOU'VE FORGOTTEN SHE'S YOUR DAUGHTER, BECAUSE YOU MADE HER INTO SOMETHING ELSE IN YOUR HEAD...
SHE DID THAT HERSELF! SHE LET ME DOWN! LET HER RACE DOWN! SHE--
SHE SURVIVED! THAT'S HER REAL CRIME, ISN'T IT?
YOUR SON, YOUR PRIDE AND JOY, DIED, AND JAZINDA LIVED, AND THAT'S WHAT YOU CAN'T FORGIVE HER FOR!
EVERY TIME YOU LOOK AT HER, YOU SEE THE SON YOU LOST!
DON'T PRETEND THIS IS ABOUT HER! IT'S ABOUT YOU!
YOU'RE TOO GUTLESS TO LIVE WITH THE DAUGHTER WHO WAS RESOURCEFUL ENOUGH TO SURVIVE!
BECAUSE YOU KEEP THINKING THAT MAYBE IF YOU'D TRAINED YOUR SON BETTER, HE'D STILL BE ALIVE! YOU SEE YOUR OWN FAILURE IN HER!
SO INSTEAD OF PUNISHING HER FOR THAT, WHY NOT BE THANKFUL THAT--
ZWAKAAAM

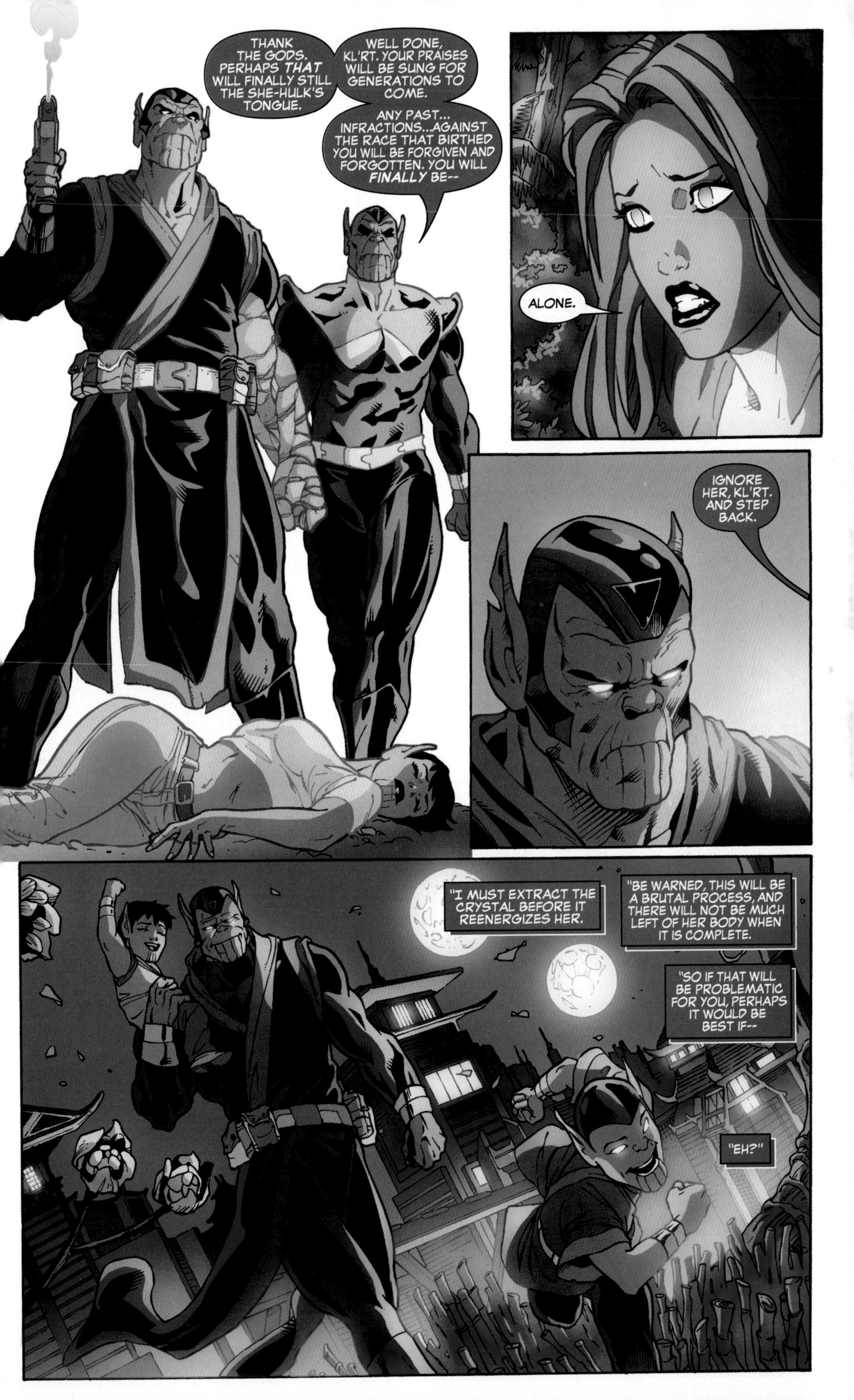
THANK THE GODS. PERHAPS THAT WILL FINALLY STILL THE SHE-HULK'S TONGUE.
WELL DONE, KL'RT. YOUR PRAISES WILL BE SUNG FOR GENERATIONS TO COME.
ANY PAST... INFRACTIONS...AGAINST THE RACE THAT BIRTHED YOU WILL BE FORGIVEN AND FORGOTTEN. YOU WILL FINALLY BE--
ALONE.
IGNORE HER, KL'RT. AND STEP BACK.
"I MUST EXTRACT THE CRYSTAL BEFORE IT REENERGIZES HER.
"BE WARNED, THIS WILL BE A BRUTAL PROCESS, AND THERE WILL NOT BE MUCH LEFT OF HER BODY WHEN IT IS COMPLETE.
"SO IF THAT WILL BE PROBLEMATIC FOR YOU, PERHAPS IT WOULD BE BEST IF--
"EH?"

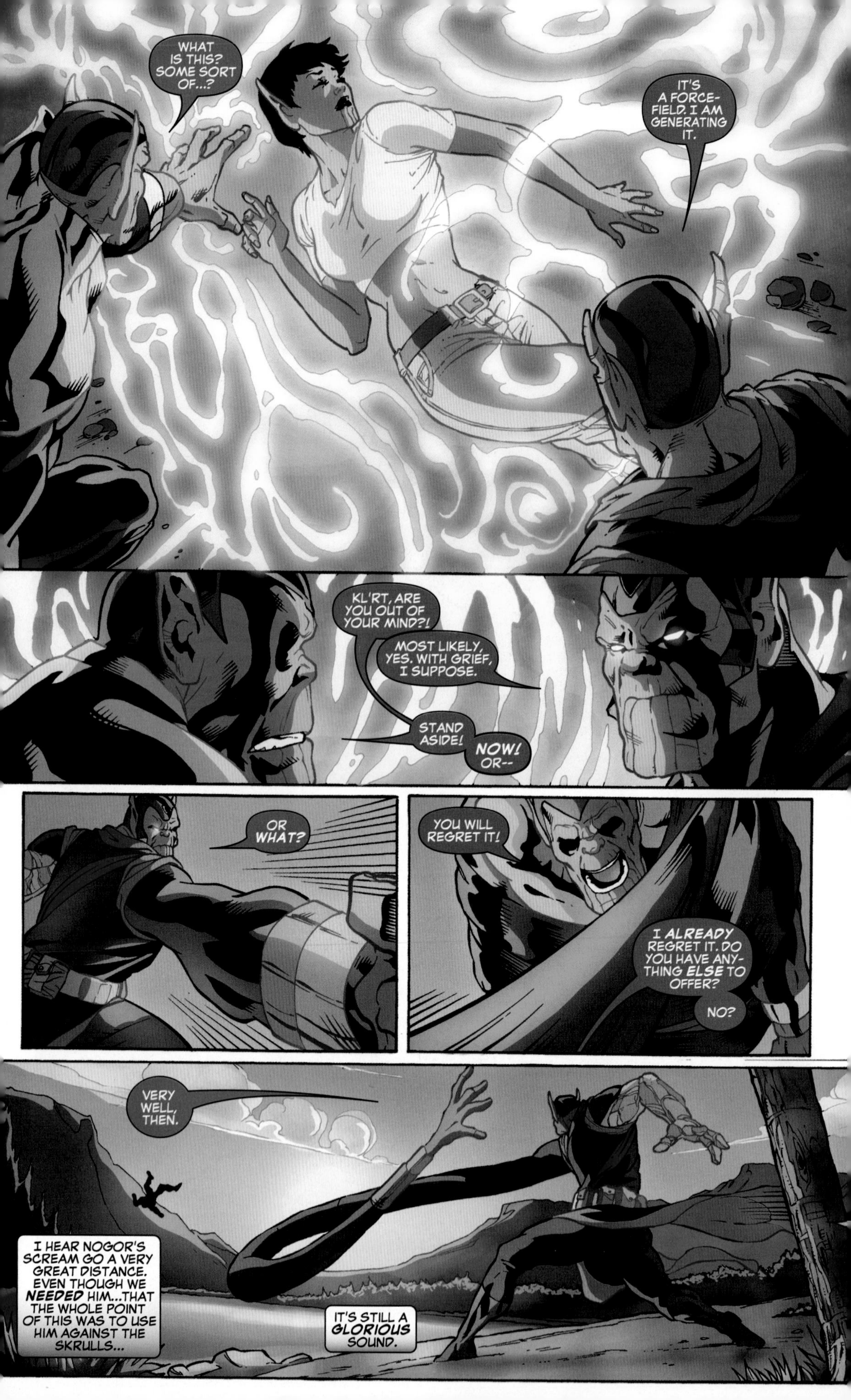
WHAT IS THIS? SOME SORT OF...?
IT'S A FORCE-FIELD. I AM GENERATING IT.
KL'RT, ARE YOU OUT OF YOUR MIND?!
MOST LIKELY, YES. WITH GRIEF, I SUPPOSE.
STAND ASIDE! NOW! OR--
OR WHAT?
YOU WILL REGRET IT!
I ALREADY REGRET IT. DO YOU HAVE ANY-THING ELSE TO OFFER?
NO?
VERY WELL, THEN.
I HEAR NOGOR'S SCREAM GO A VERY GREAT DISTANCE. EVEN THOUGH WE NEEDED HIM...THAT THE WHOLE POINT OF THIS WAS TO USE HIM AGAINST THE SKRULLS...
IT'S STILL A GLORIOUS SOUND.

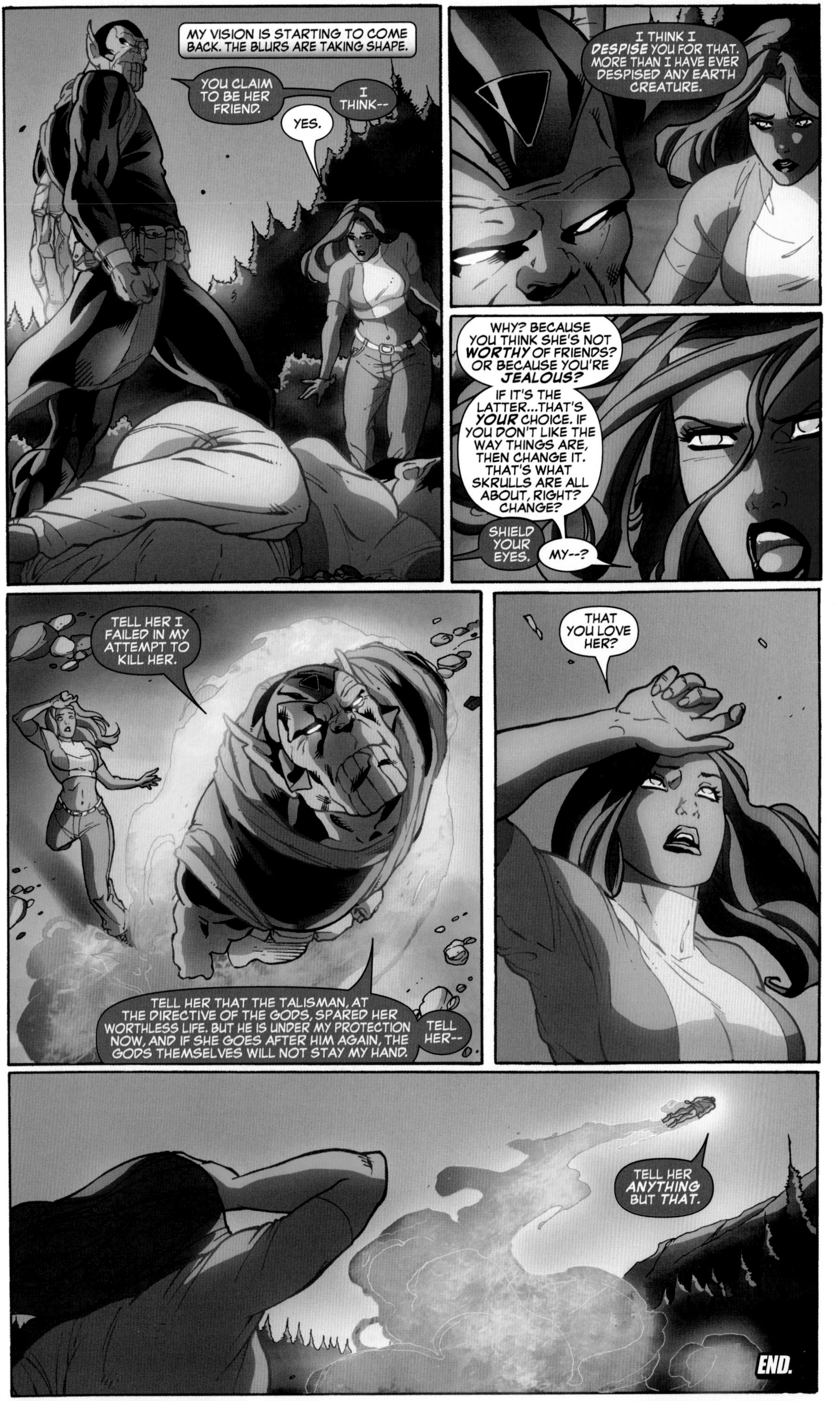
MY VISION IS STARTING TO COME BACK. THE BLURS ARE TAKING SHAPE.
YOU CLAIM TO BE HER FRIEND.
I THINK--
YES.
I THINK I DESPISE YOU FOR THAT. MORE THAN I HAVE EVER DESPISED ANY EARTH CREATURE.
WHY? BECAUSE YOU THINK SHE'S NOT WORTHY OF FRIENDS? OR BECAUSE YOU'RE JEALOUS?
IF IT'S THE LATTER...THAT'S YOUR CHOICE. IF YOU DON'T LIKE THE WAY THINGS ARE, THEN CHANGE IT. THAT'S WHAT SKRULLS ARE ALL ABOUT, RIGHT? CHANGE?
SHIELD YOUR EYES.
MY--?
TELL HER I FAILED IN MY ATTEMPT TO KILL HER.
TELL HER THAT THE TALISMAN, AT THE DIRECTIVE OF THE GODS, SPARED HER WORTHLESS LIFE. BUT HE IS UNDER MY PROTECTION NOW, AND IF SHE GOES AFTER HIM AGAIN, THE GODS THEMSELVES WILL NOT STAY MY HAND.
TELL HER--
THAT YOU LOVE HER?
TELL HER ANYTHING BUT THAT.
END.

ISSUE #32 APES VARIANT

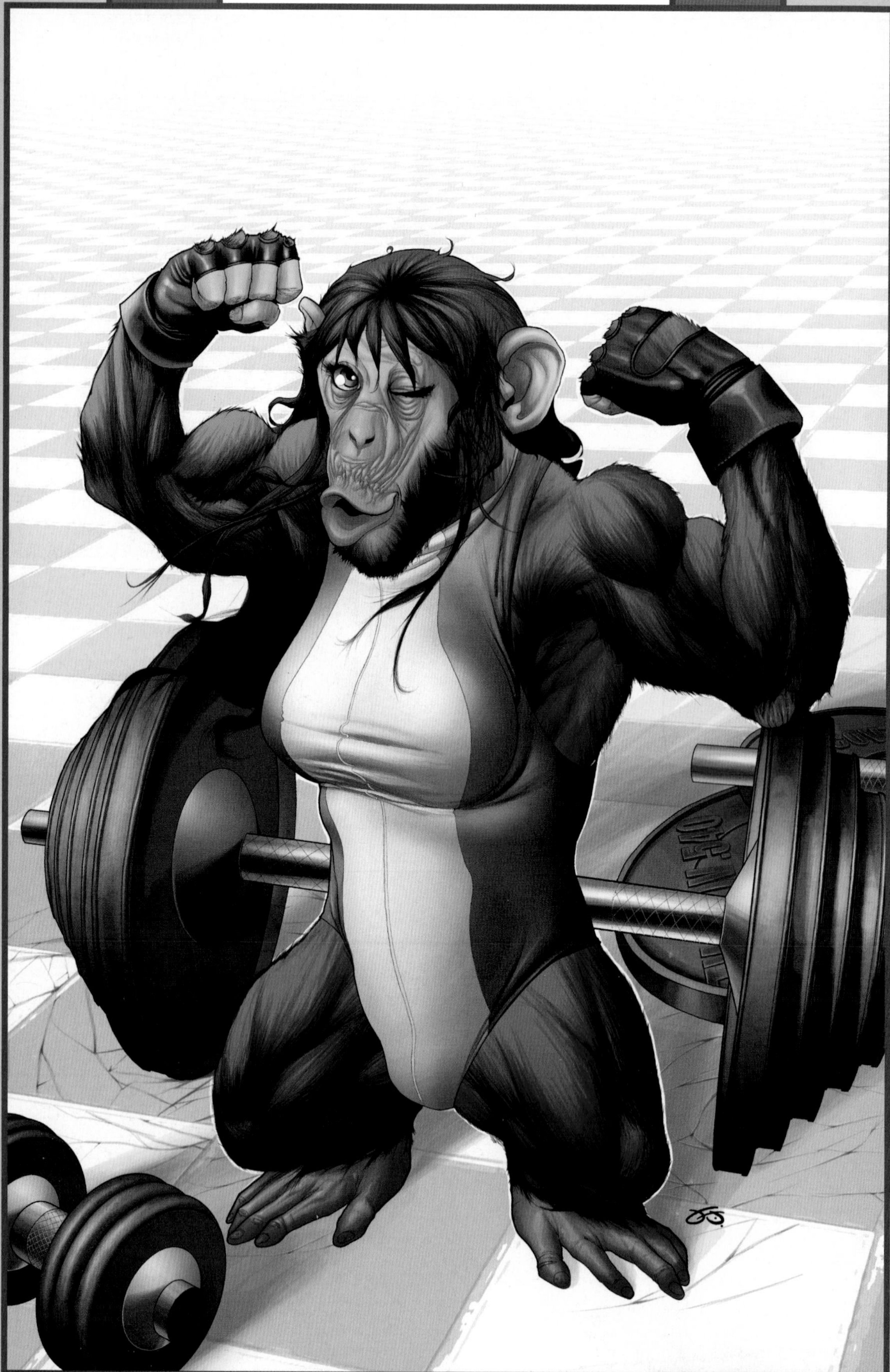

by Frank Martin Jr.